The Belt and Road Initiative

The Belt and Road Initiative

Legal Risks and Opportunities Facing Chinese Engineering Contractors Operating Overseas

Permanent Forum of China Construction Law

 Wolters Kluwer

Published by:
Kluwer Law International B.V.
PO Box 316
2400 AH Alphen aan den Rijn
The Netherlands
E-mail: international-sales@wolterskluwer.com
Website: lrus.wolterskluwer.com

Sold and distributed in North, Central and South America by:
Wolters Kluwer Legal & Regulatory U.S.
7201 McKinney Circle
Frederick, MD 21704
United States of America
Email: customer.service@wolterskluwer.com

Sold and distributed in all other countries by:
Air Business Subscriptions
Rockwood House
Haywards Heath
West Sussex
RH16 3DH
United Kingdom
Email: international-customerservice@wolterskluwer.com

Printed on acid-free paper.

ISBN 978-94-035-1440-6

e-Book: ISBN 978-94-035-1443-7
web-PDF: ISBN 978-94-035-1450-5

© 2019 Kluwer Law International BV, The Netherlands

Printed in the United Kingdom.

List of Contributors

Panel of Chinese Experts

(in alphabetical order of names, unless specifically indicated)

Name	Organization	Position
Qin Yuxiu (convener)	China State Construction Engineering Corporation Limited	General Legal Counsel
Cui Jun	Beijing Overseas Junhe Engineering Consulting Co., Ltd.	Chairman
Li Zhiyong	POWERCHINA International Group Limited	General Manager of Department of Law and Risk Management
Lu Xiaopin	Beijing DHH Law Firm	Partner
Qian Wuyun	China Civil Engineering Construction Corporation	Former General Manager
Sun Yiwen	China Railway Construction Corporation Limited	Legal Counsel
Sun Wei	Zhong Lun Law Firm	Partner
Wang Jiaguo	China Railway Construction Corporation Limited	Deputy General Counsel, Director of Legal and Compliance Department
Xu Qianqian	China State Construction Engineering Corporation Limited	Senior Manager of Department of Legal Affairs
Zhang Xiaoxia	Beijing Tiantai Law Firm	Partner
Zhao Shanshan	China ENFI Engineering Co., Ltd.	Director of Department of Project Management
Zhou Xianfeng	Jun He LLP	Partner

List of Contributors

Name	Organization	Position
Tang Lei (Secretary of the Panel)	AllBright Law Offices	Partner

Panel of International Experts

(in alphabetical order of names)

Name	Organization	Position
Alexander Gunning QC	One Essex Court	Queen's Counsel
Alexis Mourre	ICC International Court of Arbitration	President
Anthony Houghton SC	Des Voeux Chambers	Senior Counsel
Gordon Tregaskis	Quantum Global Solutions	Executive Director
Jakob Ragnwaldh	Arbitration Institute of the SCC	Vice-Chair
	Mannheimer Swartling LLP	Partner
Jeremy Nicholson QC	4 Pump Court	Queen's Counsel, Arbitrator, Adjudicator
Johan Granehult	Mannheimer Swartling LLP	Partner
John Bishop	Arbitration Chambers	Member, Independent Arbitrator
Kim Berry	Currie & Brown	Chief Operating Officer, Asia Pacific
Laura Abrahamson	AECOM	Senior Vice President
Michael E. Schneider	Swiss Arbitration Association	Honorary President
	LALIVE	Founding Partner
Michael Tonkin	HKA	Partner
Mohamed S. Abdel Wahab	ICC International Court of Arbitration	Vice President
	Zulficar & Partners LLP	Founding Partner
Nikolaus Pitkowitz	Vienna International Arbitration Center	Vice President
	Graf & Pitkowitz Rechtsanwälte GmbH LLP	Founding Partner
Omar Aljazy	Aljazy & Co	Managing Partner
Professor Khory McCormick	Griffith University	Professor of Strategic Law
Sam Boyling	Pinsent Masons LLP	Partner
Sally Roe	Freshfields Bruckhaus Deringer LLP	Partner

Name	Organization	Position
Sir Vivian Ramsey	Singapore International Commercial Court	Judge
Terence Wong	Winston & Strawn LLP	Partner
Thayananthan Baskaran	Baskaran	Partner
	Crown Office Chambers	Associate Member
Tony Dymond	Debevoise & Plimpton LLP	Partner
Tunde Fagbohunlu	Aluko & Oyebode	Senior Partner

Table of Contents

Forewords

It is a privilege for me to be invited to write this foreword for *The Belt and Road Initiative: Legal Risks and Opportunities Facing Chinese Engineering Contractors Operating Overseas* (the Book).

The Permanent Forum of China Construction Law (PFCCL) conducted a study (the Study) on the risk analysis and management that Chinese engineering contractors which operate overseas are facing. As an outcome of the Study, PFCCL successfully presents Chinese readers this Book, which comprehensively covers the topics of political, social and market environment of host countries, legal environment in host countries, risks of project stakeholders, project risks and internal risks of contractors, which will serve as a very useful guidance for Chinese engineering contractors when operates construction and engineering projects overseas. Its importance to Chinese contractors operating overseas becomes even more significant in the context of the Belt and Road Initiative (BRI) because BRI is such a dynamic project that involves the global flow of hundreds of billions of dollars, many of which are and will be used in engineering and construction projects delivered by these leading Chinese contractors.

Furthermore, looking from another perspective, the Book could also perfectly serve for two additional purposes: (1) the perspectives on risk analysis and management from Chinese engineering contractors presented by the Report may help their counterparts to better understand the worries and concerns of the Chinese engineering contractors and the Chinese business culture and philosophy behind them; (2) more broadly speaking, some of the risks that Chinese engineering contractors are facing in their overseas operation are in fact the same as those faced by the contractors from other countries and thus may serve as a general guidance to the same, both of which will eventually help the improvement of business practice in the captioned sector in real life practice. I understand that PFCCL will work with multiple international organizations towards an updated report in the future from a more global perspective to benefit the general international arbitration practice in the captioned field, to which I am looking forward.

Being the world's leading arbitral institution, with more than 20% of its caseload in engineering and construction sector, ICC International Court of Arbitration (ICC

Court) has devoted itself to more effective and efficient dispute resolutions in the field. Having supported the Study by providing the Working Group with several anonymized arbitral awards for case study, ICC Court will continue contributing to the global engineering and construction community with its flagship arbitration services, as it has done in the past 96 years, and, through its BRI Commission and Africa Commission, continuing working with PFCCL and other friends to update the engineering and construction community the latest international arbitration practices via conferences and trainings and improve the overall quality of arbitration for engineering and construction disputes.

Congratulations again to PFCCL on the successful publication of the Book!

Alexis Mourre
President of ICC International Court of Arbitration
28 May 2019

The spectacular development of China in recent years is largely reflected in its booming construction industry. Buildings, civil, industrial and other engineering works designed and implemented in China are most impressive.

It is only natural that the experience and expertise developed by Chinese engineering contractors are now playing an increasing role in China's exports. Exporting engineering services however require that contractors familiarize themselves with international contractual practices and with the various legal environments in which they will have to operate. These may indeed differ considerably from one country to the next and from those applied in China. Chinese engineering contractors turning to export their services, thus, face new risks, in addition to those inherent in engineering projects in general.

In this context, the PFCCL can only be congratulated for having established its Sixth Working Group and mandated it to examine the Legal Risks and Opportunities Facing Chinese Engineering Contractors Operating Overseas.

The complexity of legal and contracting issues that arise in international engineering projects and the diversity of systems that must be considered, made this project daunting. The task was made even more challenging considering the broad scope adopted for the study. Yet, the Chinese group of Legal Experts completed this mission in a remarkably short period of time, gathering a large amount of materials and very useful thoughts.

Further input was provided in the form of external material, in particular from the ICC and International Council for Commercial Arbitration (ICCA), and from the Panel of International Experts to which I made a modest contribution as one of the Panel members.

In its final form, the book provides both insight into the risks of international engineering projects facing Chinese contractors and useful advice on how to address them. As such, it is a valuable and important tool not only for Chinese contractors but also for all players engaged in international engineering projects, as contractors, employers, engineers, lenders, insurers and in the many other functions that are required for the successful design and implementation of such projects. It certainly deserves wide circulation within this broader construction circle.

Michael E. Schneider
Co-Chair, Expert Advisory Committee of PFCCL
Geneva, 28 May 2019

Preface

In recent years, Chinese construction engineering companies have been vigorously expanding their overseas operations, and their presence has spread all over the world. Despite the great number of prosperous projects, cases that resulted in dissatisfaction or even failure are not rare.

With the continued progress of the BRI, Chinese companies are bound to play an even more prominent role in overseas construction engineering. Risks tend to come hand in hand with opportunities and warrant our attention. As the Chinese proverb goes, "the past not forgotten will be a guide for the future." By studying both successful cases and the less productive ones, and summing up both good practices and painful lessons, we aspire to help Chinese contractors manage the legal risks of overseas business, improve the management of overseas construction projects and, ultimately, safeguard their interests while going global.

PFCCL has long focused on studying pertinent and difficult issues in the field of construction law. In October 2017, PFCCL began preparations for establishing a Sixth Working Group (the "Working Group") to conduct a themed research on *The Belt and Road Initiative: Legal Risks and Opportunities Facing Chinese Engineering Contractors Operating Overseas*.

In November 2017, the Working Group was formed after recruitment and selection procedures. Its Members include 13 Chinese experts and 23 international experts. Some of the Members are general legal counsel or senior managers of overseas projects in Chinese engineering contractors, some are revered judges and arbitrators who have tried/arbitrated numerous international construction disputes, some are lawyers who have stood the test of many battles in assisting Chinese contractors in overseas dispute resolution. The profound knowledge base and extensive practical experience of the Members are a strong endorsement to the expertise and authority this book embodies.

Since the establishment of the Working Group one and a half years ago, in the pursuit of producing superb research product, each expert has conducted extensive case studies, refined their practical experiences, drawn on academic literature and improved their research results time and again with the spirit of craftsmanship. After the completion of the first draft, the Working Group translated it into English and submitted the English version to the international experts to be reviewed in groups and in chapters, to ensure that the book is comprehensive, accurate, substantive, of firm basis, and of practical value.

In terms of the structure of the book, the Working Group adopted a problem-oriented approach and fully explored the risks facing Chinese overseas contractors from the following aspects: the host country's integrated environment (political, social, market, legal environment); the behavior of other relevant parties in overseas construction projects; the overseas construction project itself (such as natural environment, construction works and finance); the contractor's own management (such as internal management decision-making, compliance, organizational management) and so on. The aim is to provide more targeted and more practical risk prevention and response strategies for stakeholders in overseas construction projects.

The Chinese version of this book is to be published by Law Press China, and the English version is to be published by Wolters Kluwer. Due to limitations of time, energy and capacity, there will inevitably be inadequacies in this book. Your comments and suggestions are appreciated. We will also continue to closely follow the industry developments and update the book accordingly.

At this juncture, I would like to express my heartfelt gratitude to all of the experts of the Sixth Working Group for devoting their enthusiasm and precious time into this research book. It is precisely because of their dedication that the PFCCL has been continuously gaining momentum. I believe that our efforts and achievements are bound to contribute to the development of China's overseas engineering and construction industry, and further to the implementation of the BRI.

I am also most grateful to the ICC and the ICCA for their constant attention and robust support to this research project. ICC provided the Working Group with several anonymized arbitral awards as case study materials, and ICCA recommended reputational international experts in the construction dispute resolution sector to join the Working Group, both of which have greatly helped the successful completion of the project.

I am deeply in debt to the Committee of Chairs, the Expert Advisory Committee and the Secretary-Generals' Meeting of the PFCCL for their high regard and solid support of the research project. They are undoubtedly the strong backing of the Sixth Working Group.

Editors at Wolters Kluwer Ms. Eleanor Taylor and Ms. Kiran Gore have assisted throughout to bring this book to print, to whom I would like to express my sincere gratitude. In addition, many thanks to the following persons for their careful review of the book: Ms. Charmelia Sugianto, Mr. Xingyu Huang, Ms. Jia LI, Mr. Yingfu Zhao, Mr. Guolin Li, Ms. Ziyue Wang, Ms. Huilanzi Gong, Mr. Xi Tao and Mr. Alex Kamath.

Publication of this book benefited substantially from the warm support of many colleagues and friends. Due to the limited space, I am unable to list them one by one. On behalf of PFCCL, hereby I would like to pay them all my respect and deep appreciation.

As China's ancient poet Qu Yuan put it, "the way ahead is long, I see no ending; yet high and low I will search with my will unbending." PFCCL has been trying its best to deliver its goal and will keep trying with unrelenting passion!

Wei Sun
Secretary-General of PFCCL
16 June 2019, Beijing

Introduction

With the development of global economic integration and the implementation of China's "going-global" strategy, more and more Chinese enterprises have begun to expand their businesses to overseas markets. The "Belt and Road" Initiative has aided this expansion, providing more opportunities (and appetite) for Chinese contractors to operate outside China. In expanding their business offerings, and in order to successfully deliver on their project obligations, Chinese contractors will need to be aware of: (a) the risks of working on international projects and in foreign jurisdictions, (b) how these risks will affect a Chinese contractor (and its ability to operate overseas) and (c) how these risks may be mitigated.

Importantly, Chinese contractors should be aware that the risks that arise on international projects or in other jurisdictions (as well as how these risks can be managed or prevented) may be different to the risks and/or solutions that Chinese contractors are accustomed to on China-based projects. For example, complying with regulatory or legal requirements of a foreign jurisdiction may have cost and scheduling impacts on a Chinese contractor that it might otherwise not have experienced in China. Similarly, solutions that may be readily employed in China may not be available in other jurisdictions, or may otherwise be too time-consuming, expensive or difficult for a Chinese contractor to implement overseas.

This book is intended to assist Chinese contractors in identifying the risks that they may face on international construction projects, including those risks that arise due to the political, social, economic or legal context of the foreign jurisdiction, the risks that are inherent to a particular project and finally the internal business risks that may arise for the particular Chinese contractor.

CHAPTER 1
Political, Social and Market Environment of the Country

The external environment of a project is comprised of the specific political, social, marketing and legal factors of the host country of the project investment. Correspondingly, these factors can cause a wide variety of risks in these foreign countries that can prevent the successful and timely implementation of international construction projects. This section explores the widely diversified set of political, social and market risks that Chinese contractors might encounter in overseas markets.

§1.01 POLITICAL RISKS

Political risk is the most special risk in international projects of investment and is also the chief soft element that influences the international project. Generally speaking, political risk refers to the changes that take place in the political condition, international relationships or influential strength of the host country in the internal affairs. For example, political events such as war, regime change, labor strikes and democratic protests that take place in the host country can lead to substantial damage to or even the failure of a project, the change of project credit structure, the reduction of project solvency or other consequences.[1]

Political risk has strong national and regional characteristics. Most of the countries along the "Belt and Road" are developing countries in Asia, Africa and Latin America, and quite a few of them are experiencing economic transition or regime change.[2] As a consequence, the political situation in those countries is not only unstable but also nontransparent and incoherent. War and civil strife can happen at

---

1. Zhipeng Qiu, "Reasonably Avoid Investment Risks to Help Power Enterprises", China Power Enterprise Management, October, 2017.
2. Jian Huang, "China and One Belt and One Road Countries Project Docking Risk and Response Strategy", *Journal of Beijing Technology and Business University (Social Sciences)*, November 2017 (6).

any time there. When having problems of economic slowdown or financial constraints, some countries may even declare the contracts of government projects invalid and refuse to pay the debt. The following sections will give some analysis of various political risks.

[A]   War

War and other similar forms of hostility might be the most extreme form of political risk. Many of the projects undertaken by Chinese contractors are in less developed areas, where the World Bank, Asian Development Bank and multinational corporations are reluctant to invest and step in. Most of these countries and regions are in a period of economic transition or undergoing regime change. The backward state of their economy and political upheaval make the future full of uncertainty. In addition, many countries like these are also faced with the problems of ethnic conflict, religious conflict, narcotrafficking, terrorism, territorial disputes and resource disputes, all of which have a significant impact on the regional state of politics.

In recent years, economic and trade cooperation between China and Gulf Cooperation Council (GCC) members has developed rapidly. But many of the Arabian countries in the Middle East are undergoing profound changes in social systems and structures, which are placing the engineering projects there in a high political risk state. For example, the Iranian situation had caused much trouble to the safety of international oil transportation there.

In South Asia, Pakistan has a lot of trade with China. But Pakistan has consistently faced local terrorism threats as well as the terrorist threat from the Afghan Taliban. In August 2008, two Chinese engineers were kidnapped by armed assailants in Pakistan. In 2013, a total of 1,717 terrorist attacks occurred in Pakistan, with 2,451 people being killed and 5,438 people injured.[3]

In Central Asia, some countries get entangled in the disputes between some other big countries over the right for oil and gas pipelines. When Armenia and Azerbaijan argued strongly over the issue of *nagorno-karabakh*, some other countries were entangled with the problem of migrant labor conflicts, partisan fighting, military conflict, refugee issues and drug trafficking. This reflects the complicated and diverse conflicts and political risks that Chinese contractors are faced with in countries in Central Asia.[4]

Africa has been an important market for Chinese companies going abroad owing to its rich resources, low labor cost and favorable policy toward foreign investment. Moreover, ever since the implementation of the "Belt and Road" Initiative, Africa has been an indispensable participant of this Initiative.[5] However, the risks facing investment in Africa has remained at a high level, with one of the major types of them being

---

3. *Ibid.*
4. *Ibid.*
5. Yao Guimei, "Joint Construction of the 'Belt and Road' by China and Africa: Progress, Risks and Outlook", Contemporary World, October 2018.

political risks.[6] Africa's political risks have remained high. In 2009, a Chinese contractor won the bid for Libya's west line railway project. In the initial stages of the project, including the execution, engineering design, advance payment and entry to site stages, the Chinese contractor remained in control of both business operation and construction implementation which went very smoothly. However, when the project entered its second year, i.e. the stage of profit, the "Jasmine Revolution" suddenly took place. Prior to the "Jasmine Revolution" in February 2011, Gaddafi had firm control over the domestic affairs, and the political situation in Libya at that time was relatively stable. However, with the onset of the "Jasmine Revolution," Gaddafi's government encountered the military strikes authorized by the United Nations. As a result, the civil unrest in Libya developed into an international war overnight, and the situation suddenly spiraled out of control. This project and all of China's other projects in Libya, which were worth approximately USD 18.8 billion, were suspended, with all the Chinese companies in Libya suffering serious losses. As another example, a Chinese contractor working on a project in an east African country in the early 1990s was forced to terminate the contract and evacuate because of the outbreak of a war there. Although most of the project contracts have "force majeure" clause similar to Conditions of Contract issued by Federation Internationale Des Ingenieurs Conseils (FIDIC), which may in principle form the basis of the contractor's claim for compensation from the employer, it is in reality very difficult to obtain compensation for the full extent of their losses.

[B] Economic Sanctions

The economic environment has a strong influence on international engineering projects. The economic environment refers to a holistic view of a country's economic system by examining elements such as the levels of economic development, price fluctuations, financial stability and stock market maturity.

The economic condition of a country is closely related to its political situation. A nation's choice of economic policy can have dramatic effects on its economic system by affecting factors such as its level of prices, ease of obtaining financing and degree of foreign exchange freedom. We can say, to a certain degree, that the stability of a country's political environment can determine whether its macroeconomic environment is favorable or not for the Chinese contractors to contract for projects there. In analyzing the macroeconomic environment of the target country, Chinese enterprises can pass judgment based on a series of economic indicators, including economic growth rate, national budget and deficit, employment numbers and unemployment rate, rate of inflation, import and export trade and international income differentials, central bank interest rate, currency exchange rate, currency circulation and velocity, national income and consumption of the whole society, ratio of savings, investment and national income, population size and growth rate. In the countries and areas where

---

6. Dou Wei: "Political Risks Facing Chinese Companies Investing in Africa and Suggestions", Modern Economics Discussions, March 2016.

the above information is difficult to obtain accurately, enterprises can rely on the resources and platforms of professional service organizations or multinational consulting firms in order to have the maximum control and knowledge over the possible risks and plan accordingly.

In the present age of economic globalization, the economic condition is not only decided by a country's domestic political situation but also influenced by the international economic and political situation. For example, economic sanctions by a country may have a huge impact on international projects located in another country. Economic sanctions often lead to the tightness of foreign exchange reserves, freezing of funds access and reduction of financing capacity. This will not only increase the risk of foreign exchange collection by Chinese contractors in executing the projects but also significantly increase the difficulty and complexity in developing new markets for Chinese enterprises. Iran and Russia are two important market areas to Chinese enterprises seeking to execute projects overseas, but both have suffered and continue to suffer double sanctions imposed by the United States (U.S.) and the European Union (EU) in recent years.

[C]   Domestic Regime Change

A country's political environment is one of the most sensitive and important factors to be considered by multinationals making investment decisions. The political environment is directly related to the stability and continuity of political power in the host country. Political system, regime stability, policy consistency and the degree of war risk concern the security of the investment and the physical security of employees living abroad. In some countries, coups happen frequently, which significantly affects the progress of projects. If the political situation of the host country is unstable, or when regime changes take place, the new government may refuse to continue the policy of the previous government, interrupt the investment arrangements of the project or even refuse to recognize the promises made or the debt incurred by the previous government. In this case, it will be difficult to successfully implement the project and receive full payment for the project. In addition, the rise of a new party may lead to drastic changes in the market environment of the host country and even social unrest due to its policy adjustments in political, social and economic aspects. In some African and Southeast Asian countries, where political environment is relatively stable, the intergovernmental policies have a certain consistency, such that the political environment has relatively little impact on project implementation.

However, there are countries where political struggle has been getting intensified, adding a great deal of uncertainty to the investment environment in terms of political risk. For instance, in 2018, a new government of a Southeast Asian country implemented a policy to conduct a detailed and careful review of the major projects for which foreign contractors have been appointed and specifically to reexamine Chinese-backed projects. Although the head of this country expressed his support for the "Belt and Road Initiative (BRI)" at a press conference, he reiterated that there are several projects that need to be renegotiated with the Chinese counterparties, creating uncertainty over the future of such projects. Given that this country has seen a marked increase in investment by Chinese developers in its domestic projects in recent years, any proposed reforms and policy changes by the new government in the real estate sector could cause these projects to lose significant value. On July 4, 2018, the newly elected government announced the suspension of three Chinese-backed project contracts worth USD 22 billion and requested renegotiation of the project agreements.[7]

Some countries in the Middle East also face the problem of instability. Protests against monarchical systems, fight for sectarian equality and democratic uprisings are surging in the GCC countries.[8] This political instability constitutes a great threat to projects with foreign involvement. Local mass demonstrations are often accompanied with beating, smashing, looting and personal attacks. Chinese-backed companies' offices, camps and project sites have often become the targets of such attacks.

[D]   Expropriation

Expropriation can be divided into direct expropriation and indirect expropriation. By direct expropriation, a country directly deprives investors of employership of their property through processes such as nationalization. Indirect expropriation refers to the unreasonable interference in a foreigners' right in using, possessing and disposing of their properties for the period of their rightful use under investment agreements and associated contracts. Direct expropriation rarely occurs now because it is easy to identify, and once implemented, the host government usually faces the danger of both high compensation and political pressure from the investor's home country. The more common type of expropriation, therefore, is indirect expropriation. As indirect expropriation is not a direct deprivation of investor's property employership, it is extremely difficult to identify. For this reason, whether the government's behavior constitutes an indirect expropriation or not often becomes the focus of disputes among parties in investment disputes.

In the field of construction engineering, environmental protection measures, new standards for project quality and new norms of builder qualifications adopted by the host government can cause project investors and contractors to suffer loss of intended benefits under the contract. However, it is difficult for investors and contractors to prove that the government's behavior is an expropriation because the host government often denies the claims of investors and contractors on the grounds that its behavior is a legitimate act of performing government functions. For example, in the case of *Metalclad Corp v. United Mexico*,[9] Metalclad filed an arbitration on the grounds that the Mexican local government's refusal of its project construction license application

---

7. FT Chinese, *Malaysia Suspends China-Backed Projects*, http://www.ftchinese.com/story/00107 8337/en?ccode = LanguageSwitch&archive (last visited May 24, 2019).
8. Sujuan Gong: "Study on Economic and Trade Cooperation Between China and GCC Countries", Dongbei University of Finance and Economics, 2014, master's thesis, p. 31.
9. https://icsid.worldbank.org/en/Pages/cases/casedetail.aspx?CaseNo = ARB(AF)/97/1, September 11, 2018.

without any reason constitutes an indirect expropriation of its investment interests. In its defense, the Mexican government argued that its actions were legitimately within its discretion. Moreover, even if an arbitral tribunal were to find that the behavior of the government of a host country constitutes indirect expropriation, the issue of how to determine the appropriate amount of compensation payable remains controversial in practice. For example, arguments may relate to whether different compensation standards should be established according to the legality of the indirect expropriation. For another example, if the government's indirect expropriation takes the form of a series of unclear acts or omissions and has caused continuous damage to the contractor's interests, a controversial issue which may arise is how to determine the valuation period of the contractor's interests.

[E]   Bilateral Relationship

China has good bilateral relations with many countries which have largely promoted the foreign business expansion of Chinese contractors. However, at times, bad bilateral relations with certain nations have occurred with spillover effects. For example, on May 13, 2014, as the conflict between China and Vietnam in the South China Sea got increasingly heated, it triggered an anti-Chinese movement in Vietnam. As a result, Chinese companies' facilities in Vietnam got smashed, burned and looted. On July 24, 2015, anti-Chinese protests also happened in the Philippines.[10] Similar events occurred in Africa in reaction to a perceived China threat despite an increasingly optimistic China-Africa relationship. China's investment in Africa has been regarded by some as a kind of resource plunder, and this has fostered a certain kind of anti-Chinese sentiment among the people there. While the BRI has won the approval of most of the countries along the route and the general understanding by the major countries in Europe, there are also some countries which are suspicious of the BRI and refer to it a Chinese version of the "Marshall Plan."

[F]   Prevention of Political Risks

Faced with the above political risks, it is recommended to take the following preventative actions.

First, before a project is contracted, the political situation of the host country should be fully investigated and possible political risks in the country where the project is located should be fully estimated and evaluated. In high-risk areas, special care must be taken and costs of war or terrorism must be assessed in advance. Risk avoidance measures should be considered if the risk is sufficient to threaten the implementation of the project, while at the same time, no effective measures can be taken to transfer the risk. For example, after the Libyan war broke out in Libya, the Gaddafi regime was

---

10. Dan Ma: "CJIC's Internationalization Strategy Research", Jiangxi University of Finance and Economics, 2016, master's thesis, p. 21.

overthrown and the situation became very chaotic. Under this circumstance, the Libya North-South line coastal railway project had to be aborted.

In recent years, the Chinese government has increased its support for the international engineering industry and actively promoted bilateral infrastructure cooperation by entering into bilateral investment agreements with some developing countries.[11] Generally speaking, cooperation with countries which have good bilateral cooperation with China can reduce political risks.

Second, an important measure in mitigating the political risks is insurance. Due to certain features of international engineering projects such as its long cycle, the complexity of the environment and the multilateral participation involved in these projects, project investors and contractors have to face various risks including political, social and economic risks and risks relating to the natural environment. In view of the above risks, it is extremely difficult for investors and contractors to achieve comprehensive risk control without efficient risk transfer through professional insurance institutions.

According to the common risk categories of international projects and the classification of insurance types of major insurance companies, common international engineering insurance can be classified into the following five categories: (1) investment insurance which provides risk protection for cross-border investment activities by providing medium or long-term political risk insurance and related investment risk advisory services to cross-border investors; (2) credit insurance which can be divided into short-term and medium-term export credit insurance according to different coverage periods—in this regard, the short-term export credit insurance covers the credit risk of export within one year, while the medium- and long-term export credit insurance covers the risk of export credits with a credit period of 1-15 years. In view of the long period of international engineering projects, there are many enterprises that insure the medium- and long-term export credit insurance in practice; (3) engineering insurance, which mainly relates to engineering risks, including construction machinery and equipment insurance, third-party liability insurance, motor vehicle insurance, ocean transportation insurance, professional liability insurance, employer liability insurance; (4) personnel insurance, the most common type of which is life insurance and mainly covers personal accident insurance, medical transfer insurance; (5) security insurance, which comprises of (among others) corporate security insurance and terrorist attack insurance that are intended to address risks of terrorist attacks and kidnapping.

If investors and contractors of overseas engineering construction insure the corresponding risks on the basis of accurately identifying the project risks, they can make up for the losses caused by the risks. For example, in investing, considered the political situation in that country and a Chinese company insured its investment in a photovoltaic power generation project in a country in Eastern Europe with China's Export Credit Insurance Co., Ltd. for three basic political risks of war and political riots,

---

11. Zhenyu Zhao, Jiahui Yao, "Regional Environment Identification of International Project Contracting Market", Construction Enterprise Management, January 2016.

expropriation and exchange restrictions. Later, the National Energy and Water Resources Regulatory Commission of that country issued two decrees to impose a 39% additional network transmission and distribution fee and a 20% income tax on all new energy power generation companies in the country, causing huge losses to the company. When this happened, the company made a claim to China Export Credit Insurance Co., Ltd. Upon finding that the levy of additional network access fees from the government of the host country had triggered the loss clause of the policy on "levy" behavior, China Credit Insurance Co., Ltd. immediately paid on the claim, which helped the company to come out of the dilemma caused by the impact of taxation.

Third, it is important for enterprises to conduct sufficient safety training to dispatched employees so as to improve their safety awareness and cultivate their ability to identify risks. For employees working in high-risk areas, it is necessary to give them trainings against anti-terrorism to improve their ability to respond to emergencies.

Fourth, a feasible safety emergency plan should be made according to concrete local situations. Suggestions for safety emergency plan include: (1) in high-risk areas, it is advisable for project enterprises to strengthen perimeter blockade and inspection to prevent armed personnel from sneaking in; (2) issue risk assessments and risk levels regularly and implement armed guards for daily construction services and maintenance operations within the scope of the project; (3) implement 24-hour armed patrols in the project area; (4) set up multiple garrisons in the key operating field of the project to form an effective protective network and clarify the distribution of security responsibility between the employer and the Chinese contractor to effectively implement the agreement between the employer and the Chinese contractor in relation to security; (5) at the same time, sufficient basic living materials and emergency living materials should be reserved for emergency evacuation of all employees; prepare emergency vehicles, spare drivers and oil materials and reserve emergency domestic water; each person should be equipped with a personal emergency kit, with each person carrying a small amount of cash for emergency use; and implement emergency aircraft resources and update agreements with airlines.

Fifth, contracts should pay attention to timely transmission of information so as to improve early warning capability. To avoid social security risks, enterprises should make efforts in the following areas: (1) establish an unobstructed emergency information communicating system and keep efficient communication channels open with embassy and other relevant institutions; (2) enhance security information sharing, pay attention to the early warning information released by higher authorities and communicate with each brother unit at the site of construction; (3) maintain good relations with local tribes and employees and get along well with the security and production departments of the relevant parties; (4) strengthen the unit's capacity of information collection, analysis, assessment and early warning to ensure the accuracy and reliability of security information.

Sixth, contracts should employ private security companies. The security business involves security guarantees in many areas, such as political turmoil, military conflict, personal security and property security. Chinese enterprises should formulate, according to different regions, a step-by-step strengthening security system which is composed of property protection system, security system, conflict protection system and political turmoil precaution system. Depending on the level and type of risks, enterprises in different countries can have various security plans, giving prominence to key points and taking into account the overall situation.[12] Furthermore, they can also ask the government of the country where the project is located to provide them with regular military protection and establish protective work at the construction site and transit terminals so as to strengthen the security on the spot and in transit and effectively prevent the risk of kidnapping and armed attacks.

Seventh, contractors can actively promote localization management. To develop social relations with the local people, enterprises can employ some technical managers, who are both familiar with local conditions and have certain influence, and let them be in charge of construction management in particularly sensitive construction areas.

Eighth, it is necessary to strengthen the preservation and backup of all kinds of information and to have important information transmitted back to China as soon as possible.

Ninth, contractors should strengthen the work of inspection and valuation by forming creditor's rights and debts relationship with the employer as soon as possible so that they can seek the support of economic laws and regulations during an emergency.

Tenth, in handling projects with high political and security risks, enterprises can assess and include security costs as part of their tender bids appropriately based on their risk tolerance. In contractual negotiations, clauses for exemption of the contractors' liability arising out of suspension or termination of the contract caused by reasons attributable to the employer or the security situation should be added.

§1.02   SOCIAL RISKS IN HOST COUNTRIES

The social environment is another major factor affecting international engineering contracting. The social environment refers to the state of social development in a certain period of time, which is mainly reflected in social security, cultural traditions, religious beliefs, social customs and educational level. A poor public security situation in a host country will have a negative impact on international projects and serious social security deterioration which can even lead to termination of the projects. The success rate of investment may depend on effective management of the difference between the culture of the investing country and that of the host country. Multinational corporations should respect the cultural values, religious traditions and social customs of the host country. The educational development level of the host country, which has a bearing on the behavior of the host country staff, their way of understanding and efficiency of communication will indirectly affect the investment activities of the multinational companies.

---

12. Hongyi Wang, "Compliance Construction One Belt and One Road Security Guarantee First", International Project Contracting & Labour Service, March, 2018.

11

[A]   Social Security (Terrorist Activities, Kidnapping)

Social and public security risks refer to the risks brought by sudden events such as robbery and kidnapping to enterprises in the countries or regions where the overseas projects are contracted.[13] In many cases, social security risks are controllable, but in other cases, social security risks may manifest in social unrest caused by or intensified by changes in the political system. For example, a large-scale mass protest against the new government policy in the Ecuadorian elections in 2015 brought hidden security dangers to the stability of the political situation in Ecuador. At the same time, in recent years, due to the deteriorating economic situation in Ecuador, social security problems have become particularly prominent. Various incidents of gun robbery and gang crimes have occurred frequently. Chinese companies, local residents and even local banks have been robbed, suffering millions of dollars in losses. On April 15, 2016, two Chinese hydropower company employees were followed to an underground garage and robbed after withdrawing money from the Pichincha Bank with two armed security guards, causing more than USD 30,000 in losses.[14] On the morning of May 2, a hydropower motorboat was robbed by eight gunmen on its way of to the dredger platform. Similar robberies plagued the project, which made it increasingly difficult for Chinese-funded enterprises to protect the personal and property safety of their Chinese employees.[15]

In the second half of 2011, in order to unite with the Qaddafi mercenaries that returned to Mali, Al-Qaida in the northern part of Mali frequently infiltrated Algeria through the southern border of Algeria and launched a number of terrorist attacks including suicide attacks, causing the death of more than 10 people. In early 2013, in the southern province of Eritrea in Algeria, Al-Qaida in the Maghreb launched a large-scale armed attack on British BP and Norwegian STATOIL, killing two people, injuring six people and injuring 41 foreigners (mainly Japanese and American citizens). With the growth of the business scope of Chinese contracting companies in Algeria, the distribution of projects becomes increasingly dispersed, which makes security risks an important factor to be considered.[16]

[B]   Religious and Cultural Differences

Religious and cultural risks refer to the unpredictable economic losses caused by the differences in religious beliefs and customs between the home country and the host country. Due to their special nature, religious and cultural risks play a very important role in international engineering risks. Different religious and cultural backgrounds

---

13. Ming Liu: "Study on Risk Management of Overseas Project Contracted by CC Group", Beijing Jiaotong University, 2012, master's thesis, p. 17.
14. Faming Tan, "Analysis of Labor Cost and Labor Risk of International Engineering Project in Ecuador", Management Observer, June 2016.
15. *Ibid.*
16. Yanjun Wang: "Study on the Market Development of Engineering Contracting in Algeria—Take a State-Owned Company in Algeria as an Example", Chengdu University of Technology, 2017, master's thesis, p. 31.

may result in people of different nationalities having different values and ethical standards. This can sometimes lead to conflicts between Chinese project managers and local staff, increase project costs, hinder the smooth operation of the project and sometimes even lead to the failure of the whole project. Important beliefs and customs may also directly or indirectly affect the normal progress of the project. For example, Muslims observe the "five times" ritual on time every day, i.e. five times of worship. In addition, Friday is a legal prayer day in Islam. Usually all government offices, companies and shops are closed for a day on Fridays, and government offices are also closed on Saturdays. A religious event is about the holy month of Ramadan, during which Muslims fast from sunrise to sunset and abstain from drinking and smoking. Most of the local industry only work half a day during the Ramadan period, and work efficiency is very low. Even foreign non-Muslim personnel are not allowed to conduct activities in public during the fasting period.

[C]   Environmental Protection Risks

Both developed and developing countries are paying more and more attention to environmental protection, which has become a sensitive issue in international engineering contracting. Environmental problems increasingly become a source of risk in the implementation of overseas projects.

At present, only some laws and regulations issued by the state council and various ministries and commissions deal directly or indirectly with the protection of the overseas investment environment. For example, we have *Decision of the State Council on Investment System Reform* (2004), *Interim Measures for the Administration of Approval of Overseas Investment Projects* (2004), *Opinions on Encouraging and Regulating Foreign Investment Cooperation of Chinese Enterprises* (2006), *Measures for the Administration of overseas Investment* (2009), *Regulations on the Administration of Foreign Contracting projects* (2008), *Guidelines on Social Responsibility of Foreign Contracting Engineering Industry* (2012), etc. These regulations are too general, simple and lack operability.

Some Chinese companies' overseas investments (in mining, oil and hydropower) had not paid enough attention to the environmental protection of the project site. The site selection of a few projects had caused damage to the local ecological environment and affected the lives of local residents. For example, the Myanmar Myitsone Hydropower Station, which is known as the overseas "Three Gorges," had caused strong protests from the local residents and environmental organizations for its failure to fully consider the ecological impact at the time of construction. The Myanmar government had to suspend the project due to the pressure from the public. For this reason, the contractor suffered huge losses. In some circumstances, Chinese companies may be compliant with local environmental standards when they made the initial investment in certain developing countries. However, these developing countries may subsequently raise their environmental standards, which create impediments to the Chinese companies' investments. In 2016, for instance, an environmental event took place in an iron and steel project invested by an enterprise in Vietnam, which led to a mass demonstration protest organized by the local residents. The Vietnamese government then began to implement measures of higher standards, stricter monitoring and heavier fines for environmental protection in this project. As a result of the new measures, many contractors were punished by the government for their failure to meet the requirements for construction of waste disposal.

[D]   Work Habits and Efficiency of Local Employees

Chinese contractors often employ a large number of local employees at the location of the project. The work habits and efficiency of local employees often have a certain impact on construction. For example, some countries have abundant labor resources, but the workers there lack labor discipline in that they are unrestrained in behavior and low in attendance in work. These local workers may have a strong sense of self-righteousness. Strikes frequently happen as a result of these factors coupled with their advantage in language communication. All of these create great difficulties in human resources management.[17]

In addition, work policies issued by the host government will also affect the progress of projects. One example is the summer's customary construction practice in the United Arab Emirates (UAE). From June to September every year since 2004, companies in the UAE are not allowed to have employees exposed to the sun from 12:30 p.m. to 3:00 p.m., or they will be fined. Companies that violate this rule and involve a large number of people will be downgraded. In some cases, for example, when large-scale concrete works have to be completed without interruption, public utilities and power networks need urgent maintenance, or traffic jams occur; it is hard to implement the lunch break system. Under these circumstances, enterprises have to get special approval from the Ministry of Labor before construction. At the same time, companies are expected to provide necessary cold drinks, salt, lemon and other summer products and emergency medicines. The Ministry of Labor will also send a number of full-time inspection staff to conduct inspections and give safety warnings to enterprises to ensure effective implementation of the summer lunch break system.[18]

[E]   Social Risks Prevention

Various types of social risks were summarized as provided in Table 1.1.

---

17. Yanjun Wang: "Study on the Market Development of Engineering Contracting in Algeria—Take a State-Owned Company in Algeria as an Example", Chengdu University of Technology, 2017, master's thesis, p. 17.
18. Dengning Hu: "Market Characteristics and Management Countermeasures of UAE Projects", Shan Dong University, 2015, master's thesis, pp. 19-20.

Table 1.1   Summary of Social Risk Performance

Number	Risk Form	Specific Performance
1	Social security	Local criminal cases such as robbery, theft, extortion of money, etc.; terrorist attacks; local bad actors deliberately harass project implementation
2	Cultural difference	Differences in ideology, corporate culture, management models and business practices; differences in customs, traditional taboos and language uses
3	Environmental protection	Damage caused by site selection of the project to local ecological environment and influence to the lives of indigenous peoples and local populations; violation of internationally accepted rules or practices in environmental protection
4	Employment risk	Industry and labor access systems; restricting foreign technicians and laborers to enter the country to work; increase in labor costs; local employees' lack of quality; difficulty and high cost in hiring competent local employees

To prevent social risks, companies can take measures in the following aspects.

First, to solve the security problem of the host country, enterprises need to improve the safety awareness of Chinese employees. For example, employees should not be allowed to leave the engineering area or residential area in the absence of protection, and their activities should be strictly within the limits of security. In particular, Chinese employees have the habit of going to the bank to collect cash before returning home so as to bring it back to China, which gives criminals convenient chances to commit robbery. In countries with serious security problems, risk prevention may refer to the prevention measures of political risks, such as the establishment of China's overseas security system.

Second, in view of the risk of cultural differences, we should mainly rely on a detailed prior investigation. Since cultural differences are not formed in one day, they will not feature unexpectedly. A proper investigation into the cultural norms and preparation in advance is essential in risk prevention and mitigation.[19] At the same time, Chinese companies should also pay attention to the efficacy of employee training in educating employees to respect local culture and customs.

Third, Chinese enterprises are better off making overseas investment which is compliant with high environmental standards in view of environmental risks. If the local economic level imposes environmental standards which are lower than in China, Chinese enterprises can consider discharging the higher environmental standards imposed in China. As for developed countries (which may impose environmental standards higher than in China), investment should be based on the environmental protection requirements stipulated by developed countries.

---

19. Jingnan Fu: "Risk Study for the International Engineering Project in Bushehr, Iran", Jilin University, 2017, master's thesis, p. 17.

Finally, the construction plan should be arranged with a consideration of local customs and employees' work habits. Take a certain Chinese contractor with a civil construction project in UAE as an example. While the Chinese contractor, as the main body of construction, basically does not rest during the construction period, water and power subcontractors and concrete suppliers need rest every Friday. To avoid the project shutdown on account of the hydropower subcontractors and concrete suppliers resting on Friday, it is advisable to prioritize the part of the construction work that requires water and electricity so that such work is completed before Thursday so that the Chinese company can carry forward the work of steel bar binding and part of formwork construction on Friday. By this arrangement, contractors can minimize the idle time of civil works and hydropower cooperation, thereby reducing the risk of slowdown.[20]

§1.03   HOST COUNTRY MARKET RISKS (THE MARKETIZATION LEVEL IN THE LOCAL ECONOMY)

[A]   Macroscopic Investigation of Market Environment and Risk

The market environment of a host country has a profound and direct impact on the activities of overseas contractors. Local enterprises of more mature and stable economies often have strong advantages in management and competitiveness that make it more difficult for foreign investors to effectively compete with them. This is why most multinational companies often tend to invest in countries with lower levels of economic development. The host country's economic policy is a series of policies adopted to develop its own economy and achieve specific economic goals, reflecting its attitudes and management methods toward foreign investment. Economic policies vary according to the host country's national conditions and will directly affect the sustainable income and reinvestment dimension of multinational investments. Usually, the host countries with loose trade tariff policies, open economic policies and fewer nontariff barriers are more attractive to multinational investors. For example, to encourage foreign and domestic capital to invest in all areas of the country, the government of the UAE follows the policies of free trade. The import and export tariffs for general commodities are only 5% at most, and all enterprises are exempt from business tax, value-added tax and profit income tax. According to a survey of the business environment of 189 countries and regions around the world conducted by the World Bank in 2014, the UAE ranked top in terms of tax payment, cross-border trade, application for building permits, registered property and access to electricity.[21] The good investment environment results in the UAE's engineering project market continued growth, which provides unprecedented opportunities for international contractors.

The UAE, powered by infrastructure construction, has quickly attracted much "hot money" from all over the world because of its liberal economic policies. However,

---

20. Dengning Hu: "Market Characteristics and Management Countermeasures of UAE Projects", Shan Dong University, 2015, master's thesis, p. 42.
21. World Bank: 2014 Business Environment Report.

due to their inherent instability, these funds can easily lead to market volatility. "Hot money" can accelerate the 'formation and expansion of infrastructure investment bubbles. Once "hot money" flees, the bubble will burst, and the capital chain of engineering projects will be ruptured, which can lead to huge setbacks in the implementation of engineering projects, and a large number of projects will end in "rotten tail" and economic disputes. In 2009, triggered by the American subprime mortgage crisis, Dubai fell into debt crisis. When Dubai World, the country's largest state-owned company, announced a debt standstill, the construction of the world's tallest building and the palm island project was faced with a "rotten tail" crisis. In addition, according to domestic media, nearly 400 construction projects have been canceled due to funding problems. Therefore, when judging the market risk in the country in which the project is located, companies should not only merely see whether it is beneficial to the contractor but also make comprehensive assessments of the economic policy of the project country in the light of local realities and the interaction of multiple factors.

In addition, as an important macroeconomic policy of each country, foreign exchange policy directly affects the interests of transnational investors and is closely related to the free flow of foreign capital and the smooth repatriation of profits and other benefits to the investor's parent country. From the perspective of investors, the lower the level of foreign exchange management of the host country is, the more favorable it is for investors to transfer their investment profits and reduce the losses caused by the violent fluctuations of the exchange rate.[22] At the same time, inflation is also a worldwide problem threatening economic stability. In some developing countries, the annual inflation rate can reach up to several hundred percent. Due to inflation, prices of materials and local labor force will rise, causing the project cost to increase significantly.[23] From the perspective of the project contractor, both the fluctuation of the exchange rate and the price change of the resource supply will inevitably increase the uncertainty of the returns of project contract and the difficulty and complexity of risk management. At present, although some big engineering firms are trying to take advantage of financial measures, such as currency swaps, to reduce risk, the results of these practices show that these measures are still immature and the risk exposure is still large.

The level of investment protection offered is another important factor to be considered. A host country which is party to a favorable international investment agreement (IIA) with the country of the investor is certainly a more attractive target than a host country without such protection. Typically, investment protection secures the investor against changes of laws or measures which result in expropriation or other losses of its investment. The IIA typically offers security by granting the investor a right to request remedies directly against the host state before an arbitral tribunal and thus reaches well beyond diplomatic support.

---

22. Liping Wang: "Study on Overseas Competition Strategy of Shandong High-Speed Group Co., Ltd", Shan Dong University, 2015, master's thesis, pp. 17-18.
23. Guoxing Chen, Jianxing Jiang: "Common Risks and Preventive Measures of International Contracting Project", Jiangsu water conservancy, No. 4, 2010.

Finally, the tax regime and double taxation treaties concluded with the host state may also impact investments. To attract foreign investments, some countries offer favorable taxation (i.e., tax-free repatriation of dividends). These should be considered.

From a practical perspective, the investor should seek to optimize the level of investment protection and taxation. This may possibly also prompt an investor to structure its investment via a third country offering a more favorable access to the host country than China. Austria, for example, which has concluded a number of favorable IIAs and double taxation agreements with many countries in the Central and Eastern Europe region and beyond, is therefore often selected as an intermediary vehicle for investments in this area.

[B]   Availability of Local Resources

In overseas projects, Chinese companies often face risks in terms of the availability of local resources. Due to the underdeveloped state of the economy of many host countries, the supply capacity of certain goods in the surrounding area can be low, the procurement price of certain materials can be too high or the cost of maintenance of equipment can be prohibitive. Some countries carry out the policy of a supply list system, requiring all construction materials to be purchased from listed suppliers.

The standard specification of building materials is usually compiled by a consulting company in bidding documents. Many building materials and equipment are assigned to the origin or brand. For example, sometimes the engineering project specifies that the origin of the steel bar must be Turkey, UAE or Qatar, or the origin of glass is designated to Belgium; elevators are designated to famous brands like Mitsubishi of Japan, Otis of the U.S., Schindler of Switzerland and Senty Kluber of Germany. These brand products are usually available only through a sole local agent.

In addition, many sales companies will not maintain high inventory in order to reduce the storage cost and capital burden. Decorative materials in extra-large demand and mechanical equipment with a higher unit price need to be booked in advance as there is often a need to wait for several months for production and shipping.[24] These features undoubtedly make it a critical requirement for Chinese contractors to make plans of rational procurement and cost control.

Specifically, the potential risks that Chinese contractors might face may be in relation to (among others) the following four aspects.

The diversity and large amount of equipment procurement and long cycle of multinational supply pose a major risk. Many materials and equipment required in overseas projects are scarce in some host countries. Limited by the low level of industry in host countries, a lot of materials and equipment have to be purchased from China or a third country. If the procurement comes from China, the time cycle from domestic organization, shipping or air transportation to the construction site is very long. For the

---

24. Dengning Hu: "Market Characteristics and Management Countermeasures of UAE Projects", Shan Dong University, 2015, master's thesis, p. 18.

materials that require a special transportation environment, the transportation time might be even longer. In this way, there is a risk of the installation schedule being affected by the supply schedule. If air transport is used, it may lead to the risk of increased cost.

Second, the process of equipment acceptance and checking is complicated, and equipment logistics takes a long time. Equipment logistics needs to go through procedures such as transportation to port, shipping, customs clearance and transportation to the site. After engineering equipment arrives at the construction site, the employer's engineers and the contractors will jointly check them. As part of the equipment acceptance process, equipment will not be allowed to be installed until passing the check. When equipment arrives in bulk at the same time, there may be a risk of installation progress being hindered by the equipment acceptance progress.

Third, fixing equipment defects is a complex and time-intensive process. If defects and missing problem are found during the installation of the equipment, there is a risk that installation schedule will be affected even if domestically procured materials are shipped as quickly as possible.

Finally, the management of equipment through sub-suppliers is complex. If the sub-suppliers' input is not enough, the quality of the equipment will not be guaranteed, and if spare parts are insufficient, there will be a risk of affecting the construction schedule and delay of the construction period.[25]

[C]   Market Risks Prevention

In order to prevent these market risks, Chinese engineering contractors should consider the following items.

First, contract terms should be made according to the specific circumstances of the project and the market environment of the host country. The prevention and resolution of market risks largely depends on the setting of the contract terms between the contractor and the employer. If at the initial stage of contract, the contractor can fully consider the various market risks that may arise and make the contract terms as complete as possible and strive for full maneuverability and enforceability, it will effectively reduce the probability of disputes. Or, when dispute occurs, contractual conditions can be used to protect the interests of Chinese contractors.[26]

Second, materials and equipment procurement should be flexible. In countries with low tariffs, if materials and equipment are unstable at local prices and stocks, direct purchases from foreign sources can be considered. For materials and equipment that cannot be imported from the parent country or can only be procured from local exclusive agents, it is advisable to transfer the risk to the local supplier when signing the contract. For the materials and equipment that have a large upward trend in market price, it is advisable to place order in advance and sign contract with fixed prices, and

---

25. Fei Su: "Project Risk and Control of International EPC Project", Yunnan Water Power, No. 6, 2015.
26. Xiangna He, "Implementation of the Project in the Sudan", International Project Contracting & Labour Service, March 2018.

it is better to have a performance bond to secure the obligation to deliver at the fixed prices.

Third, contractors should make reasonable purchasing plans. Here the first step is to decide, according to the characteristics of the project, what materials need to be used and what the arrival sequence of equipment is. The second step is to decide on the source of materials and equipment, i.e. to determine the location of material procurement based on the principle of low cost. If products are imported from China, it is also necessary to calculate the amount of tariffs, transportation fees, domestic export tax rebates, etc. Meanwhile, production and transportation time of materials and equipment should be comprehensively considered; the supply contracts should be signed in advance; and reasonable time for entering into the market should be agreed so that the site will be reasonably allocated, and storage costs will be reduced.

Finally, it is important to make reasonable and pragmatic calculations of the core data and conditions of the engineering project, such as cost, construction period, quality and technical standards and equipment and material parameters. This is the basis of effectively adapting to the market environment of the host country and ensuring the smooth implementation of the project.

From a legal point of view setting, the right contract terms for the project are certainly of utmost importance. This includes a choice of law clause as well as a dispute resolution clause. Lesser developed countries often also have less developed laws and courts. For that reason, many international investors seek to either impose their own law on courts or—more often—a neutral arbitration venue; especially when there is no bilateral recognition of court decisions, the parties have no other choice than to agree on arbitration. Under the New York Convention of 1958, which has 159 signatories, arbitral awards are enforceable practically all around the world. Agreeing on the law of a developed country can be in the interest of the investor, as it often contains statutory protections. Austrian law, for example, contains special regulations to minimize risk for (national as well as foreign) contractors. For example, section 1170b of the Austrian Civil Code entitles the contractor to claim a security of one-fifth of the contract value to protect its claim for payment.

If contractors fear delay when shipping materials or spare parts, it is advisable to include specific protection in the contract with their sub-suppliers, such as contractual penalties. At the same time, they should try to keep their own liability and contractual penalties as low as possible (a complete exclusion of liability is not possible in most legal systems). This might require good negotiation skills but can prove very valuable if disputes actually occur.

At the start of a new business relationship, parties are often overly excited and fail to pay sufficient attention to certain contract terms, such as liability and dispute resolution. Contractors might think that nothing will go wrong in any event, and even if something did go wrong disputes will surely be solved amicably. Sadly, this often turns out to be a misconception. Therefore, it is advisable to always prepare for the worst case and seek legal support already in an early phase, i.e. when drafting the contract. As several laws might apply (the law of the host country, of the home country and that of a third neutral venue), the legal consultation may be burdensome.

However, in most cases, the upfront investment is relatively minor in comparison to the significant costs which may arise in case of a dispute. Similarly, a detailed analysis of the market risk in the host country would likely be relatively minor in comparison to the significant costs which may arise in case of a dispute.

CHAPTER 2

Legal Environment in Host Countries

§2.01   WORK VISA

In order to protect local employment, host countries usually restrict foreign managers, professionals and workers who are not normally resident there ("foreign personnel") from entering and/or working thereby requiring work visas or work permits ("work visas") in respect of type of work, education, number, duration, etc. The time taken to obtain work visas is uncertain as this is determined by the laws of the host country and employment policies of state and local governments. If the work visas needed cannot be obtained in good time, the contractor cannot dispatch foreign personnel to the project at the time(s) required by the project schedule, and the project progress will be delayed.

[A]   Quota and Duration of Visa

To apply for a work visa, a contractor usually needs to comply with any quota imposed by the host country. The size of the quota and the type of work allowed to be carried out with the relevant work visa has to sufficiently satisfy the needs of the project. Usually the type of work for which the visa is sought must be urgently needed locally, and the foreign personnel applying for the visa must have relatively high professional or technical skills. The work cycle to obtain a visa is relatively long, and Chinese contractors need to plan in advance in order to comply with the project schedule.

For example, in a general contracting project for construction of a hotel in a Central Asian country, in order to obtain work visas for Chinese workers in accordance with local laws, the Chinese contractor had to comply with the following requirements: (a) the contractor first had to apply for sufficient amounts of work quota to the Ministry of the Interior. All workers introduced from abroad have to be urgently needed in that Central Asian country and must be highly skilled or to satisfy other special require-ments; (b) the workers introduced from abroad needs to have appropriate educational backgrounds and skills. Documents evidencing educational backgrounds and skills had to be obtained and double authenticated. Double authentication is a procedure to be completed before obtaining visas: Notarizations have to be obtained and submitted to the Ministry of Foreign Affairs of the People's Republic of China and the embassy of that Central Asian country in China for verification and authentication of the contents of the notarizations. This generally takes 15 working days; (c) All documents must be translated into Kazakh or Russian. If visas are needed for a large number of personnel, the translation will take about one month. In summary, the difficulties in obtaining work visas in the Central Asian country are: (1) the work quota is very limited and insufficient to satisfy the need for workers on construction sites; (2) in order to protect employment of nationals of that Central Asian country, its authorities will examine strictly the professional qualifications of foreign technical personnel. In particular, if the professional qualifications of foreign personnel do not match the openings for personnel on the project, or if that Central Asian country has technical personnel qualified in the same type of work, work visas will not be granted for the foreign personnel, and that Central Asian country strictly controls entry of personnel with professional qualifications of less than three years; (3) the cycle for obtaining work visas is generally four to six months. As a result, if Chinese personnel cannot arrive on site in good time, the construction progress on site will be affected.

For another example, in an African country, in order to protect local employment, governments impose increasingly stricter restrictions on import of labor services by Chinese contractors into the African country, and especially for personnel with low technical capabilities, who will face tough regulations on entry. Entry and visa administration issues have loomed large to become serious problems faced by Chinese contractors in Africa. As found by the "In-Depth Investigation on Project Contracting in Seven African Countries by Chinese Enterprises" published by China Council for the Promotion of International Trade, some African countries have strengthened controls over the entry of and visa administration for foreign personnel, which has constituted a very important obstacle for many foreign engineering companies. In other African countries, visas for Chinese workers are also difficult to obtain, which is regarded by some investigated enterprises as a bottleneck in development. In another African country, the expense for work visas increased to USD 2,000 per visa in 2015 and thus increased the enterprise costs. In summary, apart from some African countries where situations are better, regulations on visas in African countries are increasingly strict and this is unlikely to improve.[27]

In Europe, countries generally restrict the entry of Chinese workers by requiring work visas and specifying the maximum number of and requirements for foreign staff in contracts for the purpose of protecting local employment, labor conditions and interests of special professions. This results in failure to obtain entry of large numbers of Chinese workers or delay in obtaining work permits for them. Most Chinese

---

27. Excerpt from "In-Depth Investigation on Project Contracting in Seven African Countries by Chinese Enterprises" published by China Council for the Promotion of International Trade. Refer to http://www.ccpit.org/Contents/Channel_3430/2015/0921/489451/content_489451.htm on March 2, 2018.

contractors lack experience in managing subcontractors and teams in developed countries, and the Chinese way of managing workers does not operate well in European countries, which has adverse impact on the normal operation of projects.[28]

[B] Adverse Impact of International Politics on Obtaining Visa

To obtain work visas, applicants may need to avoid the adverse impact of international political relationships or political situations.

For example, a Chinese contractor in investment and construction in Southeast Asia faced difficulties in obtaining work visas for its engineering, procurement and construction (EPC) project because of tense international politics. The funds had been paid, and machinery had been imported, but technical and management personnel could not arrive at the site on time due to problems in obtaining work visas. In another project implemented by that contractor, technical personnel on key posts had to return to China upon expiration of their work visas, and such professionals were in short supply in the local market, so the project had to be suspended until key technical personnel obtained work visas again.

For another example, affected by changes in the political situation between China and a Southeast Asian country from 2013 to 2014, the Immigration Bureau of that country strengthened administration on visas and searched for and detained illegal workers on construction sites of Chinese contractors. As a counteraction to changes in the policies of the Immigration Bureau, a Chinese contractor applied for Special Working Permit (SWP), Alien Employment Permit (AEP), Special Resident Retiree's Visa (SRRV) and various other work permits to obtain corresponding types of visa for qualified personnel, established a good contact mechanism and relationship with the Chinese embassy in the host country and the embassy of that country in China and thus established an emergency countermeasure mechanism[29] to minimize the adverse impact of this crisis.

We suggest, first, that Chinese contractors overseas should strengthen the training of human resources, and recruit or train local skilled workers, to satisfy actual demands for workers of the project and/or of Chinese contractors. Second, Chinese contractors should take care to communicate and coordinate with the relevant government authorities of the host country, take different actions on different categories of issues and flexibly handle those issues when applying for work visas and link approval and implementation of the project with approval of work visas of the number and type

---

28. Excerpt from "Which Problems Will Chinese Enterprises Encounter in Contracting Projects in Middle and East Europe", written by Zhang Xiwei, Zhang Lihua and published in Journal of International Economic Cooperation, Issue No. 6, 2017.
29. Predict and Control Commercial Risks in International Engineering Projects, written by SHEN Weidong, assistant general manager of Shandong Electric Power Engineering Consulting Institute Corp., Ltd.; WANG Hua, manager of commerce department of Shandong Electric Power Engineering Consulting Institute Corp., Ltd., quote from China Investigation & Design, Issue No. 12, 2016, page 18.

required through coordination and interaction with the relevant government authorities. Third, Chinese contractors should also formulate in advance a contingency plan to avoid risks of difficulty in obtaining work visas as indicated in the example above.

[C]   Avoid Illegal Labor

Chinese contractors should not take part in any fraudulent or corrupt conduct in applying for work visas and should avoid employing illegal labor in host countries.

For example, a foreign enterprise investing in a Southern Asian country and undertaking international engineering projects had failed to obtain work permits for foreign employees and allowed them to work locally with only travel visas. The government of that country has now amended the law in the new Immigration Labor Law for foreign employees and employers of foreign employees such that for each illegal foreign worker employed by the employer, the employer will be fined THB 4,00,000 to THB 8,00,000 and the illegal foreign worker employed will face up to five years' imprisonment or fines of THB 2,000 to THB 1,00,000.

[D]   Other Certificates or Certifications

When granting work visas to foreigners, governments of some Middle East countries require the applicants to provide special certificates or certifications. For example, since February 4, 2018, the UAE government has required applicants for work visas in the UAE to provide an authenticated "Certificate of Good Conduct." This "Certificate of Good Conduct" is also referred to as Certificate of No Criminal Conviction, which is issued by the state of nationality of the applicant for work visa or the state in which the applicant has resided for the past five years. Upon issuance, the certificate will not become effective until it is authenticated by a UAE embassy abroad or the Authentication Center of Ministry of Foreign Affairs and International Cooperation.[30]

[E]   Prevention and Allocation of Risks Related to Work Visas

Since the abovementioned risks relating to work visas often cause delays in the construction period, Chinese contractors should conduct due diligence on the legal environment of the host country in advance and solicit help from professional institutions when necessary. So as to avoid misjudgment, this due diligence should factor in work visa processing time when calculating the project construction period. In some cases, due to political risks and other reasons, contractors encounter obstacles in obtaining work visas for their workers by themselves and must ask for the assistance of the employer. For those cases, the relevant obligations of the employer must be made clear in the contract.

---

30. *Quote from* www.dibaichina.com, website address as http://www.dibaichina.com/forum.php ?mod = viewthread&tid = 359323&highlight, visited on February 14, 2018.

In a relevant case provided by the International Court of Arbitration (ICC) for this research project, Chinese contractors contracted projects in a country that had not yet established diplomatic relations with China. The contractors, therefore, could only apply for work visas through third-country governments, which caused a great deal of inconvenience. Judging from the correspondence between the employer and the contractor, the contractor had always believed and expected that the employer would provide assistance with respect to the work visa situation. However, the contractor did not insist on memorializing this an obligation of the employer in the contract. On the contrary, the EPC contract between the parties clearly provided that the contractor was obliged to get work visa by itself.

During the course of performance of the contract, work visas and other issues caused delays in the construction period, and the employer filed an arbitration request to terminate the contract and made claims based against the Chinese contractor's liability for breach of contract. The Chinese contractor contended that the employer did not fulfill its obligation to assist with the work visa and that the difficulties in getting the visa were beyond its control which could not be attributed to the contractor.

According to the explicit provisions of the EPC contract, the arbitral tribunal determined that there was no obligation on the employer to assist in the visa application and that the absence of diplomatic relations between China and the host country preexisted the contract. This fact, therefore, could not be used as a defense by the contractor, and the tribunal found that the contractor breached the contract.

§2.02 CUSTOMS CLEARANCE

Delay in customs clearance of goods for overseas construction projects may cause demurrage, warehousing fees, and progress of the project on site may be delayed. In particular, delay of key equipment and facilities or materials will seriously prolong the construction period. To avoid delay in customs clearance, the following factors should be noted.

[A] Focus on Logistics and Customs Clearance in EPC Project Procurement

Logistics and customs clearance are two processes with the highest risks of delaying progress in procurement for overseas EPC projects since they are inherently uncertain and uncontrollable. We emphasize that the logistics and customs clearance cycle for most equipment and materials may well be longer than anticipated. The risks of delay in logistics are mainly caused by shipping schedules for transportation by sea, which are predictable but often uncontrollable. The risks of delay in customs clearance are caused mainly by two factors: first, complicated work procedures and inefficiency of customs authorities in the country where the project is located and into which goods are imported and second, the great variety of documents required for customs clearance. These two factors can be controlled through careful coordination and preparation in advance to mitigate the impact of work procedures and inefficiency and to improve control of progress. In overseas projects, contractors must take initiative to set aside enough scheduled and float time for procurement and consider risks in customs clearance in procurement, carefully formulate countermeasures, prepare for customs clearance and produce equipment and materials at the same time.[31] Particular care should be taken in obtaining and presenting documentation.

[B]   **Understand in Advance the Product Admittance Criteria of the Project Country**

At the time of customs clearance for imported project equipment and materials, some countries and regions request contractors to provide technical certificates and certificates certifying compliance with the technical standards specified in the contract.

For example, as regards the Russian Federation: (a) as a precondition for importation, all products need to have certification of satisfaction of Russian technical specifications, and such certification must be carried out by Russian institutions. In most cases, the certificates required by the Russian government for imported products are a Technical Passport and Permit to Use issued by Rostekhnadzor. For contractors, it is a heavy burden to obtain such certificates. If they are not arranged in advance, the project progress may be seriously delayed; (b) in addition, EPC contractors will be requested to engage local design institutes in Russia (Russian Design Institute, RDI) to implement certification for SRO (Self-regulating organization) permits,[32] and in carrying out certification, RDI will review and verify all design works for EPC projects. These impacts must be taken into consideration when assessing construction period and contract price. Also, it is critical to choose RDI capable in this field and experienced in cooperating with foreign contractors to avoid risks.[33]

Another example is Europe, where for many industrial projects the engineering equipment used in the project needs to have CE certification.[34] If the contractor does not understand the product admittance criteria, the equipment cannot pass customs clearance and the contractor will also be denied access to the European market. For example, in an EPC project for a thermal power station in Turkey contracted by a Chinese contractor, since the engineering equipment transported to Turkey had not

---

31. Considerations on Implementation of Overseas EPC Projects written by Liu Ying, Project Management Review, Issue November to December, 2015.
32. SRO is a self-regulating organization for construction projects. In accordance with Town Planning Code of Russia, the main obligations of contractors with respect to approval and permission for construction projects are joining "SRO" which satisfy project requirements and obtain corresponding qualification certificates.
33. Key Legal Risks in International Engineering Projects in Russia, written by Gregory Jones, a practicing lawyer in England and Wales and senior associate of Pinsent Masons LLP, London office; HU Yuanhang, senior associate of Pinsent Masons LLP, a practice lawyer in England and Wales and hold a Chinese lawyer's license. This article was published in Sailing Abroad Share SA Issue No. 33.
34. CE mark is a safety certification mark regarded as the passport for manufacturers to open and enter European market. CE stands for unity of Europe (CONFORMITE EUROPEENNE). Products with "CE" marks can be sold in Member States of EU and do not need to comply with requirements in each Member State, which realizes free circulation of commodities among Member States of EU.

obtained CE certification and could not pass customs clearance, the project progress was delayed and the cooperation between that contractor and the employer broke down. Not only all equipment was returned and the contractor subject to the employer's claim for monetary damages but also the contractor was blacklisted by EU customs, which made it more difficult for the contractor to expand into the European market.

[C] Check Whether Any Special Certificate Is Required

Some countries require special certificates for customs clearance of project materials of foreign contractors.

For example, due to restrictions in Russian laws, foreign contractors may encounter difficulties in customs clearance in Russia. The customs clearance of certain goods needs approval certificates, and in practice, these certificates can only be obtained by Russian legal entities. To avoid possible delay and expense in customs clearance, it is suggested that contractors provide in the contract that the employer shall be responsible for completing the customs clearance of all goods imported into Russia, paying all customs duty/fees and obtaining all certificates required for customs clearance.

For another example, in Southeast Asia, the customs law of some countries provides that all imported M&E equipment, tools and materials shall have a factory test report, certificate of approval, necessary quality certification and other documents. A Chinese contracting enterprise won the bid for an electrical engineering project in a country in Southeast Asia. When implementing the project, in addition to permanent equipment procured under subcontracts, the contracting enterprise produced many items of construction equipment, special tools and materials, but these products did not have factory test reports, certificates of approval or quality certification by designated institution. When the permanent equipment and construction equipment tools and materials arrived at the port of that country, the customs clearance could not be completed and the goods could not be released. Prior to the aforesaid reports being obtained and certification formalities being completed, all the equipment tools materials were held at the port, for which the contracting enterprise paid high demurrage fees and fines. Further, the construction period was seriously affected.[35]

[D] Try to Avoid Customs Clearance in Any Red Light Period

To export project materials to host countries, contractors should avoid customs clearance in any "red light period." For example, Indonesian customs are well known for strict control on customs clearance. However, generally speaking, December in each year to March in the next year is a particular "red light period" for customs

---

35. Excerpt from "Risks in Overseas Operation by Chinese Engineering Contractors—Analysis Based on Risk Cases", written by China Association of International Engineering Consultants. Please refer to http://caiec.mofcom.gov.cn/article/jingmaotongji/201705/20170502567422.shtml as of March 2, 2018.

clearance in Indonesia, during which Indonesian customs unite with other law enforcement authorities to strictly control importation and customs clearance. During this period, inspections are carried out more rigorously; more formalities have to be completed; and more time is taken, and higher expenses have to be paid if the formalities are not completed properly, for customs clearance. As such, in this red light period in Indonesia, many forwarding agencies dare not accept orders for goods transported there, Indonesian clients dare not place orders and foreign enterprises try to avoid customs clearance of goods.

§2.03   MARKET ACCESS

[A]   Qualifications

[1]   System for Obtaining a License for U.S. Contractors

In order to carry out construction activities in the U.S., enterprises must obtain the corresponding license, and contractors can only carry out construction activities to the extent permitted by the license. In most states in the U.S., the personnel involved in the construction management must have a license, and the conditions to obtain the license for the construction project vary from state to state. The respective conditions can be divided into two categories: individuals and enterprises. Individuals must have relevant proof of his/her education background, work experience and pass exams. Enterprises must take out general liability insurance and employee compensation insurance. Most states in the U.S. do not classify construction companies by different levels of qualifications for administrative purposes. Instead, construction companies are classified mainly on the basis of the size of the monetary amount insured by the insurance company. In the U.S., contractors are obliged to procure the issuance of performance bonds by local insurance companies. Construction companies can only bid to the extent of the amount of such performance bonds provided by the local insurance companies. The monetary amount which the local insurance company is willing to insure for the construction company is determined according to the performance of the construction company in local projects, while it is almost impossible for a construction company to forge its project performance or to attach their certificates to another construction company.

[2]   The Registration System for UK Project Contractor

Before taking on any subcontractors, all contractors must register with the Her Majesty's Revenue & Customs' (HMRC) Construction Industry Scheme (CIS), which applies to nonresident contractors in the same way as United Kingdom (UK)-based contractors. The scheme applies to a contractor who pays subcontractors for construction work they do in the UK or a subcontractor who gets paid by contractors for doing construction work in the UK. Under the scheme, contractors ensure that all their subcontractors are registered with HMRC and make appropriate tax deductions from payment to the subcontractors.

[3] System of License for Project Contractors in Japan

A construction license is required in accordance with the Construction Business Act in order to carry on a construction business in Japan, regardless of public or private works. However, a company is not necessarily required to register for a construction license if it carries out a business of only minor works. Minor works mean: (1) general building works less than JPY 15 million or wooden house construction with a total floor area less than 150 square meters; (2) other types of works less than JPY 5 million.

There are 30 classifications of construction works in Japan,[36] each of which represents a trade or field of the construction profession. A contractor must be licensed for each classification of work in which it intends to engage. It is possible to obtain at one time a license covering more than one classification of work, and there is no limit to the number of classifications that may be added to the original license.

In order to establish office(s) in only one prefecture, contractor needs to obtain a license issued by the Governor of municipal government. And where the contractor is to establish office in more than one prefecture, a license issued by Minister of Land, Infrastructure, Transport and Tourism (MLIT) is required. Both the MLIT and the Governor of municipal government have the authority to issue the abovementioned 28 categories of licenses.

There are two types of construction business licenses, the Specific Construction Business License and the Ordinary Construction Business License that may be issued for any of the 28 classifications of works. There are some additional requirements for the Specific Construction License in order to protect subcontractors. For example, if the price of the contract under which the construction company subcontracts to another contractor is higher than JPY 30 million, then specific license is a must.

To obtain a license, applicants are required to satisfy four "license requirements" defined by Article 7 of Construction Business Act, and not to fall under "disqualification requirements" defined by Article 8 of Construction Business Act.

The four license requirements are: (1) person responsible for management and operation. An applicant for a license must have an employee who has experience as a "responsible person for management and operation"; (2) full-time engineer attached to each office. An applicant must assign a full-time engineer attached to each office; (3) reliability. If fears for unlawful or unfaithful actions can clearly be presumed in the process of concluding a contract agreement or the execution of work, no one is eligible to operate construction business; (4) financial foundations, etc. A contractor must be

---

36. General Civil Engineering, General Building, Carpentry, Plastering, Scaffolding, Earthwork and Concrete, Masonry, Roofing, Electrical, Plumbing, Tile, Brick and Block, Steel Structure, Reinforcement Steel, Paving, Dredging, Sheet Metal, Glazing, Painting, Waterproofing, Interior Finishing, Machine and Equipment Installation, Heat Insulation, Telecommunication, Landscaping and Gardening, Well Drilling, Fittings, Water and Sewerage, Fire Protection Facilities, Sanitation Facilities.

equipped with sufficient financial foundations, etc. for contracting for the construction work that requires a license. Moreover, additional financial requirements should be satisfied to obtain a Specific Construction Business License. One of the reasons is that generally, contractors having a Specific Construction Business License carry out construction work by using many subcontractors.

A construction License is issued for a five-year period. A License must be renewed every five years within 30 days before the expiration date.

[B]   Admittance of Foreign Contractors

It is a common practice for countries to set admittance requirements for foreign contractors to enter the domestic construction market. The main purpose is to improve the management level of the domestic construction market and promote the development of construction technology. There are national characteristics to the market access system of different countries.

[1]   Kazakhstan Construction Market Access: Joint Venture System

In some countries, local laws require that foreign companies must establish joint ventures with local companies in order to participate in bids for major engineering projects in the respective country and enjoy corresponding preferential policies in that host country. By way of example, when foreign contractors participate in project bidding in Kazakhstan, given that they establish joint ventures with local companies, the joint ventures may enjoy 7.5% to 15% price preference. However, risks underlying the adoption of a joint venture structure to carry out cross-border cooperation also need to be taken into consideration. First, conflicts might arise between a foreign contractor and the local company in aspects of management philosophy, culture, language and communications. It takes a long time for the partners to finally get along. Moreover, the local companies may rely on their more convenient communication with their employers to demand more resources and more benefits. Second, shareholders of joint ventures may hold different views toward key control points in the project implementation process and thus diverging in decision-making. In addition, the members are more sensitive to changes in economic and political environment in the county where the project is located.

Therefore, foreign contractors should take measures to prevent the above risks in the selection of partners, bidding, negotiation of bids, signing and project implementation. Such as by establishing a standardized decision-making procedure, strengthening organizational capability of reviewing external contracts and striving for control status in the joint venture to ensure its voice being heard.

[2]   "Kazakh Content" System

Kazakhstan implements a "Kazakh content" system. However, until the adoption of the Law on Amendments to Some Legislative Acts on Kazakh Content, dated December

29, 2009 (unofficially called "Kazakh Content Law"), the term "Kazakh content" did not raise much attention since the Kazakh content provisions were essentially declaratory by nature. Kazakh Content Law expressly provides that the commodities, projects and services purchased from Kazakhstan shall reach a certain percentage in the procurement quantity of the whole project and specify the ratio of Kazakh employees to foreign employees among each level of executives.[37]

[3] Russian SRO System

In accordance with the Town Planning Code of Russia, if the works contracted by contractors (including foreign contractors) have impact on the safety of infrastructure, relevant works cannot be implemented until the contractor joins a corresponding (SRO) and obtain the qualification certificate issued by the relevant SRO. The code was amended on July 1, 2017, and the circumstances under which the contractors must join SRO and conditions for joining SRO were adjusted to some extent. When contractors (including foreign contractors) execute contracts with employers, supervisors and other entities on field investigation, design and construction of infrastructure projects, they cannot implement relevant works unless they join the corresponding SRO. At the same time, as the Federal Law No. 57-FZ on the "Procedure of Making Foreign Investments in Companies of Strategic Importance for National Defense and State Security" (which was enabled in April 2008 and known as the Strategic Investment Law) requires that foreign legal persons shall establish subsidiaries and branches when they operate in Russia. This is to say, in practice, SROs and Russian lawyers generally believe that before foreign contractors join the SRO, they shall first establish subsidiaries and branches in Russia.

In accordance with Russian laws, if the contractors have not joined the corresponding SRO before project's commencement, the employers will have the right to dissolve the contract and claim against the contractors for value-added tax that cannot be deducted and other losses; in which case, contractors and their senior executives may also face administrative or even criminal punishments. In practice, the claims against the contractors under these circumstances are usually supported by judicial authority. For example, in 2014 in a health-care facility expansion project in Novosibirsk contracted by a foreign contractor, the employer paid advance payment to the contractor as provided in the contract, but the contractor delayed in commencing the design works. When the employer found out the contractor did not possess design qualifications to undertake that project, it filed a lawsuit to the court claiming for termination of the contract and refund of the advance payment. The court supported the employer's claims.[38]

---

37. Encounter Legal Risks in Investment and Construction in that Central AsiaCentral Asian Country, written by Zhou Yueping, Meng Yi, Sun Yulun from Zhong Lun Law Firm, *quote from International Project Contracting Labor Services* as of April 20, 2016.
38. Excerpt from "Approval and Permission for Construction Project in Russia—Easy or Difficult? (for Contractors)", written by Tian Wenjing, Xu Yue, Ding Hongxu, *Vladislav Zinovyev, quote*

[C]   Admittance of Individuals

Countries around the world will set certain thresholds and conditions for foreign labor to enter the domestic market, in order to prevent loss of employment opportunities in the country. Generally speaking, thresholds for highly substitutable and low-tech related jobs are relatively higher than technology-intensive and insubstitutable jobs.

[1]   *License System in the U.S.*

In the U.S. construction market, managers of construction companies must have a license for an architect, engineer and contractor. Acquiring a license in one state does not necessarily enable the contractor to carry out construction activities in other states. In different states, the conditions for obtaining construction vary, but those conditions can be divided into two types: For the individual, he/she must have relevant proof of educational background and work experience and pass examinations; for the enterprise, it must provide certificate for taking out general liability insurance and worker's compensation insurance.

[2]   *Review Engineer System in Germany*

German government generally does not oversee project implementation and has no supervision system. Instead, the supervision is executed by government-approved supervision institutions, certification institutions, testing institutions or recognized review engineers. In addition, the government does not administer the qualifications of design institutions, consultancy companies and construction companies and the policies to access the market are easy and do not set any barrier. Any individual qualified for practice can establish a company to do business. However, the government entrusts associations to strictly certify qualifications of architects and engineers and administer their registration for practice to protect public interests and safety of buildings.

Review engineers are senior professionals recognized by the government: Not only they are required to have over 10 years work experience in structural design (with at least one year on-site work experience) but also they may not be employed by or have economic interests in any company. In addition, they must maintain a lack of criminal conviction and must obtain approval from the construction authority in state government. From a statistical point of view, Germany has a combination of 800 review engineers, including structural experts and professors in universities and colleges specialized in the field of engineering structure and structural mechanics who usually hold qualifications for practice as review engineers.

Germany places great emphasis on safety of engineering structure and requires under law that construction entities shall organize professional reviews on safety,

from *Blog of Research Institute of King & Wood Mallesons*, http://blog.sina.com.cn/s/blog_8f3 0351d0102wr2i.html on May 12, 2018.

stability and environmental friendliness of structure in project design. Review engineers are core to the whole technical review, who may veto the project design due to lack of structural safety. Without consent from review engineers, the approval for construction commencement cannot be obtained. Even the design made by one review engineer must be reviewed by another review engineer. But with respect to consulting engineer, the German government has no system for practice qualifications. Once a consulting engineer has graduated from college and has certain work experience, he/she may join relevant professional associations or societies, becomes a member and is qualified for providing engineering consultancy.

[3]   *Work Permit System in Kazakhstan*

It is provided in Kazakh laws that foreign citizens entering Kazakhstan to work must obtain work permits. Kazakhstan's government determines the quota for work permits to be issued to foreign employees according to the local human resource conditions. In 2008, Kazakhstan placed education, work experience and professional skills requirements on foreign workers to enter the country. However, significant investment projects signed by a legal person in Kazakhstan, relevant general contractor, subcontractor and the third party providing relevant services are not subject to quota for work permits, nor will they be subject to restrictions on application for work permits for foreign employees. The only requirement is the number and profession of foreign employees shall be expressly specified in the project investment contract. There is no prohibition against the foreign employees being the only persons in charge of the enterprise, or experts, or senior technical staff.

[4]   *Work Permit System in Thailand*

On March 6, 2018, the Thai cabinet approved the drafted amendments to the Royal Ordinance on the Management of Foreign Workers Employment B.E. 2560 (2017). The new revision aimed to facilitate better control and monitoring of the process of bringing foreign workers into Thailand, the working conditions of foreign workers and the process of obtaining jobs in Thailand, as well as adjust the terms of punishment of offenders to be in line with human rights obligations.

The new revision emphasizes the use of notification system where appropriate, instead of the permission system. This revision encompasses changes of employers, workplaces, types of work and the hiring of documented foreign workers, without having to request for permissions from the authority concerned, which is facilitative to both the employers and employees. Apart from this, the drafted amendments also remove restrictions on the accommodation zoning of foreign workers.

On the same occasion, the cabinet also approved drafted amendments to the Immigration Act, B.E. 2522 (1979) to allow foreign workers to work as laborers or to be hired to do physical work and unskilled work.

[D]   Risks in Commercial Registration

For foreign contractors entering the market of a host country, the first thing that needs to be considered is commercial registration, which breaks down into the means of entrance, the form of business entity to adopt and other key points to consider during the registration procedure. In order to establish commercial entities in host countries, the enterprises have to comply with local laws and regulations and special require-ments of employers and contractors. To avoid risks in commercial registration, the following factors should be prioritized.

[1]   *Risks Factors to Be Considered When Choosing the Form of Commercial Entity*

Choosing the suitable model to access the market is one of the key factors in deciding whether the international operation of construction contractors will succeed. The models for foreign contractors to access the market of a host country generally include: winning in bidding for international construction projects, establishing representative offices, branches, wholly owned subsidiaries or joint ventures or **acquiring** construc-tion enterprises in the host country. When choosing to access the construction market of a host country, we shall consider the following factors:

(1) The size of the target market and strategic positioning. If the market is large with promising prospect, it can be nurtured as a potential strategic market of the company. When we enter the market, we shall think and invest strategi-cally and choose to register the permanent establishment in the host country by all means.

(2) The market operation and satisfaction of demands in the bidding process. For example, some host countries may request foreign contractors to operate in the name of their parent companies. Consequently, the contractors may choose to register representative offices or branches in those host countries or choose to register subsidiaries for the convenience of visa application for employees or influx of funds. If some host countries make it compulsory for companies to register subsidiaries but request them to bid in the name of parent companies, it will cause both the subsidiary and the parent company of contractors to exist in one project. The contractors shall keep the accounts separated to avoid both increase in tax that may be caused from confusion in accounting and the risk that shareholders may undertake unlimited liability. For example, a Chinese contractor contracted a hotel project as a general contractor in Kazakhstan. In accordance with laws of Kazakhstan, before foreign contractors carry out construction activities including temporary construction works in Kazakhstan, they must register an entity locally and apply for certification of their construction qualification and obtain a con-struction permit in the name of that entity. In order to commence construction as soon as possible, the company transferred its wholly owned subsidiary

registered in Almaty to Astana and then established a branch of that wholly owned subsidiary in Astana. In so doing, a certificate of construction qualification and construction permit could be obtained in the name of that wholly owned subsidiary or the Astana branch of that subsidiary. In addition, the parent company would issue a power of attorney to entrust the management of the project and performance of contract to the entity concerned. The investors objected to this arrangement on the basis that the Chinese contractor had sought to unilaterally novate the contract to the entity concerned. In the end, the Chinese contractor had to register a representative office in Astana and obtained contraction qualification, tax registration certificate and construction permit in the name of that representative office. This delayed the commencement of the project and delayed the construction of the foundation slab until winter, as such, increased difficulties and costs in construction.[39]

(3) Tax planning. Different corporate forms assume the tax burden in a wide variety of ways. At present, the income tax collection of a partnership enterprise usually takes the approach of first distributing the profit to the partners and then having the partners pay income tax in the partners' individual names. This avoids a situation where the shareholders still have to pay tax when the company has already paid the tax under the company model, or double taxation of personal income. However, in some countries such as the U.S., where certain conditions are satisfied, some types of companies may calculate and pay income tax as partnerships. As another example, in Indonesia, PT is the short form of Perseroam Terbatas, which means "limited company" and is usually used in the name of local companies or used in the name of joint ventures where the equity is shared by local persons or companies and the joint venture operates at scale while BUT means "office," which is the branch office registered by foreigners locally and not qualified as legal persons. As provided in Indonesian tax laws, for year-end tax returns, PT shall calculate and pay income tax at 3% tax rate, whereas BUT needs to return the operating profits to its parent company in addition to paying 4% income tax, and it is required to pay 10% of after-tax profits as departure tax. In respect to income tax only, the tax burden for PT is 1% less than that for BUT. Hence, the level of tax burden for foreign contractors operating in Indonesia is directly determined by the form of entities registered in that host country.[40]

(4) Consideration on limitation of liability of parent company. If the enterprise operates in the name of its subsidiary in the host country, it shall undertake limited liability to the extent of all properties of the subsidiary. If the business of the local subsidiary is not good or it is liable for material breach, the parent company will not be directly implicated, but when undertaking construction projects, the subsidiary may be restricted with respect to its qualifications,

---

39. A Guide on Management of Overseas Legal Risks, 2013 Version published by China State Construction Engineering Corporation, p. 59.
40. *Ibid.*, p. 58.

credit, performance bond, financing, control of foreign exchange and other factors.

(5) Limitation on the number of companies to be set up by foreign companies. There is an unwritten rule within the Abu Dhabi government of the UAE that the same foreign company may not register two companies in Abu Dhabi for the same or similar business, in order to prevent different entities from evading economic legal liability and engaging in unfair competition. For example, a Chinese contractor entered the oil and gas construction market in Abu Dhabi, registered a subsidiary in Abu Dhabi and applied to the Abu Dhabi Supreme Petroleum Commission for the qualifications for construction of oil and gas construction projects. However, since a Middle East company affiliated to the contractor has registered a branch in Abu Dhabi, according to the abovementioned Abu Dhabi internal regulations, the company is not allowed to register a second one. Therefore, to enter the overseas construction market, it is necessary to know the local laws and practices regarding the establishment of branches to ensure the body to be registered is a legal entity.

[2]   Procedural Risks in Completing Entity Registration in Host Country

Commercial registration in host country is not complicated, and the procedures of entity registration in various countries are very much the same. Documents that ought to be provided include the articles of association or articles of incorporation or board resolutions of the parent company. However, in some developing countries, whether the local procedure of commercial registration has been completed by foreign contractors may determine the effectiveness of the general contract executed with that contractor. For example, dispute over whether the project general construction contract executed with a foreign contractor is effective arose due to failure of that contractor in completing commercial registration in Tanzania. It is provided in contractor Registration Act, 1997 in Tanzania that unless an individual or company has registered with the registration committee and obtained effective registration certificates, it shall not carry out and complete any construction works. After entering the Tanzanian construction market, the foreign contractor started to handle the registration of representative office. However, it only paid the registration fee and did not submit the application for registration with the Tanzania Registration Committee. In international arbitration proceedings, the employer insisted the contract was void *ab initio* on the ground of such failure to submit the application for registration:[41]

(1) Requirements on the number of shareholders. The laws of some host countries provide that to register a company locally, foreign contractors need several shareholders. For example, laws of Algeria require that to register SPA

---

41. *Ibid.*, p. 60.

(joint-stock company) locally companies will need seven or more shareholders. This requires foreign contractors to plan for investors or shareholders of their local company before registration of the same to ensure compliance with local laws.

(2) Requirement on the nationality of shareholders. It is provided in the laws of some host countries that a local company to be established must be controlled or shared by natural or legal persons of the host country. For example, under the new UAE Commercial Companies Law (Federal Law No. 2 of 2015) ("CCL"), to establish a company in the UAE (except for the Free Zone), percentage of foreign shareholding shall not be higher than 49% of total share capital and the remaining 51% must be held by nationals of the UAE or legal persons wholly owned by nationals of the UAE ("Local Guarantors"). Although foreign investors may hold 100% of equity interests in the companies established in the Free Zone, the scope of business that can be operated by such companies is restricted. For example, companies established in the Free Zone may engage in consultancy, catering, supermarket and other businesses, but they cannot obtain the qualifications for operating construction business. To satisfy the foregoing compulsory provisions in the CCL and at the same time realize control over 100% equity in the company, foreign companies entrust Local Guarantors to hold the shares.[42]

(3) Difference in type of company. For example, to undertake construction projects in Singapore, companies may choose to register as local companies or local branches of foreign companies. In Singapore, if a foreign contractor wishes to register as a local company, it needs to have at least one local resident above the age of 21 as its director. Local residents include citizens of Singapore, permanent residents and holders of valid pass for residency. The applicants may apply with Work Pass Division of Ministry of Manpower (MOM) for a relevant valid pass for residency. If a contractor intends to register a local branch of foreign company, it needs to designate two local residents as its agents to operate its daily business. The definition of local residents and relevant conditions for application are the same as above. If a contractor chooses not to rely on any professionals (or institutions) and register a local company on its own, all directors and secretary of such company must be citizens or permanent residents of Singapore.[43]

§2.04 CONTROL OF FOREIGN EXCHANGE

In order to prevent the outflow of limited foreign exchange, maintain balance of international payments and guarantee independent development of national economy,

---

42. *Ibid.*, p. 62.
43. Excerpt from "Features of Project Contracting Market in Singapore on Going Global Public Service Platform of Ministry of Commerce". Please refer to http://fec.mofcom.gov.cn/article/ ywzn/xgzx/zlyj/201511/20151101181900.shtml as of March 2, 2018.

the government of the host country generally has control over foreign exchanges. The contents and means of foreign exchange controls management include control of export proceeds; control of payments in import trade; control of inflow and outflow of capital; control of nontrade foreign exchange payments; and control of inflow and outflow of gold and cash. The following risks exist in control of foreign exchange: (1) liquidity risk. The funds cannot be remitted to foreign countries, and transfer of funds is also restricted locally on many aspects; (2) risk in fluctuations of exchange rate. In the case of specific currency, enterprises must review the history of its exchange rate to see whether it is stable. If it is unstable, to exchange USD into local currency may cause certain risks in currency devaluation; (3) risk in fluctuations of foreign exchange policies; (4) the foreign exchange policies in different countries vary greatly. This is especially so for countries implementing partial exchange controls which have particularly special foreign exchange policies.[44]

[A]   Compliance with the Laws of the Host Country

Attempting to transfer foreign exchanges by conducting the exchanges alone in person does not solve the problem of transfer of large amounts of capital due to limited amounts of foreign exchanges which can be carried about and possible confiscation by customs of the foreign exchanges—in this regard, the carrier may even be punished with imprisonment. For example, in accordance with Algerian customs laws and foreign exchange administration regulations, at the time of departure, foreigners may carry cash in local currency in the amount up to DZD 3,000. At the time of entry, the amount of cash in foreign currency and traveler's check that can be carried is unlimited but it needs to be declared to the customs. At the time of departure, the aforesaid declared cash and checks can be taken to exit the country, and for foreign exchanges consumed locally, currency exchange certificate issued by foreign exchange banks that is authorized by Algerian government and relevant receipts for consumption shall be provided. The maximum amount of declared cash in foreign currency that can be carried by residents at the time of departure is EUR 7,600 per person. If anyone violates the foregoing provisions, and takes large amounts of foreign exchanges or cash in local currency at the time of departure without declaration, once discovered, not only the foreign exchange or cash in local currency will be entirely confiscated but also the offender will be subject to high amount of fines and in some serious cases be detained or sentenced to jail. As another example, an executive of the company of a Chinese contractor in Algeria took a large amount of cash in local currency at the time of departure and was discovered by airport customs, and the customs entirely confiscated the cash he took in the amount equivalent to several hundred thousand Dinar and imposed a fine. Afterward, the local court sentenced the executive in the first instance

---

44. Excerpt from "The 'Belt and Road' and Legal Risks Faced by Chinese Enterprises Investing Overseas and Prevention Measures", Gulf Information Website: Please refer to http://www. gulfinfo.cn/info/show-6812.shtml as of March 2, 2018.

to one-year imprisonment, confiscated the carried cash and issued a fine of twice the amount of the cash carried.[45]

[B] Try to Obtain an Appropriate Proportion of Transferrable Contract Amount at the Time of Execution of Contract

The transferrable contract amount can prevent foreign exchange control risks. However, this does not mean the more the transferrable portion in the contract amount, the better as this has to be subject to considerations of the business needs. If an overseas Chinese contractor wants to transfer foreign exchange by increasing the fee quote by purchasing equipment and materials from the home country, it is necessary to estimate the difference between the increased customs duty and the profit tax saved and generally evaluate whether the corporate tax burden will be reduced overall.

[C] Be Prudent When Considering African Projects

Some African countries have strict management over foreign exchange remittance, complicated procedures and special requirements. In practice, since the economic bases of African countries are mostly fragile and the infrastructure is very poor, most of the currencies are soft coins that are easy to depreciate, the industry is underdeveloped and the relevant industrial chains are incomplete or even missing. This brings many problems to contracting enterprises. For example, the exchange rate of Ethiopian Currency Birr to U.S. dollar dropped to 1:13 from 1:9 in the financial crisis. Further, Ethiopia's foreign exchange reserves are very scarce, the management over foreign exchange remittance is rather strict and the procedures thereof are complicated; therefore, corporate financial risks are quite huge. In Tanzania, when converting U.S. dollar to Tanzanian shilling, U.S. dollars printed after 2006 need to be provided; otherwise it will not be converted.[46]

[D] Pay Special Attention to the Countries Sanctioned by the U.S.

Countries subject to U.S. sanctions are stricter with foreign exchange control. For example, at the end of 2014, given sharp drop in foreign exchange earnings resulting from the fall in oil prices and the massive capital flight caused by Western sanctions, Russian foreign exchange reserves faced tremendous pressure and Russia was forced to adopt de facto exchange restrictions. Chinese contractors in Russia experienced

---

45. A Guide on Management of Overseas Legal Risks, 2013 Version published by China State Construction Engineering Corporation, p. 31.
46. Excerpt from "In-Depth Survey of Chinese Enterprises' Project Contracting in Seven African Countries", China Council for the Promotion of International Trade, *see* http://www.ccpit.org /Contents/Channel_3430/2015/0921/489451/content_489451.htm, visited on March 2, 2018.

varying difficulties in currency exchange and repatriation, and investors in the trade and retail sectors were particularly affected.[47]

§2.05   TAXATION SYSTEM

[A]   Double Taxation Treaties

[1]   Implementation of Double Taxation Treaties

Some host governments fail to strictly implement the double tax treaties executed with China. For instance, a taxation authority of a host country ignores the tax treaty signed with China and imposes a high withholding tax on the income of dividends and royalties remitted by a Chinese contractor in accordance with the laws of that country.

[2]   Difference in the Judgment of the Nature of Income or Source of Income

There are often differences between the host country's tax authorities and foreign companies in determining the nature of income or the source of income, for example the determination of the source of labor income, the division of the domestic part and the overseas part. Such disputes often occur between businesses and local tax authorities.

[3]   Tax Discrimination

Foreign contractors are often subject to tax discrimination in the host countries. In terms of tax treatment, some host countries may make a difference between their own resident enterprises and the nonresident companies and impose discriminatory treatment on the nonresident companies. For example, if a Chinese contractor has a permanent establishment in a host country, it needs to pay the income tax on its operating revenue according to a certain approved profit rate. The local tax authority sets a higher approved profit rate for the Chinese contractor than the approved profit rate applicable to its domestic resident enterprises engaged in the same industry and undertaking similar business projects.

[4]   Designation of a "Permanent Establishment"

Domestic laws of host countries sometimes are very strict with the designation of "permanent establishment" of foreign contractors. Among Chinese contractors in expanding overseas markets, those engaged in construction projects or providing labor

---

47. Excerpt from "Report Digest | Blue Book on Foreign Investment and Risk: China's Foreign Direct Investment and National Risk Report (2017)", Social Science Literature Publishing House, *see* http://www.ssap.com.cn/c/2017-04-12/1053144.shtml, visited on March 2, 2018.

services account for a considerable proportion. Therefore, the designation of permanent establishment has become a key factor in the taxation impact on these going-global enterprises. When tax treaties are not strictly implemented, laws of some host countries have their own definitions of a "permanent establishment," which are often more stringent than those of the Organisation for Economic Co-operation and Development (OECD) model or common tax treaties for a permanent establishment, under which Chinese overseas contractors are easily to be treated as "permanent establishment."

[5] Collection of Engineering Equipment Income Tax

Most countries, including China, usually impose import duties and value-added tax on the imported equipment as part of the trade of goods. However, some other countries withhold and require payment of withholding income tax on the technology transfer of equipment, especially the high-tech equipment, or collect tax by treating all of the price of the equipment as the profits of the permanent establishment. These practices are not consistent with international practices. Without the approval of the Chinese tax authorities, the income tax paid by the "going-global" enterprises overseas for export equipment cannot be offset in China, resulting in double taxation.

[6] Denial of Global Transfer Pricing Policy

In general, "going-global" companies have multinational businesses or global businesses. Most multinational companies formulate global transfer pricing policies so that companies can allocate resources within the group to ensure the efficiency of the overall operation. However, tax authorities of some countries do not recognize the global transfer pricing policy of companies and also impose unusual and special requirements on the transfer pricing policies of local group companies. This often becomes the focus of disputes between Chinese contractors and tax authorities of host countries.

[B] Stability of Taxation Regime

Tax laws and regulations of host countries change frequently, which brings significant risks to the expansion of foreign construction enterprises' overseas markets, especially in countries which are in a period of economic change such that the tax policies are especially volatile. Change and update of tax policy occur fast, and the information transmission channel is not smooth enough. This makes it difficult for taxpayers to accurately learn the current regulations in time, which may result in taxpayers' misunderstanding of the new policies and failure to ensure timely follow-up such that the tax payments become illegal. These are tax risks which should be kept in mind. As such, foreign investors should pay close attention to the changes in tax laws and regulations of host countries to minimize the risk of losses due to changes in tax laws.

[1]   Tax Laws in Central Asian Countries

Given that some Central Asian countries are in a transitional period, the taxation legal systems are not sound, the taxation environment is complex and tax law enforcement is not standardized. During a period of social transformation in Central Asia, the system is not perfect: The legal system is not sound; law enforcement is not standardized; policy intervention is more random; economic transparency is relatively low; and the binding documents related to international cooperation and development are not robust. There are still many obstacles and problems in infrastructure, investment environment, financial services and government management. When solving specific problems, Central Asian countries often use the "presidential order" or cabinet regulations to adjust and regulate the economic activities of foreign-invested enterprises in their countries. Since policies are changeable and law enforcement is arbitrary, it is difficult for enterprises to determine whether the tax planning activities carried out are within the scope permitted by local laws. It is impossible to distinguish whether the conduct of enterprises is attributable to tax planning or illegal tax evasion, and therefore corporate tax planning faces various risks.

The tax environment in Central Asian countries is very complicated, and the tax laws are updated frequently. The fiscal policies and taxation are not separated, the tax burden is heavy and the types and items of tax regulations related to enterprises are numerous. For example, the tax law of a Central Asian country has been revised 12 times since 2005. Tax burden has been increased after each revision. The comprehensive rate of various taxes is relatively high, the calculation of tax is complicated and heavy taxation is imposed on profits. In addition to normal taxes, there are many additional apportions, sponsorships, donations, etc. imposed.

The complexity of the tax system increases the likelihood that tax authorities will abuse their power. Tax collection departments are complex, tax collection and management is strict and each invoice needs to be inspected. Banks, customs, statistics bureaus and other departments can conduct tax supervision on enterprises. Tax administration is also very complicated, and tax laws and tax regulations are constantly updated. In some Central Asian countries, the tax policy is rather arbitrary. In order to enrich the fiscal revenue with tax revenue, these countries often impose various additional taxes, which becomes payable as a matter of convention. Tax payment planning in Central Asian countries is difficult, and the legitimacy of tax planning needs to be confirmed by the tax authority of the country where the enterprise resides.[48]

[2]   Tax Laws in African Countries

Tax systems of some African countries are also unstable and the tax burden is increasing. In an African country, noncompliance with tax law is common. The court's

---

48. Excerpt from the "Tax Planning for EPC Engineering Enterprises' Operation in Central Asia", Author: Xiao Feng, see chinaacc.com, http://www.e521.com/sssw/nsch/410722.shtml, visited on March 2, 2018.

judgment procedure is complicated and greatly affected by extra-case factors. Preferential measures that have been promised are often not honored. Some tax bureau staff even require enterprises to give a certain amount of rebates. In an African country, given government corruption and inefficient work, issues are often not handled within the time frame stipulated by the government for the handling of those issues and the requirements imposed on foreign companies are particularly strict. In some other African countries, the political and economic environment is very unstable and taxes are increasing. Companies are often faced with inspections by various government authorities, but the procedures for inspection are often incomplete, the process is not transparent and tips are often requested. For example in the African country, the tax authorities previously canceled the tax reduction and exemption policy of tariffs on certain imported goods and prepaid income tax in July 2013 and added an infrastructure construction tax of 1.5% on all imported goods.[49]

[3] Tax Laws in South Asian Countries

The domestic legal status of South Asian countries is also not optimistic. As an example, one South Asian country which has a taxation system formed only a short while ago has many types of taxes, frequent changes to laws and regulations, and the content of such laws and regulations is not rigorous. Further, the interpretation of laws and regulations may also be inconsistent. Therefore, foreign contractors need to pay close attention to the dynamics of their tax policies when investing or conducting business in these countries, so as to avoid unnecessary losses resulting from the failure to make timely adjustments to their own business strategies due to changes in tax law.

[4] Tax Discrimination

Foreign companies are subject to tax discrimination or unfair treatment by host countries, resulting in failing to enjoy the tax benefits that they should enjoy in accordance with the law. China has signed bilateral or multilateral tax treaties with 54 countries along the "One Belt, One Road" route. However, the tax collection and management systems and taxation environments vary widely; for instance, the implementation of local tax collection and management and taxation treaties, methods of tax dispute resolution and the channels of communication with tax officials are intermingled with many noninstitutional factors, posing great uncertainty to foreign companies.

---

49. Excerpt from "In-Depth Survey of Chinese Enterprises' Project Contracting in Seven African Countries", China Council for the Promotion of International Trade, *see* http://www.ccpit.org /Contents/Channel_3430/2015/0921/489451/content_489451.htm, visited on March 2, 2018.

[5]   New Risks from BEPS Action Plan

Countries around the world actively respond to the BEPS (Base Erosion and Profit Shifting) action plan, update anti-tax avoidance regulations and continuously strengthen cross-border tax management and measures, which has become a new risk for foreign investors in the host countries. For example, in the process of investing abroad by foreign companies, countries (regions) such as Hong Kong, Singapore and Luxembourg are usually selected as the location where the intermediate holding company resides in order to fully enjoy the policies of these countries (regions) that do not levy or impose relatively low-income tax on the passive income that meets conditions. However, notwithstanding that Central Asian country tax authorities have listed Hong Kong on a "blacklist" of tax havens, foreign companies still set up companies in Hong Kong or Luxembourg based on the old method. According to that Central Asian country's current tax laws, if a foreign nonresident, as an intermediate holding platform for holding that Central Asian country's investment, transfers its shares (equity) in that Central Asian country company, the capital gains obtained must be subject to a 15% withholding tax in that Central Asian country. However, a 20% tax rate applies to the capital gains obtained through companies established in tax haven countries or regions (such as Hong Kong), which has the effect that foreign companies will bear additional tax costs.

§2.06   ADMINISTRATIVE PERMIT

[A]   Obtaining Construction Permits

In the international engineering practice, it is necessary to obtain the construction permit to be issued by the competent government authority of the host government before the commencement of construction. If the construction is commenced without the construction permit, the project will be exposed to the risk of being illegal. The government may impose fines and order the work stoppage. Serious violations of the law may result in criminal liability.

Although it is usually the responsibility of the employer to obtain the approval documents required for the commencement of construction, if the contractor enters the site for construction before the employer obtains the construction permit, the contractor may face legal obstacles and bear legal liabilities. Once subject to the punishment imposed by the government authority of host countries, neither the contractor nor the employer can absolve itself from the blame. In many international investment projects, after the initial investor obtains the permission for development of the project, it often needs to establish a joint venture company as a project company with other powerful foreign investors and influential local partners of a host country. Before the construction of the project starts, the legal requirements are met only if all kinds of licenses required for construction are held by the project company. However, for some reason, the project often "jumps the gun" when the construction permit has not been processed or transferred to the project company such that serious violations of the applicable law could result. For example, in the EPC general contracting project of a coal-fired power station in the Philippines, the plant unit of the project was constructed by phase. During the construction of the second phase, the major problem of the first-phase project that had not been approved by the Environment Impact Assessment (EIA) was exposed. The Philippine environmental protection authority immediately ordered the project to stop working after it found the issue, resulting in a passive situation for both the employer and the Chinese contractor, and the Chinese contractor was faced with a significant risk that the paid project funds could not be recovered.

[B]   Confirm the Requirements of the Project Entity as Soon as Possible

For projects that need to establish a joint venture with local partners or other investors as the project development vehicle, the content of the joint venture agreement should be agreed upon as early as possible prior to the execution of the project development agreement or sales agreement. This enables the project company to be established as the subscriber of the loan agreement and permits the project company to obtain various licenses for the projects in its name.

  If the various licenses of the project are held by the initial investor, before the execution of the joint venture agreement, sufficient due diligence shall be conducted on whether the initial investor legally holds all of the licenses and approvals required for the project development and construction so as to know whether the licenses and approvals can be transferred to the project company. Some licenses also need to obtain transfer approval from the local government authorities to avoid delays in financing due to the inability to obtain the required licenses and approvals for the project on time. For example, in a large thermal power project in Bangladesh in South Asia, Chinese investors originally planned to set up two project companies as the executor of the two power station projects respectively, and as the signing party of the power purchase agreement and execution agreement respectively. Upon execution of the agreement, the two project companies merged into one project company, and the merged project company was the executor of the two power station projects. Although the merger of the project company was approved by the Bangladesh Power Development Board (BPDB) and other government authorities, it was delayed and so the approval documents such as the EIA approval which needed to be transferred to the merged project company, within nine-month period stipulated in the power purchase agreement and execution agreement, was not adhered to and led to failure to start commercial operation as planned. Investors are at risk of termination of the agreement.

§2.07   LABOR ISSUES

Labor issues encountered by foreign enterprises in host countries mainly occur at three points, namely, the establishment of employment relationship, the continuation of the employment relationship and the dissolution of employment relationship. Labor disputes often occur in the process of the continuation of the employment relationship and the dissolution of employment relationship, such as strike, trade union movement and disputes arising from revocation of labor contract, and the cost of solving such problems is usually high. When establishing employment relationship concerning foreign affairs, foreign companies should fully evaluate and control the legal risks, which can minimize the probability of serious labor disputes during the continuation of employment relationship and the termination of employment relationship. From this point of view, before investing abroad, Chinese contractors should conduct detailed legal due diligence on the employment legal system, employment environment and employment legal risks of the host country and form a comprehensive and sufficient understanding of the labor risk of the host country and conduct risk control and preventive work.

[A]   Labor Issues Vary from Region to Region

Labor issues vary across regions. For instance, the labor issues encountered by foreign companies in Asian and African countries are mainly large-scale strikes and demonstrations, work-related injury compensation disputes, employment environment and poor labor health conditions. In developed countries like Europe and Australia, foreign companies are often faced with difficult trade unions, difficult access to visas, employee benefits and welfare disputes and the brain drain of senior executives and high-tech talents. A great number of Chinese contractors have suffered losses due to various labor issues in the process of foreign development. For example, a Chinese contractor failed in a Peruvian iron ore M&A project due to frequent strikes in Peru while the other Chinese contractor solved the labor disputes with the powerful local labor union at the cost of huge compensation. In the case of M&A between a Chinese company and a French company, the Chinese company's and the French company's management and technical staff had great differences in corporate culture and management methods, resulting in frequent brain drain and labor disputes. Therefore, enterprises should develop different preventive measures for labor issues based on different investment environments in the process of foreign investment.

[B]   Risk of Employment Relationship Termination

In some countries, protection of domestic workers by law is complete, strict and highly enforceable, which increases the construction costs of foreign contractors and increases the cost of foreign contractors in terminating employment relationship with local labor. For example, Indonesia has a very comprehensive labor law and is highly enforceable. Supported by this law, the local staff is very aggressive. Key precautionary considerations include the following: Fixed overtime pay can be arranged for specific positions, settled on a monthly basis, and included in salary. The corporate system plays an important role in the process of dissolution of the employment relationship. The finer the preparation of company system, the more standardized its implementation. For those who plan to have a long-term development in Indonesia, in order to increase the sense of belonging of employees, it is recommended that employers retain talents in accordance with the labor law and develop a detailed corporate system to take the initiative. The corporate system should be prepared in accordance with the requirements of the Indonesian Labor Law and be followed upon submission to the Indonesian Ministry of Labor for filing. The more detailed the preparation of the corporate system, the more standardized its implementation, provided that the company's system standards should not be lower than the current labor law standards. The corporate system can be more detailed on the basis of the labor law and more favorable to be executed. For a collective contract executed between the employer and the trade union, the collective contract is of the same effect as the corporate system. The corporate system plays an important role in the process of dissolution of the employment relationship and is also the basis for termination of the employment relationship in accordance with laws and regulations. For employees who meet the conditions for termination of employment relationship, specific matters and procedures can be identified in the corporate system.[50]

[C]   Risk of Labor Policy Limit

Restrictions on foreign labor lead to an increase in labor costs. For example, in a highway project in Eastern Europe undertaken by a Chinese contractor, the host country is an EU member country, and the labor of the project is subject to the dual restrictions of the country's labor policy and EU labor law. As a result of these restrictions, a large number of claims resulting from engineering delays have arisen. In addition, because many equipment requires qualified local workers to operate and cannot hire Chinese workers, many professional projects have to be subcontracted to local contractors, resulting in a significant increase in labor costs.[51]

[D]   Risk of Strike

Strikes are also one of the risks often encountered in foreign investment. For instance, in a copper mine project in Zambia invested by a Chinese investor, the Chinese company suffered the longest strike, and if the requirements of workers on strike are to be met, the workers' salary must be more than doubled, which undoubtedly made the investment untenable for the Chinese investor and may cause the company to go bankrupt.[52]

---

50. "Investing in Indonesia, don't let yourself become vulnerable group! Detailed Interpretation to Labor Law Practice" Author: Yang Huan, graduated from Indonesia's President University, majored in Human Resources Management, now working at Administration and Human Resources Dept. of a Indonesia-based Chinese central enterprise. Excerpt from "LOOKE" magazine, published on July 25, 2016.
51. Excerpt from "Legal Risk in International Project Contracting from Two Failures", Author: Zhu Shuying, from *Construction Times*, April 13, 2018.
52. Excerpted from the "Survey Report on Cases of China's Investment on Africa", Heinrich Boell Foundation-China National Promotion Association Project Cooperation Office, the Development Research Center of the State Council, http://d.drcnet.com.cn/eDRCNet.Common.Web/DocSummary.aspx?chnid = 4145&docid = 3260928&leafid = 16128&uid = 32&version = worldeconomy, visited on May 4, 2018.

§2.08   OCCUPATIONAL HEALTH, SAFETY AND ENVIRONMENT

Due to the nature of the project itself, many projects are operated in hazardous locations. Failure to ensure the safety of workplaces and equipment may result in environmental disasters, employee casualties, reduced profits, project losses or litigation risks.[53]

[A]   Strict Environmental Protection System of Oil-Producing Countries in Central Asia

Some host countries have very strict requirements for environmental protection during the process of construction. Foreign contractors must fully consider environmental protection plans in the project design and planning at the early stage of the project and strictly enforce the environmental protection requirements during the implementation of project. For example, Central Asian country's *Environmental Protection Law* stipulates that trees are not allowed to be cut down at will. In the process of construction, it is necessary to obtain a permit in accordance with the statutory procedures before cleaning up the trees on the site or along the way. For oil and gas exploration projects, the country bans the burning of associated gas during the process of oil and gas exploration. For projects such as thermal power plants that are highly polluted, the government will require an environmental assessment in advance. Therefore, Chinese contractors should fully understand and abide by Kazakh local environmental protection laws and regulations, fully consider environmental protection plans in the engineering design and planning at the early stage of the project and strictly implement environmental protection requirements during the implementation of the project. For example, a Chinese oil company that has entered the Central Asian country market attaches great importance to environmental protection and safe production and is widely recognized for its strict compliance with various environmental protection requirements of the government.

[B]   Risks from Strict Environmental Protection Systems in Central and Eastern European Countries

There are many farmland and vegetation protection areas in Central and Eastern Europe. The environmental protection regulations are very strict and the system is complex. There are strict regulations on the project occupation of land, dust, noise incurred during land obtention and construction and vegetation protection. For instance, in a highway project in Eastern Europe undertaken by a Chinese contractor, there are seven species of amphibians that live along the route, including a tree frog, two species of toads, three species of frogs and an animal called the common newt. After the project started, the local design subcontractor dispatched a designated person

---

53. Excerpt from the 2017 "International Project Consulting Giant AECOM Annual Report", Author: Li Ling, *quoted from Survey and Design Cutting-Edge*, published on June 26, 2017.

to the project department to train and suggest moving the rare frogs to a safe area before cooling. In order to relocate the animals, the project had to be shut down for two weeks, causing delays in construction and increase of costs.[54] As another example, a Chinese company invested in a small ironworks in Brazil, mainly using Brazil's rich iron ore and forest resources. However, shortly after the factory was put into production, the Brazilian Congress passed a law protecting forest resources such that is strictly forbidden to slash and cut forests, causing the ironworks to lose energy. Also, Brazil lacks alternative energy coking coal, so the ironworks was forced to be abandoned.[55]

§2.09 DISPUTE RESOLUTION SYSTEM

The core issue of dispute resolution for overseas construction projects is the choice of governing law for the contract and the dispute resolution mechanism. It involves a consideration of the host country's legal system as it relates to foreign investment, and also the applicable law, jurisdiction and approaches to sovereign immunity and judgments of foreign courts and awards of international arbitration tribunals relevant to the agreement signed according to such investment.

[A] Selection of Dispute Resolution Method

[1] The Right of the Parties to Select

According to the principle of freedom of contract, the parties to the contract have the right to choose the way to resolve the dispute, whether it is a sales contract, a construction contract, an insurance contract, a shipping contract, etc. In international construction projects, dispute resolution usually involves one or several of the following methods: friendly negotiation, adjudication, mediation/conciliation, arbitration and litigation. It is also common for parties to construction contracts to agree on a multitiered disputes resolution mechanism. However, the lack of a cross-border mechanism for the enforcement of settlement agreements with or without involving a mediator is said to be a long-standing barrier to the willingness of disputants to use alternative dispute solutions (ADR).

---

54. Excerpt from "Approval and Permission for Construction Project in Russia—Easy or Difficult? (for Contractors)", written by Tian Wenjing, Xu Yue, Ding Hongxu, *Vladislav Zinovyev, quote from Blog of Research Institute of King & Wood Mallesons*, http://blog.sina.com.cn/s/blog_8f3 0351d0102wr2i.html, visited on May 12, 2018.
55. Excerpt from "Report Digest | Blue Book on Foreign Investment and Risk: China's Foreign Direct Investment and National Risk Report (2017)", Social Science Literature Publishing House, *see* http://www.ssap.com.cn/c/2017-04-12/1053144.shtml, visited on March 2, 2018.

[2]   Friendly Negotiation

Considering the enormous capacity, tight project timeline, prolonged performance period and huge investment in labor and equipment involved in international construction projects, if both parties jump to a fierce confrontation at the early stage of disputes, the whole project may be severely hampered which could lead to the full suspension of work. One of the distinctive features of the 2017 FIDIC forms of contract on dispute resolution is to promote and encourage the two sides to resolve disputes gently.

We also suggest Chinese contractors opt for negotiation as the preferred method for dispute resolution while undertaking overseas projects. By this means, not only there would be time and cost savings but also the cooperation relationship between the parties would be preserved. For employers, negotiations would not impact the progress of construction and employers could avoid being trapped in prolonged disputes. For contractors, arbitration would be costly in terms of time and cost, while huge uncertainties exist as to the final outcome. Even if the contractor obtains a favorable award, full payment of the arbitral award is not guaranteed. By contrast, negotiations may lead to timely and convenient settlement of the disputes, as the parties may agree to incorporate the agreed amount of damage into the progress payment certificates so that the contractor would receive the payment within the time limit set in the contract.[56]

[3]   Mediation

Mediation is a dispute resolution mechanism in which the parties negotiate a settlement to their dispute with the assistance of a neutral third party, i.e. a mediator. For construction disputes, the mediator usually has experience in the construction industry. Further, in mediation, the parties are the decision-makers and only they can reach a mutually satisfactory agreement. The mediator cannot bind the parties to any outcome, by contrast to litigation and arbitration, where control of the dispute is relinquished to a court or arbitrator.

There are two major advantages of mediation as compared to arbitration and litigation apart from the obvious advantage of preservation of a cooperative relationship. The first is efficiency and being able to maintain low cost. Mediation sessions usually take no more than a day or two, compared to a court trial or arbitration hearing that can take weeks. Mediations can be scheduled as soon as the parties are ready, while arbitration hearings and court trials often take years to be scheduled. This time advantage is particularly important when the mediation takes place while a project is ongoing because resolution of disputes clears the way for further subsequent cooperation between the project participants.

The second is confidentiality. Everything discussed during the mediation and any settlement offers that are exchanged cannot be used in court or an arbitration if the

---

56. Resolution of Disputes under International Construction Contracts, https://www.wenkuxiazai
    .com/doc/a21507a519e8b8f67c1cb9e7.html.

parties do not settle their dispute. This issue is particularly important to an employer of a project who makes a payment to a contractor and does not want other contractors on future projects to see the employer as an easy target. Similarly, a contractor making a settlement payment to a subcontractor does not want to appear to be an easy target for other subcontractors it frequently hires.

[4]   Adjudication

Adjudication is a form of dispute resolution that is fairly unique to the construction industry. The UK was the first country to make adjudication a statutory right in disputes arising under construction contracts with its implementation of the Housing Grants, Construction and Regeneration Act of 1996 (Construction Act), followed by Ireland, Singapore, Australia, Malaysia, New Zealand and Ontario Province of Canada.

One of the golden principles of the FIDIC suite of contracts, which enshrine FIDIC's core contracting philosophy, is that all formal disputes being referred to the dispute adjudication board is deemed a condition precedent to arbitration. Parties are therefore discouraged from amending a FIDIC form to agree otherwise. The increasingly important role of dispute avoidance in construction project has led to the change to enhanced role of the Dispute Avoidance/Adjudication Board (DAAB) in FIDIC 2017. The default position is that all DAABs are standing, i.e., appointed at the outset of the Contract and throughout its lifetime. The parties may jointly request DAAB assistance in relation to any issue, and the DAAB may also invite the parties to make such a request. Upon termination of the Contract, the DAAB will expire 28 days after the DAAB has given its decisions on all Disputes referred to it or (if earlier) when the parties reach final agreement on all matters in connection with the termination.

The DAAB is obliged to complete its decision within 84 days or in such time as otherwise decided by the parties. Unless a party gives a Notice of Dissatisfaction (NOD) with a DAAB's Decision, or in respect of DAAB's failure to give a Decision within 28 days, such decision becomes final and binding. However, the parties shall promptly comply with it irrespective of NOD.

Under Sub-Clause 21.6 [Arbitration], any Dispute in which the DAAB's decision has not become final and binding shall be settled by arbitration. There is no mandatory time limit for arbitration once the NOD is given in time. The arbitral tribunal shall have the full power to open up previous Engineer's Determinations and DAAB's Decisions, as long as they are not final and binding.

[5]   Arbitration

In the event that parties fail to solve the disputes via ADR mechanism, such as negotiations, DAABs and amicable settlement, they may ultimately submit the disputes for arbitration or litigation. Parties generally prefer arbitration to litigation to solve disputes arising in international construction projects. The following two points account for the preference for arbitration. First, parties can appoint arbitrators from experienced engineers and surveyors to adjudicate the disputes, who are more capable of addressing the professional technical issues involved than judges in national courts. Second, arbitral awards are easier to be recognized and enforced in foreign jurisdictions than judgments issued by courts. It is not uncommon that, in international construction projects, the primary assets of the losing party in the arbitration or litigation are situated outside the seat of the arbitration or the jurisdiction where the judgment is issued, which highlights the importance of recognition and enforcement of awards or judgments in foreign jurisdictions. Recognition and enforcement of arbitral awards via the New York Convention in a foreign jurisdiction is obviously more straightforward and promising than enforcement of judicial judgments which greatly depends on whether bilateral or multilateral judicial cooperation instruments exist between the two countries and the content stipulated therein.

If arbitration prevails over litigation as the ultimate dispute resolution method, Chinese contractors should cautiously consider the following factors:

> Seat of the Arbitration: As parties to international construction projects normally come from different countries, they often pick a neutral third country as the arbitration seat. For future successful recognition and enforcement of the arbitral award, the third country should be a party to the New York Convention. It is worth noticing that along the "Belt and Road," only five countries are not among the New York Convention's contracting states by now, which are East Timor, Maldives, Turkmenistan, Iraq and Yemen. Besides, as the procedural law of the country where the seat is located may apply to the arbitration, parties should choose, as a seat, a country with an advanced arbitration law.

> Number of the Arbitrators: In disputes involving complex factual and legal issues, a tribunal of three arbitrators may reduce the possibility of wrong judgment while more costs would be incurred.

> Language of the Arbitration: The arbitration clause shall specify the language for arbitration, an important factor in international construction disputes, as two parties probably speak different languages. In the meantime, the language of the arbitration will likely influence the selection of the arbitrators. Language of arbitration is further expounded in subsection b of this section.

> Institutional or ad hoc Arbitration: The arbitration clause should also identify whether the arbitration is institutional or ad hoc, with preference for choosing institutional arbitration. The former is administered and overseen by an arbitral institution in accord with its own arbitration rules, whereas the latter lacks the assistance and supervision from an institution, although it still needs to follow a set of arbitration rules such as United Nations Commission on International Trade Law (UNCITRAL) Arbitration Rules.

[a] Arbitration Agreement

Chinese contractors should ensure the arbitration clause is explicit and clear. Otherwise, it may be perceived as pathological, which may affect its validity or enforceability. For example, in a project conducted in Iran and undertaken by a Chinese enterprise from steel industry, the arbitration clause in the contract provided that the parties agree to submit relevant disputes to an arbitral institution in Switzerland for resolution.[57] The institution stated in the contract, however, does not exist in reality, which may cause national courts to find the arbitration clause void and the parties, as a result, have to solve the disputes before national courts. In addition, Chinese enterprises also need to explicitly choose arbitration as the only dispute resolution mechanism to ensure the validity of the arbitration clause. If the contract includes an arbitration clause and stipulates competent courts at the same time, it may be found invalid.

In addition, most jurisdictions impose certain form requirements when entering into an arbitration agreement, notably the requirement that the arbitration agreement must be concluded "in writing." Attention should also be paid to ensure that all relevant parties are covered by the arbitration clause.

[b] Selection of Arbitration Language

It should first be noted that the language of arbitration differs from the official language of the country. For instance, while the courts in the UAE and the individual Emirates such as Dubai proceed in Arabic, arbitration in this country (under local rules such as those of the Dubai International Arbitration Centre (DIAC) and Dubai International Financial Centre (DIFC)) is often conducted in English. It is only when the courts get involved, for example, in setting aside or local enforcement proceedings that the Arabic language becomes relevant.

Also, try to choose a single arbitration language. Choosing two or more arbitration languages will not only generate additional costs in the arbitration process but also magnifies the disputes between the two languages in translation and interpretation, which will bring extra burden to the arbitration process. Finally, try to choose a widely used and popular language, rather than a minority language, as the arbitration language. Since only a small number of arbitrators, experts and lawyers may speak the minority language, on the one hand, the pool of arbitrators who can be selected will be limited, and, on the other hand, the arbitrators selected are also easily affected by the country of nationality.

---

57. The Arbitration Clause is "… If after 60 days from the start of such negotiations the parties cannot reach an agreement, then the case will be taken to the Council of Arbitration of Swiss Chamber of Commerce to be settled under … ."

[c]   Choice of Arbitration Institution

For international commercial disputes, the choice of arbitration institution is not limited to major arbitration institutions in China. The parties may also consider choosing other arbitration institutions around the world that both deliver high-quality dispute resolution service and have a long-standing good reputation. To just name a few: Hong Kong International Arbitration Centre (HKIAC), Singapore International Arbitration Centre (SIAC), ICC, the Arbitration Institute of the Stockholm Chamber of Commerce (SCC), International Center for Dispute Resolution (ICDR) of the American Arbitration Association (AAA), London Court of International Arbitration (LCIA), the Cairo Regional Centre for International Commercial Arbitration (CRCICA), Swiss Chambers' Arbitration Institution (SCAI).

[d]   Risk of Convenience in Extraterritorial Enforcement of Arbitral Award

Arbitral awards made in a jurisdiction which is a signatory to the New York Convention can also be recognized and enforced by other countries which are signatories to that Convention. The procedures and conditions for applying for recognition and enforcement of arbitral awards where the New York Convention applies are simple. By March of 2018, the number of Member States and regions of the New York Convention reached 159. As long as the contracting parties have agreed on a valid arbitration agreement or arbitration clause, the arbitral awards made by arbitration institution of a Member State may be recognized and enforced based on the New York Convention in other Member States. China is a Member State to the New York Convention, and arbitral awards made by Chinese arbitration institutions can be recognized and enforced in the other Member States of the New York Convention.

[e]   Expert Witnesses

Although Chinese contracting enterprises are extensively engaging in overseas construction projects nowadays, the prevalent arbitration-related rules in the international construction field still mainly originate from Western developed countries. Those rules match the mature management practice of contractors from Western countries, which leaves the less mature Chinese contractors at a disadvantage. For example, Western enterprises keep records, data and detailed documents during the construction process, and the commonly adopted analytical methods on delay calculation are developed on that basis. In contrast, most Chinese enterprises only have an idea of when to finish the project, but no specific daily plans are in their mind. Also, they keep limited construction management data on record. As a result, Chinese enterprises find it hard to adapt when Western rules on delay calculation apply. If disputes arise in relation to delay calculation, Chinese contractors either lose the case entirely or retreat from participating in the dispute resolution process.

    In order to deal with the above issues, besides improving project management, Chinese contractors should consider selecting professionals more familiar with the management modes adopted by Chinese construction enterprise as the expert witnesses during the international arbitration process. Such expert witnesses will strike the right balance between the Western analytical methods on delay calculation and the management capability of Chinese contractors. For instance, an ICC arbitral award was issued recently, where the international expert witness originally engaged by the Chinese contractor chose the analytical method on delay calculation according to the American standard, which impeded the analytical work as a result. The Chinese contractor later turned to a Chinese expert specializing in delay calculation, who abandoned the analytical methods used by the industry associations in the UK and U.S.. Instead, this Chinese expert adopted an analytical method consistent with the actual work conditions of the Chinese contractor and came to the conclusion that the Chinese contractor should not take any responsibility for the delay. In the end, the arbitral tribunal agreed with this conclusion and denied the claim for enormous damages caused by the delay brought by the employer against the Chinese contractor.[58]

Similarly, in a case provided by the ICC for this research project, the Chinese party relied primarily on the testimony of expert witnesses to analyze the responsibilities under the common law governed contract relating to the number of pumping stations and change orders. However, the expert witnesses relied on did not have the requisite law background, and the delay expert witness did not consider all possible methodologies in calculating the effect of a delay on progress, resulting in adverse inferences from the tribunal.

[f]   Actively Participating in the Arbitration

In several cases provided by the ICC for this research project, all of the Chinese parties had the problem of not actively participating in the arbitration to a certain extent. In one of the cases, the three Chinese companies respondents did not participate in the drafting of the Terms of Reference and ignored the time limit for submitting the statement of defense and accompanying evidence set by the arbitral tribunal. Consequently, the evidence was not submitted until the day of the hearing, and the statement of defense was submitted after the hearing. In another case, the arbitral tribunal indicated that the Chinese contractor had delayed the arbitral proceedings, that a large portion of its claims were not supported by evidence and that there existed double recovery. Such behavior cannot only lead to loss of substantive rights in a proceeding but also feeds a tribunal's dissatisfaction toward a Chinese party, making it more likely that the tribunal will rule in favor of the other party on discretionary issues.

---

58. First Appearance of Chinese Expert Witness Specializing in Delay Calculation Before the International Arbitral Tribunal. http://news.eastday.com/eastday/13news/auto/news/china/2 0180129/u7ai7388588.html.

[B]   Choice of Law

When conducting due diligence on the legal environment of a host country, Chinese contractors need to clearly and accurately understand the provision of the host country's law on the scope of choice of law through local legal counsel. If the host country's law allows the project agreement to apply Chinese law or a third country's law, priority shall be given to choose the Chinese law and Chinese standards so as to better forecast and control risks. If a third country's law is applicable, the specific third country's laws need to be determined while taking into account factors such as the legal system of the host country. For projects implemented in Commonwealth countries such as Pakistan, it is relatively favorable if English law can be chosen as the law of the contract. For example, in an EPC construction general contracting project in a country in the Middle East between a consortium formed by a Chinese contractor and a European multinational company and an energy company, the clause of contract providing the applicable law and dispute resolution is as follows: "The validity, the interpretation and performance of this Contract and the legal relationship between the parties are governed by the laws of the Kingdom of Saudi Arabia. Any dispute between the parties concerning the validity, interpretation or performance of this Contract, if not resolved through friendly negotiation, shall be resolved according to the Arbitration Rules of Kingdom of Saudi Arabia by binding arbitration through one or more arbitrators appointed in accordance with the Arbitration Rules of Kingdom of Saudi Arabia." Later, the disputes between the parties were submitted to the Arbitration Institute of the Stockholm International Chamber of Commerce. Since there is no so-called Arbitration Rules of the Kingdom of Saudi Arabia in Saudi Arabia, they were unable to select arbitrators and form an arbitral tribunal according to the clause above. The purpose of early agreement on selection of arbitrators and formation of the arbitral tribunal was lost.

Although foreign laws such as English law are often used as the applicable law for international engineering contracts, the host country's laws may still provide for the mandatory application of host country's laws in certain areas for reasons such as protection of public interest. For example, some host countries make mandatory provisions that the project agreement for some of the country's infrastructure projects must apply the local laws of the host country, or at least require that the guarantee document that provides the guarantee with the assets of the host country apply the local law of the host country. For example, in Russia, if the construction project involves a "foreign element" (e.g., the contractor is a Chinese company), English law can be chosen as the applicable law, but even so, in certain circumstances, according to the "super mandatory clause" in Russian law, the selected applicable law will also be excluded in favor of Russian law. For example, Article 1192 of the Russian Civil Code stipulates that no matter whether the applicable law of the foreign-related engineering contract is Russian law, it is mandatory to apply the relevant Russian laws and regulations. This article does not clearly stipulate which provisions are super mandatory provisions, and the Russian court cases did not provide too much in the way of practical guidance. In addition, as provided in Article 1210.5 of the Russian Civil Code, if a contract is only related to Russia, its applicable law cannot conflict with the mandatory provisions of Russian law. Given that the Russian Civil Code includes numerous provisions that may apply to engineering contracts, the contractor may need to have a basic understanding of the content of Russian law to better develop the negotiation strategy and so as to make necessary preparations for the possible claims/reverse claims that the employers/contractors may raise in the future.

[C] Risk Prevention in Choosing the Dispute Resolution Method

There are four key points that should be taken into account when choosing a dispute resolution method for a construction engineering contract.

First, whether the host country is a member of the United Nations Convention on the Recognition and Enforcement of Foreign Arbitral Awards (i.e., the New York Convention) or the Convention on the Settlement of National Investment Disputes between States and Other Countries (i.e., International Centre for Settlement of Investment Disputes (ICSID) Convention). Did the country make any reservations at the time of signing the Convention? Are there any obstacles to the enforcement of arbitral awards by international arbitration institutions under the host country's legal system? These are important issues to consider when choosing a dispute resolution method.

Second, in the choice of arbitration institution, arbitration rules and seat of arbitration, it is necessary to fully consider the fairness, convenience, cost level of the arbitration institution and the arbitration rules, as well as the effect of any mandatory provisions of the local law of the seat of arbitration on the effectiveness of the arbitration agreement and the arbitration proceedings. Negotiation of the arbitration clause should be completed as soon as possible subject to the understanding of similar project practices in the host country and the main concerns of the counterparty. Regarding arbitration institution, priority should be given to choose one of the well-known international commercial arbitration institutions.

Third, if a series of agreements are signed under the same project, the same dispute resolution methods should be chosen in those agreements to avoid inconvenience and conflict in determining the jurisdiction of arbitral tribunals and to avoid potential conflicting decisions. Additionally, a favorable and fair method of dispute resolution is the last amulet of a foreign company in the host country, which can protect foreign companies from the adverse effects of extraneous factors in the event of a dispute with the host government or entity. It is not recommended to easily give up the right to choose the dispute resolution method—instead, one should choose a system that is understood to be objectively fair. For example, in a highway project in a country in Eastern Europe, the executed and effective FIDIC agreement excludes the arbitration clause of the FIDIC contract and replaces it with the provision that "all disputes shall be adjudicated by the local court and cannot be arbitrated," which clause lost the international consortium undertaking the project the opportunity to protect its legitimate interests before an international commercial arbitration tribunal in the event of dispute.[59]

Fourth, the Islamic Quran is the fundamental source and conversion of all secular laws of some Middle East countries. The influence of religious law is deeply rooted in the arbitration practice of certain Middle East countries. An arbitral award may only be enforced after it has been recognized by the court and judicially reviewed to determine that it does not violate the Quran. As such, non-Arab parties should be cautious about choosing or accepting local judicial litigation or arbitration in the Middle East as a means of dispute resolution. In the trial of construction and engineering disputes, judges of the courts in certain Middle East countries often rely heavily on expert reports issued by expert witnesses; therefore, these courts mainly conduct written trials instead of hearing a case in court. In addition, the courts of first instance in some Middle East countries do not publish their judgments, and courts at the higher level may only publish part of the judgment occasionally, which reduces transparency, and to some extent may make the trial fairness more open to doubt.

§2.10   INVESTMENT DISPUTES RESOLUTION

[A]   The Impact of International Conventions on the Enforcement of Judgments

Contracting status to international conventions is a key factor affecting the extraterritorial enforcement of judgment. Taking China and the U.S. as an example, neither China nor the U.S. has acceded to the Convention on the Recognition and Enforcement of Foreign Judgments in International Civil and Commercial Cases, nor have they concluded bilateral or multilateral treaties on mutual recognition and enforcement of the judgments. Therefore, the U.S. courts mainly determine whether to recognize and enforce Chinese judgments based on the principle of comity and the domestic law of the U.S.. As far as domestic law is concerned, the relevant laws applicable in the U.S. states are not completely consistent one with another, which directly leads to the high uncertainty in the recognition and enforcement of judgments rendered in China in the U.S. and poses obstacles to the recognition and enforcement of Chinese judgments in the U.S..

To meet the increased need for enforcement of foreign-country money judgments, the Uniform Law Commission of the U.S. has promulgated a revision of the 1962 Uniform Foreign Money-Judgments Recognition Act with the 2005 Uniform Foreign-Country Money Judgments Recognition Act (UFCMJRA). For a foreign judgment to be enforced, it must first be recognized. Under the UFCMJRA, it must be shown that the judgment is conclusive, final and enforceable in the country of origin. Certain money judgments are excluded, such as judgments on taxes, fines or criminal-like penalties and judgments relating to domestic relations. Domestic relations judgments are

---

59. Excerpt from "Legal Risk in International Project Contracting from Two Failures", Author: Zhu Shuying, from *Construction Times*, April 13, 2018.

enforced under other statutes already existing in every state. Second, a foreign-country judgment must not be recognized if it comes from a court system that is not impartial or that dishonors due process, or there is no personal jurisdiction over the defendant or the subject matter of the litigation. There are a number of grounds that may make a U.S. court deny recognition, for example, where the defendant did not receive notice of the proceedings or the claim is repugnant to American public policy. A final, conclusive judgment enforceable in the country of origin, if it is not excluded for one of the enumerated reasons, must be recognized and enforced. The 1962 Act and the 2005 Act generally operate similarly.

[B]   The Impact of Host Country's Domestic Law on Investment Dispute Resolution

The laws of the host country also affect the resolution of investment disputes to some extent. For instance, in a Central Asian country, the Investment Law stipulates that for investment disputes (mainly disputes concerning investment contract between investors and state institutions when conducting investment activities), international treaties or that Central Asian country law shall apply, and the international treaties to which that Central Asian country is a party prevail national laws of that Central Asian country. Therefore, if domestic laws and regulations conflict with international treaties concluded or participated by the investing country, international treaties shall apply, and where neither domestic laws nor international treaties contain any specific provision on the relevant issue, international practice shall apply. The Investment Law of the country stipulates that investment disputes can be settled through negotiation. If a dispute cannot be settled through negotiation, the dispute shall be resolved in the domestic courts in accordance with any relevant international treaties or domestic law. The dispute may be heard before an international arbitration tribunal if so agreed in the treaties. If the agreement does not stipulate arbitration, then generally Kazakh courts shall have jurisdiction. As such, foreign investors should clearly agree that disputes related to investment and contracts, such as the interpretation of contracts, disputes over performance of contract, investment compensation are included in the arbitration agreement to avoid exclusion from arbitration jurisdiction due to unclear agreement in the arbitration agreement. The arbitral tribunal can only have jurisdiction over matters which the parties have agreed shall be referred to arbitration for decision.

[C]   The Act of a Foreign Contractor Providing a Performance Bond or Importing Equipment to the Host Country Employer May Be Considered an Investment

Where the ICSID Convention or the bilateral investment protection agreement between the domestic government and the host government is applicable, even if the construction of overseas contracting project has not started, the act of the foreign contractor providing the performance bond or importing equipment for the construction according to the contract is an investment as provided in the ICSID Convention such that the

ICSID has jurisdiction over disputes arising out of or relating to such investment. For example, in the case of a dispute arising out of an international airport new terminal project between a Chinese contractor and the Yemen government, the ICSID determined that, based on either the ICSID Convention or the Treaty of Governments of the People's Republic of China and Yemen on Encouragement and Mutual Protection of Investment, the provision of "performance guarantee" and "import of equipment and materials for construction" by the Chinese contractor is "eligible investment in compliance with the laws and regulations of the host country" that occurred in the "territory of Yemen," with the effect that the ICSID has the jurisdiction over the dispute, and therefore the ICSID dismissed the Yemen government's objection to jurisdiction.

Chinese contractors should attach great importance to such of the commercial agreements which are relevant to the definition of investment and which may substantially affect the dispute resolution institutions and methods. They should also study and skillfully apply international investment laws and dispute resolution rules in overseas operations. It is advised that they predetermine the dispute resolution mechanism and risk prevention and control measures before the dispute arises and conform to rules of international law after the dispute occurs.

[D]   In the Expansion of Overseas Markets, State-Owned Enterprises Are Also Eligible Investors

Chinese contractor's state-owned enterprise status does not deprive it of protection under the ICSID Convention or any bilateral investment agreements. In the event of a dispute with the host country, it has the right to apply for investment arbitration in its capacity as the contractor before the ICSID in accordance with the said Convention and agreement. For instance, in an ICSID arbitration between a Chinese contractor and the Yemen government regarding a new international airport terminal project in Yemen, although the contractor is a state-owned enterprise, the ICSID tribunal decided that the contractor is within the jurisdiction of the ICSID Convention or bilateral investment protection agreement, and in a jurisdictional award, ruled in favor of the contractor. The abovementioned principle regarding jurisdiction established by the ICSID arbitration tribunal enhanced the protection of Chinese state-owned enterprises in overseas project contracting, investment and financing from the perspective of international convention.

[E]   Restrictions of Host Country on Choice of Law

Laws of some host countries stipulate that the state authorities and state-owned enterprises have the additional obligation to choose the laws of the host country as the applicable law. If they choose a foreign law as the applicable law, they need consent from the country's parliament. For example, Article 27 of the Iranian Arbitration Law (promulgated on September 17, 1997) provides that in terms of choice of foreign applicable law, the parties are allowed autonomy in the field of commercial contracts, but if the party to the contract is an Iranian state authority or a state-owned enterprise, then the authority or the enterprise is obliged to choose Iranian law as the applicable law, and if they choose a foreign law as the applicable law, approval of the Iranian parliament is required.[60]

[F]   Suggestions to Chinese Contractors in Investment Arbitration

Chinese contractors should be cautious about the relevant issues in investment arbitration when applying for arbitration before the ICSID. First, the applicant should clarify the basis of arbitration on the dispute which could be a bilateral investment agreement, a regional treaty or an investment agreement and clarify the conditions of application for each basis of the arbitration. In this regard, a table is attached at the end of this book that contains information about whether there exists a Bilateral Investment Treaty (BIT) between China and a certain "Belt and Road" country. A complete list of BITs China has concluded can be found at United Nations Conference on Trade and Development's (UNCTAD's) website.[61] Second, in the event of a dispute, the procedures specified in the dispute resolution documents such as bilateral investment agreement should be strictly followed, and the requirements of dispute resolution documents in respects of form of notice (such as written notice) and negotiation period should be met in order to avoid being rejected by the ICSID due to procedural problems in the process of communication. Finally, the applicant should carefully choose the arbitrator. Before selecting an arbitrator, the arbitrator's attitude on relevant issues should be fully understood by searching the cases previously handled by the arbitrator, and the arbitrator's understanding of the policies of the host country's government and investment environment should be considered as well.

---

60. Quoted from [Korean] Shi Guang Xian, page 21, footnote 59, *see* http://www.clydeco.com/insight/articles/new-arbitration-law-in-saudi-arabia, visited on April 23, 2018.
61. https://investmentpolicyhubold.unctad.org/IIA/CountryBits/42#iiaInnerMenu.

CHAPTER 3
Risks of Project Stakeholders

International projects usually involve multiple stakeholders, including employers, contractors, suppliers and subcontractors. Often, the project stakeholders have different priorities and agendas, and such tensions may affect the outcome of the project. Throughout the duration of a project, the risks associated with stakeholders' differing priorities and agendas may lead to project cost increase, project delays and even failures. Chinese firms operating in the construction space are often responsible for the EPC of projects. They need to improve their management skills and get familiar with the norms, practices and operating methods in local markets in order to effectively manage the risks associated with project stakeholders' differing priorities and agendas. Knowing the game rules well is vital to success.

§3.01 CREDIT AND MANAGEMENT LEVEL OF EMPLOYERS

Chinese contractors win overseas projects usually through competitive bidding. The leading role played by employers in public bidding naturally puts contractors in an unfavorable position during the project execution. In addition, Chinese contractors are often involved in EPC projects which use the 1999 edition of the FIDIC Silver Book as a template. As a typical "pro-employer" form of contract, the Silver Book places most of the risks on contractors. Since an employer typically owns the project and awards the engineering contract, its credit and management level determines whether the project will be a success or not.

From previous experience, Chinese contractors typically have to deal with the following types of risks because different stakeholders often have different priorities and agendas.

[A]   Transferring Risks to Contractors in Contract Conditions

Employers in international construction projects are often in a strong negotiating position. When drafting a contract, it is natural for a contracting party to seek to introduce terms which protect its interests and reduce its risks, at the expense of the counterparty's rights and interests. The strong negotiating position that employers enjoy means that very often they are able to delete standard contract terms that are beneficial to contractors, and to unreasonably transfer the risks that are better undertaken by employers, given their acquaintance with the political, economic and natural conditions in the host country.[62] When contractual rights and obligations are skewed in this way, disputes often arise that may culminate in project failures.

In most international construction projects undertaken by Chinese enterprises, the employers are usually the government of the host country, state-owned enterprises or private enterprises. With years of engineering practice, many employers have accumulated rich experience in contract design. For example, the unique natural resources and geographical conditions of countries in South Asia attract numerous international contractors. Consequently, contractors from a few developed countries have entered the engineering market in South Asian countries as early as the 1970s. The public procurement department of the said countries, based on years of experience in claims and counterclaims in international projects, has made targeted adjustments and revisions of standard contract documents to eliminate what are perceived to be contractual defects which give contractors better chances of success when making claims. In addition, a series of factors increase the risks borne by the international contractors when performing a contract. For example, the employer adds terms in the project contract such as terms which oblige the contractor to execute the instructions of the engineer, including changes to the work program, immediately after receiving such instructions, notwithstanding that the engineer and contractor may not have reached a consensus on the new price of the project. Such contractual provisions encourage the employer to be tardy in approving price changes in case of variations. After completion of the project, the price approved by the employer is vastly lower than the actual cost incurred, causing losses to the contractor.[63]

An employer who is able and intent on skewing contract provisions against a contractor is surely a serious risk to the contractor. The "contract trap" designed by the employer aims at elaborately "setting up" the contract in such a manner that the contractor assumes maximum risk while the employer assumes minimal risk. The common contract traps take the form of one-sided text description, vague language and deletion of necessary procedural protections. In order to reduce or avoid risks and losses, a contractor must pay attention to contract appraisal and risk identification before signing a contract.[64]

---

62. Zhao Pixi, "Key to Contract Review—Risk Identification", *International Project Contracting & Labour Service*, 2018 (3).
63. Liu Zeqin, "Common Contractual Risks in Nepal International Projects", *International Project Contracting & Labour Service*, 2017 (3).
64. Zhao Pixi, "Key to Contract Review—Risk Identification", *International Project Contracting & Labour Service*, 2018 (3).

[B]   Employer's Payment

The ultimate purpose of project contracting is profit. Any risks or problems affecting an employer's fulfillment of its payment obligations will negatively influence the project.[65] According to Article 2.4 [Employer's Financial Arrangements] in the 1999 edition of the FIDIC Red Book, the employer, after receiving the contractor's request, shall provide reasonable evidence proving his financial arrangement and such arrangement shall be continuously maintained so that the employer will be able to pay to the contractor according to the contract provisions. This article emphasizes the employer's obligation in guaranteeing payment to the contractor. In practice, however, the employers of many government projects are reluctant to provide such evidence of financial arrangement to the contractor. The employer usually deletes this article, and the contractor's interests cannot be protected.

Most Chinese contractors' businesses are located in developing countries or regions. The economy of the host country may be such that the employer cannot provide sufficient funds due to difficulty in financing. This leads to high probability of a default by the employer in relation to its payment obligation. Alternatively, there may be constitutional or legal constraints on the employer's ability to meet its payment obligations as and when they fall due. A case on point is a government project in an African country ("country A") funded by a bank loan agreement signed between China and country A. The financial support offered by the local government was limited to the loan amount, which did not include the employer's proprietary fund. As it transpired, lots of changes occurred during construction and the accumulated cost increased by about 10% of the original contract price. While the bid price was USD 150 million, it is estimated that the final contract price will be in the order of USD 180 million (including the approved changes, the subsequent possible changes and the contractor's claims). Although the employer probably has access to other sources of financing, the increase of a project budget is regulated by the Public Procurement Law and relevant regulations, which stipulate elaborate and time-consuming procedures for increasing a project budget, including a requirement that the cost increase should be incorporated into the national construction budget and approved by the legislature. The contractor may suspend construction according to the contract, but the problem still remained.[66] In this project, the employer was willing to pay but lacked the ability to pay within a reasonable time due to objective factors, which puts the contractor in a dilemma. In practice, the employer's ability to pay is a key factor which needs to be considered by the contractor while preparing the proposal.

Besides, contractors must also pay close attention to the payment terms in the contract to avoid the risk of employers' nonpayment due to loopholes in the contract. Another case in point involves an African project with loans offered by the World Bank. The contract made no specific provision for the timing of the advance payment, putting

---

65. Liu Junying, Li Zhiyong, "Risk Management of International Project", China Architecture & Building Press, 2013.
66. Yang Yunkai, "Case Analysis: Prepayment and Change Risks in International Projects", *Journal of International Economic Cooperation*, 2015 (2).

the contractor at risk of delayed payment. According to the contract, the commencement date was August 25, 2004. The contractor provided advance payment guarantee on August 9, 2004, and the employer paid the installments of advance payment on August 17, September 3, September 4 and November 5 of the same year. The contractor believed that according to the contract, it ought to have received all advance payments as start-up fund immediately after signing the contract. The contractor therefore initiated a claim against the employer for interests due to delayed payment. The resident engineer disapproved the claim for the following reasons: (1) there was no provision in the contract which specified a time for making the advance payment; payment at any reasonable time was acceptable, and there was no payment delay; (2) there is no provision in the contract which stipulates that interest will be paid for delay in making the advance payment; (3) the provisions on interests for delay in interim payment in the contract only applies to the interim payment and cannot apply to the advance payment since interim payment and advance payment are two different things. The two parties failed to settle the dispute and submitted it to the dispute settlement committee. The committee presumed that the advance payment guarantee provided by the contractor on August 9 satisfied the preconditions for the employer to make advance payment on August 10 according to the provisions on preconditions for advance payment in paragraph 60.7 of the project contract. According to paragraph 60.8 of the contract, the contractor shall receive the interim payment within 42 days after submitting the interim payment request and the employer shall be obliged to pay interests to the contractor in case of delayed payment. As for the counterargument made by the engineer that advance payment was different from interim payment, the committee considered that advance payment is a kind of interim payment due to its inherent characteristics, although this is not clearly prescribed in the contract. According to the final verdict, the employer shall make advance payment within 42 days from August 10 and shall pay interests for delay. This case reflects the importance of specifying terms and time of payment in the contract. Where the employer defaults in its advance payment obligation, express contractual terms increase the contractor's chances of success when it commences a claim to protect its interests.

[C]   Employer's Credit Risk

Employers in international projects often enjoy a favorable position arising from instruments provided by contractors to secure advance payments.

A case in point shows how an employer can abuse the leverage afforded it by advance payment security instruments. In 2010, a Chinese contractor undertook a homeless shelter project promoted by a company in "country A." The contractor applied to the bank for advance payment guarantee and performance guarantee in favor of the employer. By the end of 2013, the Ministry of Labor in country A had changed its policy in relation to illegal immigrants from a policy of sheltering them to a policy of repatriating them. Consequently the project was terminated. At the time of termination, the contractor had received about USD 7.2 million advance payment from the employer. The contractor initiated a claim against the employer for USD 13.3

million. However, the employer recognized only about USD 2.8 million as payable to the contractor. Since the advance payment guarantee provided by the contractor was about to expire, the employer requested the contractor to immediately return the remaining USD 4.4 million advance payment, failing which the employer would enforce the advance payment guarantee. The employer also requested the contractor to sign a written agreement to waive its claim as a precondition for returning the advance payment guarantee and performance guarantee. However, the contractor thought that the project was slowed by the employer's delay in making the advance payment, the USD 2.8 million recognized as payable by the employer to the contractor was not the full extent of the amount due to the contractor and about USD 2.1 million worth of works completed by the contractor had not been recognized as payable by the employer to the contractor. In the above situation, the contractor suggested that the advance payment guarantee be extended so that the two parties could negotiate a settlement of the dispute. The employer turned down the suggestion. Given that the two guarantees held by the employer were on-demand, it was easy for the employer to make a demand on the guarantees. The contractor could try to obtain a restraining order, but the process would be long and probably complicated. Further, if the employer called on the guarantees, the contractor would suffer economic loss and a loss of its credit rating. The two parties subsequently reached an agreement by which the contractor returned the sum of the advance payment claimed by the employer and signed a memorandum of understanding on claims with the employer. In this case, the employer threatened the contractor with its potential demands on the guarantees which put pressure on the contractor and constrained the contractor to accept unreasonable conditions.[67]

Currently, most guarantees involved in international projects are on-demand guarantees. If the employer fails to act in good faith and demands the guarantees maliciously, huge risks and losses will occur to the contractor. In practice, the employer's credit status may impose risks on the contractor, so the contractor should review the employer's credit during the bid process.

[D] Employer's Excessive Interference

Contractors are responsible for EPC in international EPC projects. Compared with DB (Design-Build) projects, EPC projects, generally speaking, give more independent choices to the contractor in engineering and construction. According to our survey, employers' day-to-day management and control of the project have been increasingly severe in the past five years. In order to seek advantages, employers excessively interfere with the project construction, leading to many variation instructions and even delay and cost increase, which the employer is often reluctant to assume responsibility for. Under such circumstances, it would be difficult for the contractor to claim for compensation. Some employers delay approving the claim documents submitted by

---

67. Zhang Qian, "Discussion on Risk Prevention in Guarantee Management Based on an International Project Case", *Practice in Foreign Economic Relations and Trade*, 2017 (5).

contractors while requesting that contractors do not suspend the project. Ultimately the final approved amount is often far less than the amount claimed by contractors, causing huge losses to them. In practice, employers' excessive interference with the project is commonplace to the disadvantage of the contractor and even causing failure.

In March 2013, tests of all the units of a power plant project undertaken by a Chinese contractor in country A were completed and the conditions for handover were satisfied,.but the employer was slow to perform the handing-over procedures. Later, the employer, without issuing the interim taking-over certificate according to the contract, started up the generator units repeatedly without the permission of the contractor for the reason that the state grid had suffered power shortage and had failed. On March 19, the project manager of the employer took soldiers to the project department of contractor and forced the electromechanical management personnel to start the generator units, on pain of being arrested. The contractor continually remonstrated that the operation safety could not be guaranteed because the employer did not have enough skillful operating personnel, while the contractor's technicians could only provide technical guidance. The contractor also requested the employer to take over the project since the conditions for project handover had been satisfied. The employer refused to take over the project for a variety of reasons and forced the personnel to start the units for power generation. Finally, the senior leaders of the contractor agreed to start the units under such duress and out of concern for the safety of their personnel.

This incident put the contractor at huge risk. The employer's delay in project takeover and the duress it exerted compelled the contractor to perform acts that imperiled project safety against the contractor's better judgment. Although contracts give employers the right to exercise some control over the project, the improper or excessive exercise of the right will hinder project implementation and bring many unforeseen risks to both parties.

[E]   Assignment of Contract by the Employer

Contracts governing international construction projects usually clarify the rights and obligations of the parties. In most cases, the assignment of rights and obligations is either prohibited outright in the contract or subject to multiple restrictions on assignment. An improper assignment of obligations which violates the contract conditions may lead to contract termination.

In a case on point, a railway project in a North Asian country was taken over by the government due to changes in national policy. The original employer of the project had to transfer rights and obligations under the subcontract to the new general contractor selected by the government, and the original contractors of each section would continue construction as subcontractors. The original general contractor believed that if it accepted the transfer of agreement, it would be at risk of liquidated damages for project delay since the construction period was shortened, and the loss caused by this force majeure would not be compensated. The contract stipulates that "[the original general contractor's] refusal or delay in accepting the transfer of contract shall be deemed as breach of contract, and the contract shall be terminated." Given the original general contractor's concerns, it decided to refuse the transfer notwithstanding the express provisions of the contract, leading to contract termination. In this case, the employer had to assign the contract due to a force majeure event and the terms on assignment in the contract are obviously favorable to the employer. During contract negotiation, both parties should consider whether restrictions on assignments of contracts need to be set in the contract.

[F]   Management of Risks Related to the Employer

In general, the risks caused by employers in international projects are diverse and unforeseeable, and the contractor may take the following measures to manage such risks.

First, the contractor should enhance internal contract management and improve the negotiation skills of business personnel. Some experienced employers in international projects entrust professional consultants to design the contract terms who are skilled in introducing terms favorable to the employer and deleting terms favorable to the contractor, or designing terms containing loopholes to transfer risks to the contractor as much as possible. This worsens the situation of EPC contractors who already bear most risks. Therefore, contractors should improve the skills of their contract management personnel, and such specialized personnel should carefully review the contract terms designed by the employer and communicate with the employer in time as soon as they spot any term which is unfavorable to the contractor's interests. This helps to protect the interests of the contractor to the maximum extent without violating the relevant laws and regulations.[68] In addition, the contractor should improve the negotiation skills of its specialized personnel and, when necessary, hire professional lawyers and contract specialists to participate in contract reviews and negotiations to avoid risks being unreasonably transferred by the employer.

Second, as for the employer's payment risks, the contractor should analyze and assess the credit of the investor and employer during the bid process. Credit risks vary with different investors. Where a project is financed by an international financial institution, the contractor should pay attention to the possible impacts of political and economic risks in the host country on the policies of the international financial institution and the proprietary funds of the employer. As for projects funded by the employer itself, if the employer is a governmental agency or public enterprise, the contractor should analyze the policy stability and economic development of the host country and assess the employer's ability to pay; whereas if the employer is a private institution, the contractor should fully analyze and assess the financial situation and capability of the employer. If the project involves material variations, with the consequence that the final payment at the conclusion of the project will substantially exceed the cost budget, the contractor should analyze the procedure for variations and

---

68. Wang Haichao, "Problems in Contract Management of International Project and Countermeasure Analysis", *Science & Technology Association Forum*, 2013 (7).

the employer's ability to adjust the budget, so as to avoid the employer's delay or the risk that the employer will either not pay the additional project cost or will pay less than the full amount of the additional cost.[69] During contract negotiation, the contractor may request the employer to increase the proportion of the advance payment, select a more favorable and secure method of payment, raise the interest rate for employer's late payment and include or enhance the terms on the rights of the contractor to slow down the project progress or terminate the contract in case of the employer's late payment. During the implementation of the project, the contractor should communicate with the employer, pay attention to changes to employer's credit status and strictly monitor the possibility of the employer's failure to make payments on schedule. Once any payment risk is found, the contractor should take measures to prevent or mitigate losses as soon as possible, such as preserving the evidence for the employer's late payment, contacting the employer in written form according to the contract, suspending the work or initiating a contract claim when necessary.[70] In addition, Sinosure and Multilateral Investment Guarantee Agency (MIGA) offer insurance services on the employer's nonpayment or late payment. The contractor can purchase insurance to transfer the employer's payment risks or sell receivables to the banks under factoring (short term) or forfeiting mode, transferring the risks to the financing institutions.

Third, as for the employer's credit risks, the contractor should review the employer's credit and qualifications and the recorded litigation against the employer in recent years and as much as possible only work on projects involving employers with good credit and records. Depending on the severity of the employer's breach during the implementation of the project, the contractor may suspend or terminate the contract. In the event that the employer encounters difficulties—including financial difficulties—after the conclusion of the contract, the contractor must timely decide a countermeasure. In a case provided by the ICC for this research project, the employer had in a relatively advantageous negotiating position when the contract was drafted resulting in an EPC contract between the two parties that favored the employer over the Chinese contractor. Afterward, the employer ran into financial difficulties and notice of commencement of work by the employer was long overdue. As a result of renegotiation, the Chinese contractor agreed to provide project financing for the employer. However, despite such a major change, the Chinese contractor failed to take the opportunity to negotiate for a modification of unreasonable terms in the contract. When the dispute arises, the employer still has an advantage based on the terms of the EPC contract. This result is very regrettable, considering the competitive position of the contractor after the employer had financial difficulties.

Since the employer's intervention in day-to-day management and control of the project has increased in recent years, the contractor may limit the employer's intervention through negotiation. If the employer is too aggressive and the contractor

---

69. Liu Junying, Li Zhiyong. "Risk Management of International Project", China Architecture & Building Press, 2013.
70. Wu Xuan, Jiang Yao, Shen Qinyan. "Financial Risk Management of International Power Station Project Based on Whole Process Management", *Power System Engineering*, 2014 (4).

cannot avoid excessive employer intervention in management and control, the contractor must diligently document and keep evidence of variations made at the instance of the employer and instances of disruptive interference with the construction in order to maximize the chances of success in the event of a claim.

§3.02 THE EMPLOYER'S REPRESENTATIVE/ENGINEER

In international EPC projects, the employer usually establishes a project team at an early stage of the project as the employer's representative to supervise, manage and coordinate the progress of the project. According to Article 3.1 of the 1999 edition of FIDIC Silver Book, the employer's representative shall carry out the duties assigned to him/her and shall exercise the authority delegated to him/her by the employer. Unless and until the employer notifies the contractor otherwise, the employer's representative shall be deemed to have the full authority of the employer under the Contract, except in respect of Clause 15 ["Termination by Employer"]. The employer's representative is assigned by the employer to exercise the rights on behalf of the employer, while under the FIDIC Yellow Book or Red Book 1999, the engineer is entrusted by the employer to supervise the project quality as an independent third party. The engineer shall strictly control every work in progress, approval of materials and approval of drawings during the project. The engineer's requests on details, his/her impartiality and his/her working methods and efficiency have a direct impact on the contractor's work schedule. Whether the engineer approves drawing according to time schedule, handles monthly payment applications and the efficiency of his/her decision-making have an impact on the project. In practice, the risks that may be caused by the engineer are listed below.

[A] Low Efficiency in Examination and Approval

The FIDIC contract aims at establishing an engineer-centered model. The engineer is independent of the employer and the contractor. Forming a triangular relationship between employers, contractors and engineers and achieving mutual balance is essential to complete projects.[71] Engineers are at a connection point between employers and contractors and responsible for the approval, inspection and supervision of payment applications submitted by contractors as well as the approval of suggestions on value engineering related to employers. Engineers' efficiency in approval has significant influences on the contractor's work schedule. In an international airport project in an African country, the engineer was extremely slow to approve the payment application, seriously impacting the recycling of the contractor's funds and leading to project disruptions.

---

71. Ren Xing, Liu Junjun, Zeng Yanhui. "Discussion on Communication with Supervising (Consulting) Engineer under FIDIC Conditions", *Sichuan Building Materials*, 2016 (9).

[B]   Inadequate Capability and Experience

It is important that the engineer must possess adequate professional skill to enable him/her to provide effective supervision. Lack of professional skills will subject the project implementation to risks. In the process of inspection and supervision of project progress, some engineers with low skill levels fail to find defects in a timely manner, leaving hidden dangers with the project, which may cause safety accidents and project defects.[72] Besides, the experience of the engineer has a great impact on project progress. If the engineer is unfamiliar with the project, he/she will possibly disapprove reasonable proposals made by the contractor, which will not be conducive to project implementation and may lead to disputes.

[C]   Engineer's Fairness

The supervising engineer plays the role of a judge when disputes occur between employers and contractors under the FIDIC contract. According to Article 3 of 1999 edition FIDIC of Red Book ["Engineer"], the engineer is independent of employers and contractors so as to ensure his/her impartiality. However, engineers are engaged and paid by the employer, and sometimes disputes occur because contractors believe engineers are biased. Most contracts provide that contractors shall be entitled to object to the decisions made by engineers and initiate a claim or even apply to dispute settlement committees for resolution, but the opinions of engineers may affect results of claims and dispute settlement.[73] Once engineers are partial to employers in the process of claims and dispute settlement, contractors will be treated unfairly and bear the responsibilities and losses.

[D]   Worsening of Relations

If a contractor has had an unpleasant experience with an engineer in the past, this may affect the implementation of other projects undertaken by the contractor. For example, a Chinese contractor failed to get along with the engineer in a domestic project and prompted the employer to replace the engineer. When the contractor subsequently bidded for an overseas project and met with an engineer from the same company, this was unfavorable to the bidding and the subsequent project implementation. A good cooperative relationship between the project participants helps the project implementation, while an antagonistic and competitive relationship will lead to project failure.

An engineer acts as a bridge connecting the employer and the contractor. As an intermediary, the engineer will inevitably bring risks to the contractor. Contractors may take the following measures to prevent risks associated with the manner in which the engineer performs his/her function during the project construction.

---

72. Ye Wenzheng, "Discussion on Prevention of Supervising Engineer's Liability Risks". *Fujian Building Materials*, 2014 (7).
73. Ren Xing, Liu Junjun, Zeng Yanhui, "Discussion on Communication with Supervising (Consulting) Engineer under FIDIC Conditions", *Sichuan Building Materials*, 2016 (9).

First, engineers' efficiency in approval greatly influences the construction period. The contractor must insist on the terms guaranteeing engineers' efficiency in approval during the implementation of the project. A case in point comes from Ethiopia. In this project, approval of design was a primary risk that could potentially impact construction duration and the contractor had gained satisfactory results in the negotiation. The employer agreed to the proposals made by the contractor that only the main drawings need to be approved by the engineer and that the contractor was at liberty to submit any part of drawings completed to the engineer for approval at any time; the engineer was required to give comments on the drawings within 14 days or, at the latest within 21 days; the employer can approve or agree to the contractor's requests on submission and approval of drawings via e-mail; after the drawings submitted were approved, the contractor was required to provide a sufficient number of drawings in hard copy to the employer and the engineer respectively according to the requirements in the bidding documents. The above agreements significantly improved the engineer's efficiency in approval and enabled the contractor to control the design approval risks.

Second, contractors should investigate the background of engineers during the bid process. If the contractor's administrative costs are increased due to strict requirements by the engineer, the contractor should reflect the risks in the contractor's proposal. If a contractor finds that an engineer is not sufficiently skilled for the project, the contractor should ask the employer to replace such engineer with a more experienced and skilled engineer.

Third, contractors who expand their operations overseas for the first time may be inclined to implement overseas projects based on their local experience. This may lead to disagreements with engineers. Contractors should be familiar with the contract terms and relevant practices and standards to make the project meet the requirements and reduce disputes with engineers. Correspondence is the main means of communication between contractors and engineers and also the evidence of claims lodged by the contractor. Contractors should keep the correspondence with engineers on record and enhance the management of the correspondence, which would facilitate the settlement of disputes.[74] If engineers behave unfairly in the claim and dispute settlement, contractors may use the correspondence in aid of a claim for interests.

Fourth, contractors should endeavor to keep a good relationship with engineers during project implementation. Since engineers are engaged by employers to supervise and inspect contractors' work, contractors should show respect to engineers, work strictly in accordance with contract terms and reasonable requests made by engineers and communicate and actively cooperate with engineers during construction to avoid disputes. However, if engineers are obviously partial to the employer and behave unfairly, contractors should deploy evidence and contract terms to protect their rights and interests.

---

74. Chen Mingbao, Liu Zuguo, Xu Lijun, "How to Deal with the Relationship Between the Contractor and the Supervising (Consulting) Engineer", *Anhui Buildings*, 2010 (5).

§3.03   FINANCING AND GUARANTEE AGENCIES

[A]   Financing Agencies

International projects are mainly financed by banks. In project financing, banks rely on the project revenue to take back the principal and interest, so the success of projects directly affects the repayment of the debt. At the same time, banks have a certain impact on the implementation of the project: (1) banks will set a series of requirements for contractors' qualification, determination of the construction period and cost, project insurance and guarantees. Banks will ask employers to pass these requirements on to contractors by integrating them in project contracts and thereby transfer the risks to contractors; (2) some banks will also appoint independent consultants to supervise the execution, quality, completion testing, completion certificate, claims and other aspects of the project and strictly review contractors' performance. The system of double checks implemented by the employers' and banks' engineers may lead to the risk of project delay; (3) in project financing, banks will set a number of preconditions for loan disbursement in the loan agreement in general. Where contractors or other parties fail to meet such preconditions, banks will not approve the loan. As a result, the project cannot be started; (4) banks may require a "takeover agreement" with employers and contractors. The agreement stipulates that in case of a specific situation, especially when it is difficult for employers to perform the contract, banks will intervene and take over the EPC contract. A project involving bank financing will bring great benefit to the bank. However, the bank will have a significant influence on the project, and this may bring associated risks. Therefore, contractors should manage and prevent the risks that may be associated with the actions of financing agencies.

In projects financed by banks, contractors need to recognize that the requirements for the cost and construction period in contracts are likely to be proposed by a bank. This has the effect that contractors' bargaining powers are weakened in negotiation. In order to reduce risks, on the one hand, a risk assessment and quotation must be fully carried out in the bidding process; on the other hand, contractors should prepare their claim plans ahead of time and establish a good procedure to avoid losing the right to claim due to noncompliance with the contract requirements. In addition, in a project financed by banks, the bank usually has the right of final confirmation of the payment for the project. Without approval of the bank, the contractor cannot acquire the corresponding funds. The bank itself does not understand the actual operation of the project, and its payment management process is very strict and formal. The bank agrees to pay only when the submitted payment applications fully comply with the contract requirements. In this case, any ambiguity in the contract regarding payment terms and procedures may hinder the payment, resulting in delayed payment. This requires the contractor to carefully review the payment terms before signing the contract, to ensure that the conditions and procedures for payment are clear and free of ambiguity to reduce the risk of payment delay.

[B] Guarantee Agencies

Guarantees are a necessity for international projects. A contractor can hardly win a bid without obtaining the guarantees required by employers. Organizations that are capable of providing guarantees include banks, guarantee companies, insurance companies, other financial institutions and business groups. Although contractors can win the bid for the project smoothly by relying on the guarantee issued by guarantee agencies, those agencies may also bring risks to the acquisition and implementation of the project.

In international projects, some employers will include a requirement in the bid documents that contractors should provide a guarantee in a given format. Banks and other guarantee agencies, as guarantors, are willing to issue a guarantee in their own guarantee format. Unless a contractor is able to prevail on a bank to issue a guarantee in a form acceptable by the employer, the contractor may end up with a form of guarantee issued in a format prescribed or accepted by the bank but not acceptable by the employer. The risk of not being able to obtain a guarantee in the employer's preferred format may cause the contractor to waste time, effort and money and may even lead the contractor to miss the opportunity to become the successful bidder.

In international projects involving financing, employers often need to provide guarantees to banks to reduce the political, economic and other risks of banks, which include the sovereign guarantee, the resource guarantee and the financial institution guarantee. The first two can transfer risks of banks to a large extent, which can be approved by banks more easily. A railway project with a total investment of several hundred million U.S. dollars in a country in East Africa illustrates the point. In order to improve the project's chances of success, the employer initially insisted on using a sovereign guarantee from Chinese financial institutions. However, the foreign debt of the country was close to its national ceiling, and it was impossible to obtain the sovereign guarantee, and this threatened to cause a suspension of the project. It became difficult for contractors to continue to obtain bank loans. Through multilateral consultation, a joint guarantee of the African Trade Insurance (ATI[75]) Agency and China Export & Credit Insurance Corporation was adopted for the project. Although this guarantee was also approved by China's banks, the procedures were complicated.[76] The choice of guarantee methods is also an important factor in the successful operation of a project.

---

75. African Trade Insurance Agency: Established by a number of African countries in 2001, and headquartered in Nairobi, Kenya, the African Trade Insurance Agency acquires technical and financial support from the World Bank. It is the only international multilateral institution designed to provide African countries with guarantees of political risks and commercial loans.
76. Fu Jianjun, "Some Comments on the Operation of Buyer Credit for International Project Export", *International Project Contracting and Labor Service*, 2014 (1).

§3.04   LOCAL CONSULTANTS

In international projects, it is often necessary to track projects through local consultants. These agencies usually have a wide range of information channels to get the latest news of bidding for major local projects, as well as to provide contractors with local political, economic, legal information and business consulting services. During construction, in case of any conflict between contractors and employers, the consultant is both a local person familiar with the situation and a stakeholder of the contractor. This dual identity allows consultants to mediate and coordinate, thus properly and efficiently resolving conflicts.[77] However, local consultants can also be closely connected to employers, which creates a danger of conflicts of interest if they play a dual role. A well-chosen consultant will facilitate project implementation and the development of a new market in a good manner. On the contrary, choosing the wrong consultant can pose significant risks to Chinese contractors and bring unforeseen consequences, such as preventing other employers from inviting the contractor to bid and delaying the scheduled payment of funds to the contractor in the ongoing projects. Therefore, contractors must be cautious in the selection of consultants.[78] From the perspective of engineering practice, risks of local consultants that are common in international projects primarily include the following.

[A]   Providing False Information

A local consultant usually provides contractors with project information of the project and the local conditions of the host country under the contract. However, if the consultant plays a dual role, providing services to both the employer and the contractor at the same time, it may have conflicting loyalties which the contractors must pay special attention to. In an extreme example involving a hydropower project in a country, those conflicting loyalties led a local consultant to provide false information to a Chinese contractor, which significantly harmed the contractor. The local employer initiated international competitive bidding to obtain a low bid. A number of Chinese contractors, including Company A, bidded for the project. Company A found a local consultant to obtain information about the employer and the project. That consultant, however, was also providing services to the employer. In the bidding process, the local consultant provided false information to Company A, to lower the price provided to the employer while receiving substantial fees from the employer. In reliance on the false information it received from the conflicted local consultant, Company A started a price competition with other Chinese contractors bidding for the project. Although it finally won the bid at the lowest price, Company A suffered a major loss in this non-profit-making project.

---

77. Li Bin, "A Brief Analysis of the Selection of the International Project Agency and Signing of an Agency Agreement", *Times Finance*, 2015 (20).
78. Liu Junying, Li Zhiyong, "International Project Risk Management", China Architecture & Building Press, 2013.

This is the most extreme case in which the consultant provided false information to the contractor so as to obtain lowered bid prices for the employer. As a result, the Chinese contractor won the bid at the significantly lowered price through a price competition, which benefited the employer (to the detriment of the contractor).[79]

In international projects, conflicts of interests can create moral hazards for consultants who may not hesitate to make profits from employers (who they may see as a longer-term source of business) by preferring the interests of the employers over the contractors thereby causing detriment to the contractors. While providing employers' information to contractors, consultants can also inform employers of contractors' bid status and strategy so that employers can adjust and optimize their plans to the detriment of contractors. Chinese contractors should always consider whether the consultant has divided loyalties before acting on their advice.

[B] Violation of the Confidentiality Agreement

In international projects, consultants generally have a confidentiality obligation to contractors in relation to the relevant internal information and data. The characteristics of their service determine that consultants can access contractors' core information and data. If a consultant violates the confidentiality agreement, such core information will be disclosed, which will have a huge impact on contractors. In fact, however, not all consultants will comply with the confidentiality obligations under the agency agreement. Contractors should keep an eye on this in practice as part of their due diligence in selecting a consultant and as the project progresses.

[C] Mitigating Risks of Local Consultants

In international projects, local consultants can assist contractors in successfully acquiring projects—however, they can also pose significant risks to the contractors. To mitigate those risks, contractors must be cautious when selecting local consultants. In the bidding stage, contractors must fully examine the consultant's credibility, capacity, relationship network, operational strength, etc. In order to select a suitable consultant, a contractor should: (1) select a consultant with extensive communication relationships and strong capacity: A consultant with a wide-ranging relationship network can assist contractors to quickly contact the employer, gain a good impression from the employer and win the initiative for winning the bid; (2) select a professional and experienced consultant: International projects are usually long-term and technically complex projects which require consultants to spend a considerable amount of time and energy on services. A consultant without sufficient work experience and business knowledge will affect the consulting services and thus affect the implementation of the project; and (3) select a reputable consultant: Choosing a consultant with good credentials is the key to prevent risks.

---

79. Qiang Wanqing, Agency's Role in the International Project Contracting, *Da Guan Weekly*, 2013 (3).

§3.05   PARTNERS OF THE JOINT VENTURE

With the gradual deepening of China's "BRI," an increasing number of Chinese contractors have participated in the construction of international projects. For public projects, fully foreign-funded companies are often subject to certain restrictions. A joint venture formed by Chinese enterprises and local companies will usually be exempt from such restrictions. Therefore, international contractors invest their advantageous resources and form a strategic contracting joint venture to share benefits and risks. In this way, they improve their overall competitiveness by complementing their strengths, sharing responsibilities and risks, obtaining preferential policies and in other ways.

Article 1.14 [Joint and Several Responsibilities] of 1999 edition of FIDIC Red Book stipulates that where a contractor is a joint venture, a group or other affiliated group formed by two or more parties, the abovementioned parties shall be considered to be jointly and severally responsible to the employer in the performance of the contract, and the abovementioned parties shall inform the employer of their responsible persons who are entitled to manage the contractor and each of its partners. The terms of the contract clearly define the rights and obligations of each partner of the joint venture and the lead partner and bind the behavior of the partners of the joint venture. However, due to the complicated management levels and complex relations among its partners, a joint venture also brings certain risks along with the benefits. To summarize practical cases, the joint venture risks mainly include the following.

[A]   The Risks of Noncompliance by Partners

A joint venture usually consists of two or more companies. The performance of any partner of the joint venture has a certain impact on the execution of the project. The partners' capability of compliance is mainly reflected in the following four aspects:[80] (1) project experience: A partner with a wealth of experience is an important guarantee for the success of their cooperation. If a partner lacks relevant project experience, it will be difficult for the joint venture partners to work together in a short period, thus affecting the operation of the project; (2) profitability: For a project, profit is one of the common goals pursued by partners of a joint venture. For the joint venture, the profit is determined by the profitability of each partner; (3) degree of internationalization: In international projects, internationalization mainly includes allocation of global resources and localized management. The characteristics of the joint venture partners in these two aspects have a direct impact on the quality and benefit of the joint venture; and (4) bank credit: Bank credit is one of the strengths of joint venture partners and one of the main considerations in selecting joint venture partners. In the early stage of cooperation, it is particularly necessary to invest resources in a centralized manner. Good bank credit of partners is beneficial to the joint venture to obtain bank loans.

---

80. Cheng Jian, Zhang Wei, Song Lei, "International Project Design—Internal Risk Management of the Construction Joint Venture", *Journal of International Economic Cooperation*, 2015 (7).

The Output and Performance Based Road Contract (OPRC)[81] was adopted in a World Bank-funded road upgrading project in a country. In the bidding stage, a Chinese contractor as a lead firm of a joint venture gave priority to a Chinese design institute when selecting a joint venture partner. After winning the bid and signing a contract, as the design institute did not fully understand the specifications of the American Association of State Highway and Transportation Officials which were applied to the project and coupled with language difficulties, the design work proceeded slowly, and the approval by the engineer and the employer could not be obtained in time. The lead firm of the joint venture had to terminate the joint venture agreement with the original design institute and subcontracted another local firm to finish the design. The project was eventually successfully implemented with the local firm.[82] In this project, the construction company failed to consider the capability of compliance when selecting the joint venture partner, which led to problems in the follow-up process of the project. If the Chinese design institute carefully complied with the stipulated specifications at the beginning, or if it communicated with the lead firm to make adjustments after receiving communications from the engineer, the joint venture agreement would not have been terminated.

[B]   The Risk of Improper Type of Joint Venture

Nowadays, the internationally accepted types of joint venture can be basically divided into two types: corporate joint ventures and contractual joint ventures. Corporate joint ventures are organized by establishing an incorporated company. This kind of joint venture is not organized only for a specific project but organized for a longer-term goal. A contractual joint venture is organized only for a specific project. Both types have their own advantages and disadvantages, but the improper selection of joint venture type creates risks to contractors.

In order to expand the market in a certain country, a Chinese contractor noticed that local contractor A maintained close contact with the local government and had a wide network of relationships, which the Chinese contractor hoped to utilize. Therefore, it established a joint venture with the local contractor A for a period of 20 years. Although the two companies had cooperated well in the first project, disputes occurred in the following projects due to different considerations on the way forward for the joint venture. The Chinese contractor believed that the development prospects of roads and bridges in the country were much better than that of the building construction, while contractor A held the contrary opinion. Although there was another local company with close ties to the local governments, contractor B, who was interested in cooperating with the Chinese contractor on projects relating to roads and bridges, the

---

81. OPRC, It is an innovative mode of road contract appeared in the early twenty-first century. In this contract mode, the project funds are paid on the basis of the evaluation results of the implementation results, operation and maintenance performance of the project, rather than the unit price of the completed quantities.
82. Cheng Jian, Zhang Wei, Song Lei, "International Project Design—Internal Risk Management of the Construction Joint Venture", *Journal of International Economic Cooperation*, 2015 (7).

20-year joint venture agreement with contractor A, prevented the Chinese contractor from working with contractor B on projects relating to roads and bridges. If the Chinese contractor and contractor A had chosen to form a contractual joint venture (instead of a corporate joint venture), the Chinese contractor would not have missed the opportunity to work with a more suitable company on later projects.

[C]   The Risk of Unclear Work Scope

Compared with working alone, a joint venture as a kind of multi-interested consortium may often lead to disputes in determining the work scopes of all parties in various aspects including resource input, benefit distribution, veto power, responsibility distribution and personnel management.

The work of one project which exemplifies this risk included the construction of a multifunctional dam, water transmission facilities, a water treatment plant and a hydropower station. The project was undertaken by a joint venture consisting of contractors A, B and C. The respective work scopes of the contractors were: Contractor A would undertake the construction of multifunctional dam, contractor B would undertake the construction of the water transmission facilities and water treatment plant, contractor C would undertake the construction of the hydropower station. In addition, the contract specified that "each contractor is responsible for the construction of the access road to its work site." In this project, a road between the water treatment plant and the hydropower station needed to be constructed to connect the work site of contractor B and contractor C. However, the responsibility of the road was not clearly specified in the contract, and neither contractor B nor contractor C was willing to construct the road. The dispute was finally solved through mediation, but the project duration was seriously prolonged and the completion of the project delayed.

In another example, two Chinese contractors formed a joint venture to jointly implement an overseas project. Before signing the joint venture agreement, the two parties negotiated their respective work scope and the unit price of the project but could not reach consensus. When signing the joint venture agreement, the two companies did not specify their work scopes and the unit price and did not even mention the previous negotiations in the agreement. During the implementation of the project, the two parties had a dispute relating to price. One of the parties took the view that because the scope of work and the unit price of the project were not specified in the joint venture agreement, these issues should be determined according to the previous negotiation. However, the other party took the view that if these issues were to be determined based on the previous negotiation, the two parties were not undertaking the project as a joint venture but subcontractors—given that the two parties had signed a joint venture agreement, they should share the project funds based on their own work scope and the unit price paid by the employer as a joint venture. Although the two parties reached consensus after a series of negotiations, this seriously delayed the progress of the project.

Contractors may form a joint venture for their common interest, but unclear work scopes are very likely to cause disputes, which is bad for the cooperation of the parties.

[D] The Risk of Guarantee Extension

In international projects, employers usually require contractors to provide advance payment guarantees, performance guarantees, warranty guarantees, etc. In projects implemented by joint ventures, employers may at time require the parties of the joint venture to issue guarantees respectively according to their proportions in the joint venture and may at other times require the joint venture to provide an overall guarantee issued by the lead partner, while other partners of the joint venture provide counterguarantees to the lead firm. When employers require the joint venture to provide an overall guarantee, the lead firm may face the risks relating to extending the guarantee.

In an EPC project in Africa, a Chinese Company A formed a joint venture with other three Chinese companies as the lead partner to undertake the construction of the project. As the lead partner, Company A provided a performance guarantee and an advance payment guarantee (overall guarantee) to the employer, which were valid until September 21, 2014. One partner of the joint venture, Company B, provided two counterguarantees to Company A, which would expire on December 25, 2014. At the beginning of September 2014, the employer requested the joint venture to extend both the performance guarantee and advance payment guarantee under the main contract. Company A extended the two guarantees before the expiration date with the advance payment guarantee being extended to June 30, 2015, and the performance guarantee being extended to December 31, 2017. In an attempt to avoid risks, Company A required Company B to make a commitment (signed on September 23) to extend the two counterguarantees before the expiration date; otherwise all the interests and shares of Company B under this project will be unconditionally transferred to Company A. On September 25, 2014, Company A paid an advance payment of USD 6.5 million to Company B. Afterward, Company A investigated and found that there were serious problems in the internal operation of Company B, which caused the delay of the project construction. Therefore, Company B was more likely to refuse the extension of the two counterguarantees. Once Company B breached the contract, the overall implementation of the project would suffer a great impact and risk.

In international projects contracted by a joint venture, when employers request the extension of guarantees under the main contract, the lead partner should also request other partners to extend the counterguarantees, to mitigate the risks of liability to the employer without any corresponding counterguarantees.

[E] The Risk of Impure Motives of Forming Joint Ventures

The purpose of forming a joint venture is to better complete the project by fully utilizing the respective resources and advantages of the partners. If several companies form a joint venture out of their own impure motives, disputes relating to the interests and losses distribution between all parties are likely to arise. For example, Company A had local resources, but it could not win the bid, because its qualification could not meet the requirements. Therefore, it signed an agreement with Company B to form a joint venture. With the relationship resources of Company A and qualification of Company B, the joint venture won the bid, but Company A decided to implement the project alone. After that, Company A was discovered and suspected to have violated local laws, which led to the exclusion of the joint venture from the project. After the joint venture was excluded, the two parties had a great dispute on how to divide the "pre-expenses of the project," which eventually led to a vicious group incident at the construction site, causing more than 20 injuries and adverse effects.

[F] Mitigating Joint Venture Risks

Forming joint ventures is conducive to successful bidding of contractors in the fierce competition. However, factors such as improper types of joint ventures and poor compliance capacity of joint venture partners will also bring risks to contractors. In order to fully combine the advantages of the joint venture partners and achieve the advantage synergistic effect of "1 + 1 > 2," Chinese contractors may take the following measures to mitigate joint venture risks.

First, select capable joint venture partners. Contractors should focus on three aspects.[83] The first aspect to consider is how complementary the resources, advantages and capabilities are, which is referred to as the "value of joint venture." In other words, whether a potential partner could bring additional value to the joint venture should be considered. The higher the "value of joint venture" is, the more likely the joint venture will win the bid. The second consideration is whether the members of joint venture will benefit significantly. The benefits obtained by the parties in the joint venture need to be greater than the benefits obtained by each individual party participating in the project alone, and this is the foundation of the continuity of joint ventures. The third aspect to consider is whether partners of the joint venture have the ethos of cooperation. Partners of the joint venture should be inclusive and understanding. They should have the ability to seek common ground while reserving differences and resolving conflicts. This is the basis for establishing a joint venture. Through the evaluation of these three aspects, contractors may select partners more efficiently.

Second, clearly specify the work scope and interest distribution of the parties in the joint venture agreement. Joint venture agreements set out the code for all parties of joint venture and specify the framework for coordinating the relationships of all parties. A good joint venture agreement must clearly and reasonably specify the responsibilities and rights of the parties involved so that the overall interest of the joint venture will be maintained, and the interests of all parties will be considered as well.[84]

Third, enhance the internal organization and management within joint ventures. There are differences in the organization, corporate strategy, corporate culture and other aspects among joint venture partners, so efficient organization and management are indispensable to achieve effective integration and reasonable allocation of various

---

83. Wang Wuren, "Joint Ventures—In the Name of Faith Cooperation", *International Project Contracting & Labor Services*, 2014 (8).
84. Cheng Jian, Zhang Wei, Song Lei, "International Project Engineering—Internal Risk Management of Construction Joint Ventures", *Journal of International Economic Cooperation*, 2015 (7).

resources within the joint venture. With the increasing complexity of international projects, reasonable organizations and management systems of joint ventures are very significant for the efficiency of project. All parties in a joint venture should strictly comply with the joint venture agreement to ensure the legality of joint venture decisions and the efficiency of implementation. Meanwhile, a lead firm of the joint venture should properly fulfill its responsibilities as the leader, set itself an example to others, strictly abide by the joint venture agreement, develop reasonable planning for the organization and management of the joint venture and implement the planning accordingly.

Fourth, enhance the communication among partners of the joint venture. A large number of international projects illustrate how communication is an important tool to deal with the risks within joint ventures. Smooth communication and coordination of all parties in the joint venture are indispensable to pursue synergies, so as to achieve the win-win situation. For example, an EPC road project in a certain country in Africa was jointly implemented by a Chinese construction company and a design and consulting company in South Africa. In the survey and design phase of the project, the two companies carried out an in-depth cooperation in collecting geological, hydrological and topographic data, maximized their own advantages and quickly developed a reasonable preliminary design after confirming the design principles and scheme. In their daily communication, both parties shared their technical materials as well. The Chinese company explored and researched the design documents and related software provided by the South African company, which not only strengthened its design capabilities but also deepened its understanding and application of foreign specifications.[85] In this case, the two parties maintained good communication and collaboration during the project implementation process so that their respective advantages were fully utilized and displayed, and the goal of a win-win partnership was achieved.

§3.06 NOMINATED SUBCONTRACTORS

Nominated subcontractors are those subcontractors designated in project contracts by employers and/or to be appointed by the engineers during the implementation of the project. At present, nominated subcontractors are quite common in international projects. Employers will designate some aspects of the project engineering to be carried out by specific subcontractors, and subcontract agreements will be executed by and between contractors and nominated subcontractors.

In the process of project implementation, contractors need to organize, coordinate with and manage the nominated subcontractor comprehensively, and both parties should exercise the rights and perform the obligations in accordance with the relevant clauses in the subcontract. The traditional contracting mode cannot cover all the

---

85. Cheng Jian, Zhang Wei, Song Lei, "International Project Engineering—Internal Risk Management of Construction Joint Ventures", *Journal of International Economic Cooperation*, 2015 (7).

functions as the functions of modern buildings have become more and more comprehensive and detailed.[86] Subcontracting certain professional expertise can be more conducive to the smooth progress of the project, improvement of project quality and cost saving. In one housing project in Sri Lanka, the employer incorporated the management of nominated subcontractors into the contractor's work scope in the main contract. The arrangement envisaged that the contractor, in accordance with the instruction of the employer, should subcontract some professional engineering of the project to the subcontractor designated by the employer and enter into a subcontract with the nominated subcontractor, with the main contractor collecting a percentage of management fee for the designated subcontracting work. In some examples, employers may desire professional subcontractors in a certain engineering specialty to ensure engineering quality and progress.[87]

With respect to the international projects, contractors are responsible for the overall management of the project, for coordinating the relationship among various subcontractors, and for the implementation of the whole project. The work of the nominated subcontractors is part of the project, and the progress and quality of it can impact the success of the whole project. However, nominated subcontractors are appointed by the employer, and so contractors have a lower degree of control over them than other domestic subcontractors. In light of the foregoing, the contractors should pay attention to the following risks.

[A]   Poor Compliance Capability of Nominated Subcontractors

As a result of monopoly operation or other reasons, nominated subcontractors may have poor qualifications and compliance capability, which will lead to technical risks and affect the quality of the whole project. In a bridge project in a country in Southeast Asia, the employer in the contract appointed a local consortium as the subcontractor of the construction of the ramp approach bridge in the south side. A series of technical and quality problems occurred during the subcontractor's performance. Poor construction capacity, construction without complying with the technical plans, incorrect construction methods and other problems caused the nominated subcontractor to fail to meet the requirements of standards, procedures and design documents.[88]

[B]   Managing Risk of the Nominated Subcontractors

Contractors are exposed to additional interface management risks in managing nominated subcontractors. Although project contracts usually stipulate that contractors have the responsibility to coordinate the work interface between subcontractors, it is quite difficult to specify every detail about all the interface. Much overlapping of work

---

86. Guo Haimei, "Study on the Understanding and Management of Designated Subcontracting by the Main Contractor in an International Project", *Engineering Construction*, 2017 (6).
87. *Ibid.*
88. Guo Sen, Tang Jian, Wang Yanpeng, etc., "Management of Designated Subcontractors in International Engineering Projects", *Highway*, 2011 (3).

interfaces exists between the main contractor and the nominated subcontractors.[89] Improper handling of interface problems will directly affect the quality, schedule, cost and safety of the project, which is crucial to the success of the project. In the implementation process of the project, nominated subcontractors are organized and managed by contractors, and poor management of the nominated subcontractors will have a significant impact on the implementation of the whole project. In order to improve its ability to manage nominated subcontractors, and improve the efficiency and quality of the project, contractors should pay attention to the following aspects.

First, the qualifications and capabilities of nominated subcontractors have a significant impact on the result of the entire project. Contractors should, as early as possible, exert their influence in the employers' selection process of the nominated subcontractors. A good nominated subcontractor will reduce the overall contractor's difficulty in managing the whole project and ensure the quality and schedule of the project at the same time. As a contractor, it should take advantage of its wealth of experience to help employers in the process of selecting subcontractors, reviewing subcontracting teams and providing suggestions. If a contractor is not able to exert influence in the process of designating subcontractor by the employer, it may refer to Article 5.2 Objection to Designation in the 1999 edition of FIDIC Red Book, and provide reasonable evidence to reject nominated subcontractor or make timely communications with the employer to modify the subcontract agreement, and require the employer to change the nominated subcontractors where necessary, to safeguard the contractors' own rights and interests.

Second, contractors should make sure that the subcontract terms are consistent with the project contracts and that key terms of the project contracts flow down to nominated subcontractors. In international projects, project contracts are signed by the employers and contractors. Some project contracts clearly stipulate contractors' responsibilities for nominated subcontractors. Subcontract agreements are signed by contractors and nominated subcontractors. Every subcontract agreement and other subcontract documents generally constitute a complete contract system.

In some cases, subcontract agreements are negotiated between employers and nominated subcontractors. This may also pose risks. First, the contract conditions of subcontract and the main contract may be incompatible. For example, in a civil engineering project in a Central Asian country, the employer engaged a supplier for some equipment and wished to apply the nominated subcontractor clause in the main contract. The contract form at which the employer had engaged the nominated subcontractor was FIDIC Yellow Book, while the main contract was concluded with the red book. The subcontractor refused to accept terms of the main contract that were incompatible with the subcontract on which the main contractor insisted. The problem was not resolved, and the supplies by the nominated subcontractor were transferred out of the main contract, thereby causing much delay. Second, if the obligations and responsibilities of nominated subcontractors are less than those of contractors under the project contract, contractors will bear additional responsibilities (for which there

---

89. Guo Haimei, "Study on the Understanding and Management of Designated Subcontracting by the Main Contractor in an International Project", *Engineering Construction*, 2017 (6).

are no corresponding responsibilities on the nominated subcontractors) in the event that the nominated subcontractor breaches the subcontract agreement. Therefore, contractors shall conduct a careful review of the contract terms during the contract negotiation stage, discover the loopholes and risks therein and negotiate with employers. Contractors can refer to Article 5.2 Objection to Designation in 1999 edition of FIDIC Red Book, if necessary, to exercise the right of "reasonable objection to designation" to protect themselves from adverse effects of risks assumed by the contractors as a result of a mismatch between the project contract and subcontract terms.

Third, contractors should enhance the organization, coordination and management of the project and supervise the quality, HSE (Health, Safety, Environment) of the work implemented by nominated subcontractors to ensure the effective implementation and operation of every subcontracting work. The main contractor should integrate interface management into the scope of project management, which should be organized and designed in the early stage of the project. While ensuring that the interface management system is complete and does not miss any work, it should also ensure that the interfaces do not overlap with each other, so as to avoid confusion in responsibility allocation and a series of disputes. In the process of interface management, it is also necessary to enhance the communication with nominated subcontractors, which can effectively guide the project implementation and improve the efficiency of project management.

Fourth, in the process of the management of nominated subcontractors, the possible risks should be fully considered and all evidence shall be retained for future claims. In the project of Suramadu sea-crossing bridge, the contractor minimized oral agreements, oral notices and oral instructions so that the written records prevailed. It retained evidence of all management behavior, which was an important measure to prevent loss in disputes. Specific requirements of the contractor included:[90] (1) all correspondences shall be categorized and recorded, and out mails shall be signed by the party involved after receiving, and the receipt record shall be kept; (2) all documents about contract management, quality rectification notice and measurement shall be categorized and filed after being signed by relevant nominated subcontractors; (3) in the subcontract management, all management notices, instructions and orders shall be sent to nominated subcontractors in written form; (4) all minutes of negotiation results and the working conference shall be recorded and sent to nominated subcontractors in written form after being signed by all the attendants; (5) as to the materials and machinery related to nominated subcontractors, the handover record shall be signed by relevant persons.

---

90. Guo Sen, Tang Jian, Wang Yanpeng, etc., "Management of Designated Subcontractors in International Engineering Projects", *Highway*, 2011 (3).

§3.07   OTHER SUBCONTRACTORS

With the development of international projects and the improvement of Chinese contractors' overseas contracting ability, more and more Chinese contractors are engaged in overseas market as main contractors. EPC projects, including the whole process of design, procurement, construction, installation and trial operation, are often large in scale and involve many technical specialties and complicated construction process. To ensure smooth implementation of the project, contractors usually subcontract parts of the work to several qualified subcontractors. In this way, they can reduce their input and execution cost from various aspects such as equipment procurement, human resource and management cost, so as to achieve cost saving and win-win cooperation effect. Subcontractors include nominated subcontractors and other subcontractors. Nominated subcontractors are selected and designated by employers, while other subcontractors are usually selected by contractors. Contractors should organize, manage and coordinate subcontractors in a comprehensive manner. The works of subcontractors form part of the work of contractors. If other subcontractors fail to perform the obligations under subcontract agreements, the losses will ultimately be borne by contractors. Based on case studies, risks caused by subcontractors in international projects mainly include the following.

[A]   Subcontractor's Weak Performance Capability

Subcontractors are usually chosen by contractors. If subcontractors have poor qualifications and low professional skills, and fail to complete the project on schedule, with approved quality and quantity, they will ultimately affect the performance of contractors in the entire project. In an international project, the contractor subcontracted the road and tunnel construction to three domestic subcontractors respectively. In the end, the contractor was forced to terminate all three subcontractors due to their weak construction capability and project delays. The project suffered a loss of more than ETB 30 million resulting from failure of these subcontracts alone, which doubled the losses and put pressure on the whole project.

[B]   Risk of Re-subcontract Wholly

For any project, the choice of subcontractor is very important, which will result in one honors all; one damns all. However, illegal subcontracting and multilevel subcontracting has become one of the biggest risks to Chinese contractors nowadays. Under such circumstances, it is difficult to guarantee that works carried out by subcontractors are qualified. Company A is a large international contractor, who has been listed as one of the world's top 225 engineering contracting companies by American Engineering News Record (ENR) for several years. Company A undertakes the general contracting, and completes sets of equipment, engineering consultation and engineering design, project management and engineering supervision, installation and debugging and technical services of various domestic industrial projects. A project in Country F in Southeast

Asia was developed and executed by two subsidiaries of Company A: Company B and Company C. Company B is a trading company. This was the first time that it carried out foreign projects. Previously, Company B had no overseas project experience and personnel with relevant experience. Company C is an enterprise whose main business is project design, debugging and tests. In the selection of equipment suppliers, materials suppliers and other suppliers, Company B chose enterprises that had cooperated with Company A in other projects. Problems concerning these enterprises occurred during the installation, debugging and operation process, resulting in project delay, repeated procurement and increased costs. In the stage of commissioning and trial, Company C subcontracted the work to Company K, and Company K subcontracted to Company P, which was also a subcontractor of the employer. This subcontracting mode caused many problems, which led to project delay and triggered the employer's claim. Such practices of illegal subcontracting and multilevel subcontracting have made contractors of the project less controllable on the quality and progress of the project, bringing significant risks and hidden dangers to the implementation of the project.

Compared with the nominated subcontractors, contractors can effectively control and manage other subcontractors in the selection process and the negotiation and performance of the contract to manage risks caused by subcontractors. Contractors may take the following measures to manage risks.

First, risks of subcontracting should be controlled at the beginning. In selecting subcontractors, contractors should be fully aware of subcontractors' technical strength, equipment condition, and fully investigate their qualifications, funds, reputation, engineering experience and litigation in recent years. The contractor should choose subcontractors with good credit standing, strong performance ability and high reputation instead of those offering the lowest bid price solely for cost saving. At the same time, after a subcontract risk occurs, contractors should take corresponding measures to mitigate the specific causes of the risk. For example, in an oil project in a country in Central Asia, when the subcontract risk occurred, the contractor opened the joint management account of both parties, controlled and tracked the subcontractor's payment, paid the remuneration of on-site labor on behalf of the subcontractor, and changed the subcontract's suppliers of materials, so as to reduce the adverse impact of the subcontract risk on the implementation of the project.[91]

Second, in international projects, contractors will sometimes receive payment from employers after paying subcontractors for work completed, thus bearing the risk of nonpayment by the employers. To avoid nonpayment risks, contractors could adopt the "Pay When Paid" clause or "Pay If Paid" clause under the "back-to-back" contract mode[92] to transfer the risk of nonpayment to subcontractors to the extent permitted by laws of the relevant jurisdiction. For international projects, at the beginning and end of

---

91. Chen Yanhua, "Risks and Strategies for Overseas Petroleum Engineering Contracting Projects", *Finance and Accounting (Financial)*, 2013 (8).
92. The so-called back-to-back contract refers to a contract established by the general contractor in a subcontract to obtain the employer's payment as a precondition for payment to the subcontractor.

each financial year, employers tend to lack funds, which can lead to delayed payment. The "back-to-back" clause allows contractor to be temporarily free from the obligation to make payments to subcontractors, ensuring that its own cash flow is functioning properly.

The template of "back-to-back" clause is set out in FIDIC Conditions of Subcontract for Construction (first edition, 1994) Clause 16.3 Payment Due; Payment Withheld or Deferred; Interest: The contractor shall be entitled to withhold or defer payment of all or part or any sums otherwise due pursuant to the provisions hereof where:[93]

(a) The amounts are less than the minimum amount of the subcontract;
(b) The amounts are less than the minimum amount of the general contract;
(c) The amounts included in any statement are not certified in full by the Engineer, providing such failure to certify is not due to the act or default of the contractor;
(d) The contractor has included the amounts set out in the Statement in his own statement in accordance with the Main Contract and the Engineer has certified, but the employer has failed to make payment in full to the contractor in respect of such amounts, providing such failure is not due to the act or default of the contractor; or
(e) A dispute arises or has arisen between the Subcontractor and the contractor and/or the contractor and the employer involving any question of measurement on quantities or any other matter included in any such Statement.

Meanwhile, "FIDIC Conditions of Subcontract for Construction" also stipulates that if contractors withhold or delay any payment, it shall promptly (but not later than the agreed payment term) notify the subcontractor of the reason for the withholding or postponement.

Finally, while contractors can use the "back-to-back" clause to transfer risk of nonpayment to the subcontractor, they should also pay attention to validity and legality this kind of clause under a different legal regime. Article 19.5 of China's current construction engineering construction professional subcontract (demonstration text) (gf-2003-0213) says: The subcontract payments are not related to the payment by employers. The Housing Grants, Construction and Regeneration Act passed in Britain in 1996 prohibits "back-to-back" clauses, except when the employer goes bankrupt. American and New Zealand judicial precedents also tend to protect subcontractors' rights. Australia directly prohibits the use of such provisions and the terms. Contractors should seek legal advice as to how to best avoid payment risk to subcontractors under the governing law and jurisdiction of the project.

§3.08   SUPPLIER OF MASTER EQUIPMENT AND MATERIALS

With the increasingly fierce competition in the international projects, bidding prices and overall strength have become more and more essential to achieving success in the bidding stage. For Chinese contractors going global, the procurement management of equipment and materials for international projects directly affects the bidding price,

---

93. Bao Yanping, Meng Yourui, "An Analysis of 'Pay-If-paid' and 'Pay-When-Paid' Clauses in International Project Subcontracting Contract", *International Economic Cooperation*, 2014 (11).

which determines to some extent whether contractors would win the bid or not. During the implementation of the project, management of suppliers will also affect the cost, schedule and quality of entire projects. If contractors fail to enhance the selection and management of suppliers, they are likely to face difficulties during the project execution. In practice, there are many cases in which contractors suffer losses due to improper selection or poor management of suppliers. In general, the supplier risks brought by suppliers are mainly reflected in the following aspects.

[A]   Weak Capability to Perform the Contract by Suppliers

Choosing suppliers is an important part of supplier management. The selection of suitable suppliers by contractors will not only effectively promote the normal corporate operation but also have far-reaching significance for the long-term corporate development. Different suppliers vary in strength, scale and product quality. The failure of suppliers to deliver the goods in time will not only delay the project schedule but also generate cost due to the idleness of mechanical equipment and personnel. Any issues with the quality of products provided by suppliers will greatly affect the quality of the entire project and may even lead to major safety accidents and damage the reputation of contractors.[94]

Under the EPC mode, designs are based on suppliers' data (including equipment type, specification, power, and design parameters, etc.). The data is mainly included in the documents submitted by suppliers. However, in practice, the following two circumstances often occur: (1) false or misleading technical information data provided by suppliers; (2) suppliers fail to submit technical data in a timely manner or provide multiple versions of technical data, which will lead directly to design error or delay the design progress. In a project in Africa, due to the incorrect equipment specifications and parameters presented by the supplier, the project was unable to reach the guaranteed performance value and suffered project delay and increasing cost.

[B]   Moral Hazard of Suppliers

Reviewing qualifications in writing alone cannot help contractors to avoid risks, especially under the current Chinese economy, where there is a large number of suppliers with quite different qualifications.[95] Some suppliers use various unreasonable means to guarantee their profits in the bidding and follow-up process, which will inevitably bring greater risks to contractors. The suppliers' moral hazard is mainly manifested as the followings: (1) the risk of failing to perform the contract: Some suppliers will refuse to perform the contract because the price of the product has risen sharply after signing the contract; (2) the risk of "false offer": Contractors usually choose the supplier who offers the lowest price in the bidding when the technical

---

94. Ma Haiyan, "Research on Supplier Management Based on Cost Control", *China Market*, 2014 (35).
95. Wang Shuang, "EPCI Supplier Risk Management for International Engineering Project Procurement", *Global Market*, 2017 (22).

standards are met. Once contractors win the bid, some suppliers will insist that there are some errors in the proposals and some prices, for example the short-distance transportation cost or service fees, shall be increased, which is actually a behavior to increase the bid price in disguise; (3) the risk of fraud in the performance: During the project implementation, some suppliers provide some unqualified materials by taking advantage of limited skill and carelessness of contractors' personnel or subcontractor to other suppliers if they do not have adequate production. These will bring a huge impact on the quality of the project.

[C]   Risk of Supplier's Bankruptcy

Suppliers going bankrupt will also bring risks to contractors. In an international project, Company A of Europe and Chinese contractors W signed a contract on purchasing large-scale power generation equipment and the procurement of domestic components. During performance of the contract, Company A applied for bankruptcy procedure due to disputes and accessory debts arising from the lease contract of Company B, its subsidiary, and intended to freeze the properties of Company A and its subsidiaries abroad through government takeover, in an attempt to minimize its own losses. Subsequently, Company P of a third country expressed interest in the acquisition of Company A and negotiated with the local government and the original shareholders of Company A about acquisition and cooperation agreements. During this period, the contractor W launched a set of emergency plans to make arrangements among the technical department, logistics department, legal and contract department and finance department; communicated with Company A a number of times; and coordinated the leadership of the government authorities, Company P and the lawyer representing Company A. Finally, it was confirmed that Company A's remaining obligations under the procurement contract would be performed by Company P, thus avoiding the risk of the losses caused by Company A's nonperformance.

[D]   Cost Risk

Contractors' selection of suppliers at the bidding stage and its procurement plan at the project implementation stage will influence the cost of the project to some extent. In international projects, employers will sometimes require contractors to provide the equipment of European brands or from other countries. The cooperation between contractors and some suppliers designated by the employers may be either the first time or a one-off cooperation. These factors will possibly make it hard for the contractors to obtain a reasonable price discount, thereby increasing the procurement expense of equipment and materials. Some contractors do not sign procurement contracts with suppliers in a timely manner after winning bids, which will lead to an abrupt increase in the procurement cost. In a road project in a Central European country, after an early meeting with suppliers, Chinese consortium did not respond to the suppliers because of the down payment problem and the price which was too high price. Unexpectedly, the price of sand was tripled and the rent of digging equipment also rose by more than five times within one year afterward, thereby resulting in a sharp increase in the project cost. Further, if employers designate the specific suppliers or there are no available substitute suppliers of certain products and technologies, these suppliers will have a relatively strong bargaining power and possibly increase their offer price after an inquiry. In these circumstances, the contractors will face an even bigger cost risk. As such, contractors should be prepared ahead of time to lock down committed prices as soon as possible after winning the bid.

The key to managing supplier risk is to perform rigorous qualification review, select those supplies with good reputation and strong performance ability and exert stringent control over the cost risk that will possibly arise out of suppliers. Below are concrete preventive actions.

First, contractors shall pay attention to the following aspects during supplier selection:[96] (1) review qualification certificates of suppliers, mainly including business license, ISO9000 quality management system certificate and HSE certificate; (2) review the technical level of suppliers, mainly including technical R&D capacity and equipment capacity: Only if suppliers take a leading level in the industry, can it make products to meet quality requirements; (3) review the financial status of suppliers: contractors should also require suppliers to provide a credit reference report issued by a local bank, besides examining key financial indicators, such as net cash flow from operating activities, net profit, balance sheet ratio, over the past years; (4) review trace records of suppliers, mainly relating to the suppliers' reputation and quality of products: During the review, contractors shall perform a comprehensive assessment of suppliers' performance records in the industry over the past years to prevent the supplier from having product quality problems and after-sales service problems; (5) suppliers' management level: A well-run company should definitely have a good operation and management mode. At the same time, suppliers' management level will also secure timely delivery of the product; (6) litigation history of suppliers: Contractors should review the litigation history of suppliers over the past years to evaluate their credibility level and whether they are easy to cooperate with.

Second, contractors should widen equipment and material procurement channels and build the equipment and material suppliers network. At the bidding stage of a project, contractors should conduct effective inquiry and make a reasonable procurement plan based on the project schedule. After winning the bid, contractors should sign agreements with suppliers as soon as possible. It will be a benefit for contractors to set up smooth supply channels. Taking a project as an example, the contractor set up communication with a number of local suppliers in time, and it could at the earliest time know whether it can buy required materials and parts from the local market. During project implementation, the tail lock got rusty after installation due to errors in the painting process. If it had to be transported back to China, the costs would have been prohibitive. The contractor addressed this issue by finding a local plant which completed the repair of the lock in time, with the support and help of the supplier network which it had put in place early on.

---

96. *Ibid.*

§3.09 COMPETITORS

In view of the current development of the world, no matter whether contractors are domestic or foreign, international projects have been viewed as an important direction of development. Since the international market entails intense competition, contractors not only need to face the complicated project risk and macroscopic environment risk but also need to face the competition risk. And this competition risk comes not only from foreign contractors but also from the domestic "going-global" contractors. These competitors compete with each other in the limited market, which puts a lot of pressure on others involved in the competition. In the fierce competition, if the contractor is weak, it is likely to be squeezed out and suppressed in the next competition by other contractors, or even to be expelled out of the market.[97]

In a market of fierce competition, competitors are the key factors that contractors have to consider when bidding. The risk of competitors mainly takes the following form.

[A] Low-Price Bidding Risk

In international project market, the most prominent advantage of Chinese contractors is that the labor cost of Chinese contracting enterprises is relatively low, which results in price advantage. Given that all Chinese contractors have this same advantage, these Chinese contractors initiate the price competition in overseas markets.

For example, at present, the intensity of competition for state highway projects of W country is mainly caused by the following three factors: (1) there are numerous competitors: There are more than 10 Chinese contractors and many contractors from other countries; (2) tender information is transparent: Most companies have long-term cooperation relationship with the National Highway Authority of W country. Most of them have projects under construction, and every company can easily obtain appropriate tendering information from its employer; (3) low-cost bidding is common: Most contractors are trying to open up new markets, and they are not familiar with the market in the W country. For example, it is misunderstood that the World Bank's tax-exempt provisions in other markets would also apply to the W country. In these circumstances, the contractors offer a price below reasonable market prices under the pressure of intense competition. As a further example, in response to the tender of GB project and BN project which was announced in January 2009, eight and nine contractors respectively submitted bids for these projects. Ordinarily, the bidding price for a single project undertaken by the Chinese contractors that has been operating for many years in the W state is USD 1 billion. However, in this case, A company and B company from China and C company from Sudan who just entered the market without much experience in the W country placed a bid price of below 50% of the usual price,

---

97. Wen Shengli, Chen Jianfeng, "Analysis of How to Enhance the Competitiveness of China's International Project Contracting Enterprises", *China Science and Technology*, 2016 (16).

with the effect that the employer eventually chose Company A as a contractor for two projects.

Taking another AM project, for example, in order to expand in a new market, contractor A compressed the profits and management fees when bidding. However, due to the contractor A's lack of in-depth acquaintance with the market, it bid at relatively low price. In the end, contractor A won a bid with the price of USD 6.1 million, which was significantly lower than the price of another well-known Chinese contractor ranked second, and was only 58% of the base price prepared by the Engineer. At the time of evaluation of the bidding, contractor A was the most unlikely company to be able to complete the project because of serious deviation from the base price. However, under the World Bank's lowest bid mechanism and the employer's investment strategy, after several unit price decomposition and clarification, the employer still chose contractor A as the contractor.

At present, most foreign employers still follow the low-priced bid principle to select the contractor. The existence of competitors makes contractors compress the profit and the total cost to win the project in the intense competition.

[B]   The Gap Between Chinese and Foreign Contractors

In recent years, although Chinese contractors achieved much success in international projects, there is still a deep gap between Chinese and foreign contractors in the areas of cooperation mechanism and competitiveness. Chinese contractors fall behind especially in the following aspects:[98] (1) the management capability is relatively weak: Lack of management methods of Chinese contractors makes the expenses often exceed the budget range and makes it difficult to take the advantages of Chinese labor resources; (2) the capital strength is weak: In recent years, with the gradual deepening of the "Belt and Road" Initiative, Chinese contractors have made great progress. However, compared with the foreign contractors, the financial strength of Chinese enterprises is insufficient; (3) it is difficult to satisfy technical standards: Employers of international projects generally adopt the technical standards of developed countries such as Europe and America. Due to a lack of familiarity with foreign standards, many problems occurred.

In the face of the severe competition in international projects, contractors must improve their own competitiveness, instead of winning the project by offering low prices. Chinese contractors can improve their competitiveness through the following ways.

First, optimize human resources management mechanism: Talent strategy should be put in the first place. The introduction of high-qualified staff will be better for promoting the development of enterprises and comprehensively enhancing the core competitiveness of enterprises. At the same time, enterprises should improve the internal human resources management mechanism. Providing equal employment

---

98. Bai Xiaodong, "The Competitiveness of China's International Project Contracting Enterprises", *Science and Technology Information*, 2013 (23).

opportunities and a relatively generous salary and welfare system will help to reduce the demission rate and encourage loyalty of employees, so as to maintain high-qualified talents and create value for enterprises.

Second, utilize information technology to improve the management level: In the management of international projects, contractors should combine modern information technology with management tools, through which contractors can obtain the most information at the lowest cost and realize the optimal allocation of resources.[99]

Third, promote technological innovation and improve labor productivity. Contractors could use technology as a breakthrough. Chinese contractors should integrate the concept of technological innovation into all aspects of construction from pre-construction geological survey and engineering design to mechanical operation in the construction process to the quality inspection in the later stage of construction. The promotion and application of technological innovations in international projects will not only increase the efficiency of labor productivity but also save the cost and the labor resource to maximize the benefits of enterprises.[100]

Fourth, accord priority to development of international business: Domestic infrastructure market reaches its saturation point, so international market is becoming the target market for Chinese contractors. Chinese contractors should adhere to the priority allocation of high-quality resources for international projects. They should select experienced personnel to enrich the overseas branches, establish an incentive mechanism for overseas bidding and management and mobilize the enthusiasm of frontline staffs. Further, contractors should get used to international market and enhance information communication to achieve a rapid response and improve the efficiency of overseas operations.[101]

§3.10   PUBLIC RELATIONS

With the steady progress of the "the Belt and Road" Initiative, Chinese contractors have become an important strategic force to globalize Chinese economy. It is inevitable for Chinese contractors to establish contacts with local governments, social organizations and local residents to carry out international projects. In the process, risks brought by host countries, local governments and other stakeholders have caused significant losses to Chinese contractors. At the same time, with increasingly tense competition and strict requirements of employers, corporate social responsibility is becoming the hard and fast rule that contractors must abide by. Discharging its social responsibility will not only bring benefits to contractors but also promote the good image of the country. Nowadays, the price advantage is no longer the decisive factor to win the bid—instead, the enterprise image plays an increasingly important role in winning a

---

99. Wen Shengli, Chen Jianfeng, "Analysis of How to Enhance the Competitiveness of China's International Project Contracting Enterprises", *China Science and Technology*, 2016 (16).
100. Bai Xiaodong, "A Brief Discussion on the Competitiveness of China's International Engineering Contract Enterprises", *Science and Technology Information*, 2013 (23).
101. Yang Tao, "An Analysis of the Competitiveness of Chinese Offshore Engineering Contractors", *International Economic Co-operation*, 2014 (1).

bid. The key to improving enterprise image is to deal with local public relations in the host country properly and actively. The risk of public relations is mainly manifested in the following aspects.

[A]   Host Government

In international projects, it is advantageous to establish a friendly cooperative relationship with the local government. However, not all governments are friendly in their cooperation with Chinese companies. As the scale of overseas investment by Chinese contractors expands, some governments are beginning to worry that Chinese overseas investments could jeopardize their national security. National security review imposes harsh conditions that discourage Chinese companies from investing or from undertaking mergers and acquisitions (M&A) which may result in failure.[102]

Host governments often play a critical role in international projects. It is particularly important for contractors to establish a friendly cooperative relationship with the host governments, which will help contractors to obtain not only more detailed information but also more favorable conditions. Friendly relationships between contractors and host governments are based on mutual benefits. If there is a conflict of interest between the parties, it would be difficult to achieve cooperation, which could ultimately lead to a loss in the project or even a risk of corruption.

In carrying out overseas projects, Chinese contractors should establish a good cooperative relationship with local governments. On the precondition of properly protecting interests of Chinese contractors, it is suggested that Chinese contractors try to meet the needs of the local government to the extent possible, promote the development of local economy and society and help the government to deal with the relations between stakeholders. This promotes the achievement of a win-win situation.

[B]   Political Factions

Chinese contractors tend to carry out projects in developing countries, some of which have been in civil strife for years, with fierce struggle and unstable political situations. This has a great impact on the Chinese contractors. For example, on November 4, 2014, the Ministry of Communications and Transportations of W country announced that an international consortium, led by a Chinese company, was awarded a high-speed railway project in W. It would be the first 300 kilometer per hour high-speed railway project ever built by a Chinese company overseas. Three days later, however, W country unilaterally canceled the bid. The cancellation was announced by the president and reasons for the cancellation was that too few companies submitted proposals because of insufficient time. However, in fact, the cancellation was based more on political considerations than legal issue.

---

102. Zhao Guohua, Chen Yan, "Paying Attention to the Risks of Overseas Investment Caused by the Host Government and Stakeholders", *Foreign Economic and Trade Practices*, 2015 (5).

With political tensions in some countries in recent years, contractors with close ties to governments are more likely to be passively involved in political issues and suffer loss as a result. Contractors should choose the right position and strictly comply with the local laws and regulations to ensure that they are not involved in political issues.

[C]   Community Relations

Community relations refer to the contractors' relationship with the community organization and the whole population. It is the natural foundation of the existence of the enterprise and the social foundation of the development of the enterprise. In the process of contracting overseas, Chinese contractors often ignore the establishment of community relations due to the excessive pursuit of project benefits and ultimately finds it difficult to continue the project because of opposition from local communities. Since the beginning of the twenty-first century, Non-governmental Organizations (NGO) have become important participants in the domestic and global agendas in many countries. Theoretically speaking, NGO claims to promote humanitarianism and speak for the disadvantaged. Through its own network, NGO can communicate with each other and launch lobbying activities. NGO can influence the agendas and decisions of sovereign governments as well as intergovernmental organizations such as the United Nations and the World Bank.[103] If a contractor neglects the activities and impact of the local NGO, it may suffer losses or even be forced to suspend the projects as a result of the organization's objections. For example, in 2011, a Chinese mining company invested in a South American mining project where under intense pressure from local environmental groups and societies, the government environmental agencies imposed a high fine on the company for failing to disclose environmental risks relating to the mining project.[104]

In addition to social organizations, contractors may be hindered by local residents. With the progress and development of society, the consciousness of rights is becoming stronger and stronger. Local residents often take measures to force the contractors to make changes if pollution, environmental damage and other various social problems are concerned.

[D]   Influence of Public Media

As more and more Chinese companies invest overseas, some countries are trying to propagate the "China Threat Theory" in public discourse by (among other things) accusing investment behavior of Chinese enterprises as the new types of "Neo colonialism."[105] The images of some Chinese contractors have been greatly damaged as

---

103. Sun Haiyong, "Risks and Countermeasures for Social Organizations in China's External Infrastructure Investing", *Modern International Relations*, 2016 (3).
104. Zhao Guohua, Chen Yan, "Attention to Foreign Investment Risks Arising from the Host Government and Stakeholders", *Foreign Economic and Trade Practices*, 2015 (5).
105. *Ibid.*

a result of some foreign media platforms exaggerating particular incidents, causing the contractors to have a negative impression on the local people and government. Taking the hydropower project in L country as an example, one local media platform criticized the project on account of its serious impact on the local environment and reported the local residents' protests on wages, medical care and other issues caused by the project, which resulted in a negative impression of the Chinese contractors.

Faced with the influence of public media, it is the most important for Chinese contractors to assume the social responsibility, maintain the image of the company and improve the technical reliability, economical efficiency and environmental protection. Based on the measures above, contractors should establish good relationships with local governments, social organizations, residents and other groups to avoid unnecessary conflicts, disputes and strive for the mutual understanding of local residents and organizations. At the same time, Chinese contractors may also establish a good relationship with local media and fully utilize the media to enhance the transparency of project information and to publicize the good image of fulfilling its social responsibilities.

Along with the intensification of global competition, it is significant for contractors to enhance their competitiveness by fulfilling its social responsibilities. The contractors should perform social responsibilities required by employers because fulfillment of social responsibility has increasingly become a mandatory requirement for contractors. Further, the intention to fulfill social responsibilities would also impact on business decisions and activities directly or indirectly. Therefore, daily activities are the most important behaviors which should be dealt with.[106] During the implementation of international projects, some countries pay more attention to social responsibility. An example is India, where many Indian contractors do not only take up their own corporate social responsibility but also ask their partners, including suppliers and subcontractors to actively assume their respective social responsibilities. For example, Group V, an Indian company who invests in minerals, metallurgy and energy, explicitly stipulates its requirements for corporate social responsibility in the EPC contract.[107] In fact, fulfillment of social responsibilities is not only essential in winning projects but also important in the successful implementation of the project after the successful bid. Contractor A won a project in W country. During the execution of the contract, the employer illegally obtained the land use rights of project site and destroyed local coffee trees, orange trees, banana trees, corn, soybeans and other crops and destroyed the community solar power facilities. Further, there was an ugly dispute between the employer and local residents. After entering the site, the contractor discovered the dispute. It urged the employer to seize the opportunity to settle the dispute, but the employer was reluctant to. One day, local residents shot at the contractor's camp causing contractor's personnel's safety to be seriously threatened. The contractor evacuated from the site on the same day and terminated the project contract. At

---

106. Zhang Haili, "Research on Social Responsibility of International Engineering Contracting Enterprises", *Industry and Technology Forum*, 2014 (7).
107. Li Kaoxin, Jiang Wei, "The Revelation of India's CSR Legislation", *International Engineering and Services*, 2013 (6).

present, in the international engineering market, most Chinese contractors begin to transform and upgrade and intend to participate in the investment of international projects. As employers, it is more important for Chinese companies to pay attention to the importance of fulfilling social responsibility, handle community relations and get better help and support for local residents' education, medical and other aspects. Chinese companies should establish a good corporate image through small costs in exchange for big gains.

Chinese enterprises, who are going global, have become active practitioners of "building a community of human destiny," and have not only carried forward the spirit of "dedication, fraternity, mutual assistance and progress" abroad but also conveyed to the host country the responsibility of the world's citizens. They should bear in mind the objective of promoting local people's livelihood and building a community of global common prosperity. The fulfillment of a corporate social responsibility is not only about the image of the enterprise but also about the image of a country.

Chinese contractors should adhere to the following principles to fulfill their social responsibilities in overseas projects:[108] First, establish the concept of global responsibility and integrate social responsibility into the project management mechanism to safeguard the rights and interests of stakeholders and to make responsible benchmarking. Second, strive for high-quality projects and provide employers and local communities with quality and reliable products and services. Third, pay attention to the protection of ecological environmental by consciously complying with local environmental laws and standards in order to carry out environment-friendly projects. Fourth, adhere to the people-oriented principle, protect the legitimate rights and interests of employees, satisfy the requirement of localization and improve the technical level of local employees. Fifth, take local communities into consideration, promote the long-term development of local economy and achieve mutual benefit.

In order to manage the risks of community relations, contractors should establish good cooperative relations with local social organizations and residents. Contractors may take the following measures:[109] (1) deepen comprehensive understanding of ecological environment, humanistic characteristics and community interests, carry out assessment on overall social risks and environmental risks in the decision-making stage and carry out the process control. This is to address the risks brought by social organization, which mainly arise from the issues of transparency, environmental protection, residents or labor rights and interests of the local community; (2) enhance the communication with local NGOs, local residents and so on, to prevent the negative impact of such groups on the projects.

---

108. Luo Wenjin, "The Implementation of the Social Responsibility of Large-Scale Overseas Projects-to the Four Air Bureau of the Mongolian Railway Project as an Example", *The Construction Enterprise Management*, 2017 (9).
109. Sun Haiyong, "The Social Organization Risk and Countermeasures of China's External Infrastructure Investment", *Modern International Relations*, 2016 (3).

CHAPTER 4
Project Risks

With overseas projects growing in their number and complexity, Chinese enterprises engaged in overseas construction projects are exposed to more and more risks in the international construction industry.

It is of crucial importance for enterprises to identify and manage these risks in order to survive and thrive. In the context of international construction projects, a variety of interconnected factors influence the cost and delivery of project. Cost risk is particularly prominent in lump-sum contracts. The failure to adequately address this risk would cause the contractor to be exposed to profit dilution or loss. As international construction projects face increasing challenges in assembling resources in comparison with domestic projects, delay risks must be given priority in project management. Because disputes occur most frequently in the completion and handover stage, appropriate measures need to be taken during contract negotiation and project performance stage to avoid disputes in later stages of the project. Reasonable arrangements covering defects liability and damage clauses may help to restrict the contractor's liability. Insurance is a functional instrument for international contractors to transfer risks and mitigate damages. It is a usual practice for contractor to provide on-demand performance guarantee in international construction projects. The contractor, through the whole life cycle of projects, should always stay on guard in case the guarantee is called upon by the employer/beneficiary.

This chapter analyzes the key risks of overseas construction projects and discusses risk prevention measures designed to ensure these projects progress smoothly and result in quality and sustainable developments.

§4.01   PROJECT FEASIBILITY

[A]   Technical Feasibility

The purpose of analyzing the technical proposal or a project is to enable the contractor to identify the feasibility of the design and construction of the project in respect of the project on which a contractor intends to bid. Feasibility usually has two aspects. First, the contractor must consider its own capabilities in respect of contract management, design and construction and machinery and equipment, as well as its experience in contracting for similar overseas projects. These elements constitute what is referred to as the technical capability of the contractor. Second, the contractor must formulate the technical solutions for the specific project, including familiarizing itself with the design and construction standards, project design and construction technology solutions and, in particular, the project's difficulties and detailed solutions. These elements constitute what is referred to as the feasibility of the technical implementation plans.

As far as the feasibility of the technology implementation plan of a specific project is concerned, the contractor should mainly consider the feasibility of the project plan (measured by the feasibility of the design plan, the procurement plan, the construction plan and the trial run plan, and the compliance of the design and construction standards with the required standards of the proposed bidding project and the host country where the project is located, etc.), the reliability of the project schedule (measured by the reasonableness of the schedule, machinery and equipment level and labor input, etc.), the quality assurance system, the HSE system, the main personnel of the project (including managers and technicians), the technical performance of materials and equipment, etc.

In addition, the bidding documents generally require the contractor to list the subcontractors it intends to employ, such as engineering subcontractors, design subcontractors and construction subcontractors. Therefore, the contractor needs to analyze and consider the proposed subcontractors' technical capabilities and construction experience, including its performance and reputation, both in compliance and general terms. Such matters should be monitored during the life of the project.

[B]   Differences in Technical Standards and Specifications

One of the most prominent risks arising from the technical proposal is the difference between Chinese technical standards or specifications and the standards of other nations or published by international bodies. Chinese enterprises do not have enough knowledge or mastery of foreign standards or specifications, and sometimes they seek to apply Chinese standards and specifications as an alternative, which makes them vulnerable to risks. The lack of knowledge and mastery is manifested as follows: At the bidding stage, the bidding documents cannot be prepared according to applicable foreign or international standards and specifications; at the design stage, the design cannot be drawn according to applicable standards, and the design drawings do not meet the contractual requirements; at the equipment procurement stage, the applicable standards and specifications are partially understood, and the differences in specific technical standards and technical parameters are ignored; at the construction stage, the construction cannot be carried out according to applicable standards and specifications.

In practice, for example, PetroChina Central Asia Natural Gas Pipeline Co., Ltd. has encountered problems arising from different design standards applying to overseas pipeline construction than applied domestically. While domestic projects incline to employ the national standard (GB), the American Society of Mechanical Engineers (ASME) standard is adopted in most overseas pipeline construction projects while some CIS countries tend to apply the GOST standard (Russian state standard).[110] In the Kenya Gaoluo Power Station project, some design requirements in the contract were completely different from Chinese domestic design standards. Chinese designers need to digest and absorb these local requirements before they put forward the design proposal. For instance, the contract required the design of a centralized motor control center to control the operation of the oil, water, gas and other auxiliary systems. Moreover, the contract required that everything in the metal structure design, from means of expression of the drawing to the standards to be adopted in design, must conform to the standards agreed in the negotiation. Consequently, the design, which was not complicated, took almost one year.[111] Different design standards correspond to different design specifications. In addition, the technical parameters as well as quality standards of equipment and materials are different. This means procurement management must respond to a changeable environment. Handling the differences in technical standards and specifications and the risks to which these give rise has become an important part of project management. In many countries, technical standards undergo constant review and updating and amendment.

In this regard, the contractor should, in all phases including bidding, design and construction and in combination with project requirements and site conditions, strictly ensure compliance with the current applicable technical standards and communicate with the employer in accordance with any time stipulation, unless the contract mandates a fixed standard or specification (and a mutual mandatory law does not override the contract).

In a coal-fired power plant project located in a Southeast Asian country, the contract required that the on-site transmission test of the power plant boiler must comply with the ASME standard. The Chinese contractor did not raise any objection to or potential deviation from this standard during the bidding process and ignored this requirement when implementing the test. Instead, the contractor decided on its own to apply a Chinese standard in the test. After the employer discovered the noncompliance, the construction was forced to shut down for rectification, and as a result, the Chinese contractor defaulted in its obligation to complete within the construction period and

---

110. Yin Guoliang, "Safety Management in Overseas Projects of China National Petroleum Corporation: Taking China National Petroleum Corporation's Central Asian Gas Pipeline (Hakka Section) as an Example". *Petrochemical Construction*, 2013 (35) pp. 49-51.
111. Chen Guoliang, Peng Kun, "Several Reflections on the Implementation of the Songgaoluo Power Station Project in Kenya." Construction Technology, 2015 (s1), pp. 699-703.

was fined.[112] The Chinese contractor's default is largely due to its lack of awareness of technical standard risks and lack of communication with the employer regarding technical standards. On the contrary, in another case, the contractor's timely and effective communication with the employer on the differences in technical standards accounted for the final successful resolution of a standard balance which if ignored might have exposed the contractor to liability.

In a case provided by ICC for this research project, the agreed price in the EPC contract was calculated according to Chinese standards. However, the contract provided that "unless the employer approves the contractor's application of Chinese standards, the contractor shall comply with international standards." In other words, international standards are applicable by default, and whether or not Chinese standards can be adopted completely depends on the employer. This generated uncertainty and communication risks between the parties. A dispute arose soon after the commencement of the project, in which the Chinese contractor carried out the design work according to Chinese standards, and the employer gave a great number of opinions on revision based on international standards. The contractor failed to complete the revision within the time limit set by the EPC contract, thus delaying the project at its beginning stage. Afterward the parties went into arbitration because of this and several other disputes. The arbitral tribunal found it very clear that the contractor was obliged to carry out the design work according to international standards and the large number of amendments proposed by the employer was also reasonable. The tribunal found that the contractor's failure to complete the amendments constituted a delay in finishing the design and that the contractor should be held responsible for the delay.

In a coal-fired power plant project in Southeast Asia, the invitation for bids stated that the thermal insulation technology should be implemented in accordance with Australian standards, but the Chinese contractor was not familiar with Australian standards. Therefore, the contractor attempted to persuade the employer to adopt Chinese standards, on the one hand, and, organized technicians to promptly study Australian standards, on the other hand. Although ultimately, the employer insisted on the application of Australian standards in the negotiation, the Chinese contractor, through research, had found that the differences between Australian and Chinese standards were very limited and had little impact on construction costs and schedules. At last, the Chinese contractor and the employer agreed on the application of Australian standards in the project.[113]

A large number of equipment and materials in China meet the requirements of American Standards and European Standards, but the lack of certificates on these standards has led to increased project construction costs. For example, in the Saudi Arabian light rail project, the employer asked the British design agency to design according to European Standards, which required the use of European control equipment. For this reason, the contractor had to order a large number of European control equipment whose price greatly exceeded the original contract budget, leading to a substantial increase in the construction costs. If Chinese enterprises, when contracting

112. *See* http://www.sohu.com/a/135357858_475942, last visited May 19, 2018.
113. *Ibid.*

overseas construction projects, introduce and agree with the employer on the application of Chinese standards, the costs of raw materials and equipment would have dropped drastically, which would have further increased profitability. At present, China has issued the Standard Harmonization Program under the "BRI"(2015-2017),[114] intending to harmonize technical standards and specifications with countries along the route under the "BRI."

[C] Availability of Materials and Equipment

Feasibility of the procurement plan is an important consideration when evaluating the feasibility of a technical proposal. Due to the complexity of international construction projects, the contractor should especially consider the availability of materials and equipment in the procurement plan, so as to avoid the risk of delays or cost overturns caused by shortages in materials and equipment availability after entering the construction stage. The procurement of materials and equipment is the basis of smooth construction and involves many complex aspects. If the contractor intends to use Chinese-made materials and equipment, it is necessary to reach an agreement in the contract and pay attention to whether they comply with local laws and regulations, as well as technical standards as well as specifications. If the contractor intends to purchase locally, it is necessary to become familiar with the host country's market prices and supply fluctuations and develop good relationships with local suppliers. If the contractor relies on imports from other countries, then issues such as transportation risks and exchange rate risks are sure to arise. As described in the Chapter on transportation risks, materials and equipment purchased and transported, if these materials and equipment are not in conformity with the legal or regulatory requirements of the host country, due to the absence of (e.g.) corresponding certifications or qualifications, this may result in the failure of customs clearance of materials and equipment and ultimately project delay.

For example, in recent years, Saudi Arabia's infrastructure projects and industrial construction projects have significantly increased. The permanent materials and equipment involved in those projects are basically dependent on imports. The increase in prices caused by supply shortages has led directly to an increase in project costs. During the construction of the Ghana Buhvi Hydropower Station, according to the EPC contract, equipment procurement could only be carried out with the approval of the employers, which would take a long time. In addition, the project involved various types of equipment with a high degree of integration. In order not to affect the construction schedule, the contractor had no choice but to shorten the equipment manufacturer's manufacturing cycle, which resulted in a reduction in the quality of the equipment manufactured.[115]

---

114. *See* http://www.ndrc.gov.cn/gzdt/201510/t20151022_755473.html, last visited May 19, 2018.
115. Zuo Shenglong, Tang Linhou, Li Guoqiang. "The EPC Management Practice of the Bouvet Hydropower Project". *See* http://www.360doc.com/content/16/0509/18/33075242_5576206 25.shtml, last visited May 19, 2018.

In international construction projects, the procurement or production of each item of equipment generally can be carried out only after the equipment design is approved by the employer. This in turn increases the uncertainty of the equipment manufacturing time and makes it more difficult to manufacture and supply equipment. In the Yava Hydropower Station project in Myanmar, the late ordering of equipment meant that the manufacturer's production cycle was insufficient and the scheduled delivery was postponed. In addition, because of the impact of a typhoon, the shipping schedule could not be guaranteed either. As a result of all these circumstances, the equipment did not arrive as scheduled.[116] In a construction project in Saudi Arabia, where the famous oil company Saudi Aramco was the employer, the material grades in its specifications were very strict. The higher the material grade was, the longer time it took for approval and procurement. This directly affected the progress of the project. Therefore, overseas project contractors should accurately estimate the resources (manpower, machinery and equipment, materials, etc.) that need to be invested, reasonably plan procurement channels and carefully arrange procurement plans, so as to avoid risks arising from unavailability of materials and equipment.

[D]   Credit Status of the Employer

A creditworthy employer is crucial to the construction and for the viability of an overseas contracting project. In general, whether the project employer's credit status is ideal is mainly analyzed and judged by considering the following factors including: the employer's financial status and reputation; the source, amount and availability of the funds required for the project; the progress of the project approval procedures, the employer's construction experience and attitudes toward contractors as well as timely payments; and the qualification level, working methods and position on dispute resolution of the supervisor appointed by the employer. An ideal employer must have its own funds, experience in business management, certain financing capacity, good business reputation and good relations with government authorities. In addition, the ideal employer will have gone through proper approval procedures, with complete certificates and documentation. Such an employer will have a clear idea on the progress of the project and have discussions with the contractor in a professional and meticulous manner.

Investigations of the employer's credit status can be carried out in various ways, such as conducting investigations through Chinese embassies and consulates in foreign countries, forming impressions through contact with the foreign employer, acquiring evaluations from entities familiar with the foreign employer and obtaining credit status certifications from banks or relevant professional agencies.

---

116. Zhu Huojian, Liang Rengui, "Electromechanical EPC Management for the Yiva Hydropower Project". *See* http://www.doc88.com/p-3718936019162.html, last visited May 19, 2018.

[E] Availability of the Funds Required for the Project

[1] Major Financing Methods for Overseas Contracting Projects

The common financing methods for overseas contracting projects include export credits, loans from governments and international organizations, financial leasing, syndicated loans and project financing. These methods are briefly introduced as follows.

Export credit is a type of loan with lower interest rates, supported by government subsidies, offered by commercial banks or policy banks to Chinese contractors or overseas project employers. According to whether the borrower is a Chinese contractor or an overseas employer, export credit is further divided into seller's credit and buyer's credit, and the legal relationships as well as related risks involved differ accordingly.

Loans from governments and international organizations involve a type of preferential policy loan offered by the Chinese government, the World Bank, the Asian Development Bank or other international organizations to finance specific projects. At present, the Silk Road Fund and the Asian Infrastructure Investment Bank have also started to provide financial support for projects under the "BRI."

Financial leasing refers to the contractor's cooperation with domestic and foreign financial institutions such as leasing companies and trust companies. Such financial institutions raise funds to purchase large-scale items required for construction projects and then lease the items to the contractor. The contractor pays the rent with proceeds from the project. Payment is guaranteed by the project's assets, expected returns or interests, and financial institutions usually only have limited recourse to the proceeds of the project itself.

Syndicated loan is a type of loan offered by a loan group led by one or several banks, with a group of banks and nonbank financial institutions participating in the same loan agreement, to the same borrower according to the agreed terms and conditions. Chinese commercial banks or policy banks may, for example, form syndicates with the banks of the countries where overseas and/or project's employers are located.

Project financing is a type of financing that has emerged in recent years for a specific project which is an economic entity. It requires that the project exists as an independent legal entity and the various contributors (shareholders, quasi-equity investors, creditors, etc.) all share benefits and risks. Among the contributors, the contractor may be a shareholder or just a creditor.

Of course, if the relevant conditions are met, the contractor may also finance in domestic or foreign capital markets.

Each of these financing models gives use to its own associated risks. Specialists knowledge of how each operates, especially in the event of a default on the part of a debtor/party, must be obtained.

[2]   The Choice of Financing Methods

An overseas project contractor should conduct a comprehensive analysis of the project's financing costs (for international contracting projects, financing costs usually include the interest costs of any lending and guarantee costs, etc.) and assess the financial risks when preparing its financing plan. For example, the costs of project financing at an early stage are relatively high. At the same time, because it only allows limited recourse, if the contractor is not a founder, the risks borne by the contractor to advance the funds of the project will be greater whereas if the contractor is a founder, the benefits generated from the project may also be high. Different financing methods apply to projects in different fields with different characteristics, carrying with them differences in financing costs and risks, and different requirements on the contractor's credit status, financial conditions and management capabilities. The contractor should choose financing methods according to the characteristics of the project and its own circumstances flexibly and select the optimal method or a combination of methods.

[3]   Risk Management of Project Funds

In addition to the risk of repayment under different financing methods, the funds raised by an overseas project contractor may also be subject to risks in terms of management and financial environment. The funds raised for international construction projects shall be earmarked for its specified purpose only and generally not be used for other purposes. In addition, the profitability of the project depends to a large extent on the risk management of the funds, such as foreign exchange risk. In international EPC projects, the employer may pay the contractor with a currency different from the one the contractor pays the seller of the imported materials and equipment. The foreign exchange risk mainly refers to the change in the actual purchase cost that may be caused by the exchange rate changes between the two currencies.

The following example is illustrative. A Chinese enterprise is the contractor in a construction project in that Central Asian country. In this project, the payment currency of the main contract between the contractor and the employer is Tenge (Central Asian country's legal currency), while the payment currency in the materials and equipment supply contract between the contractor and the supplier is U.S. dollars. After the contract was agreed, the Kazakh National Bank announced that the benchmark exchange rate for U.S. dollar against Tenge was adjusted from 1 to 120 to 1 to 150, and so the Tenge was devalued by 25%. This caused the contractor to suffer serious foreign exchange transactions losses.[117] In the Algeria East-West Expressway project contracted by China CITIC-China Railway Construction Consortium, when the employer signed the contract, the U.S. dollar was used as the payment currency for the international portion of the project, and a cap clause was inserted in the contract. As a result, the contractor was to bear all the risks of exchange rate fluctuations. In this

---

117. Gu Xiangbo, Ren Shu, "Exchange Rate Risk Analysis of Overseas Contracting Projects in the Post-financial Crisis". *Contemporary Petroleum and Petrochemicals*, 2010 (10) pp. 36-39.

project, the amount to be paid in U.S. dollar reached USD 3.5 billion. During the two years of project implementation, the U.S. dollar depreciated significantly against RMB. In August 2006, the exchange rate of RMB against U.S. dollar was 7,973. By August 2008, the exchange rate of RMB against U.S. dollar was 6,842, causing an increase of 14% in the exchange rate of RMB against U.S. dollar. Such large exchange rate fluctuations have caused the contractor to encounter major foreign exchange risks during both project financing and collection of the contract proceeds.[118]

In response to such risks, the contractor can at a minimum adopt strategies including the following. First, if possible, the contractor may require the employers to pay in a combination of currencies to minimize the risk of losses caused by exchange rate fluctuations. If the contractor could use the employer's payment currency as the payment currency in its contract with third parties, the said risks might be reduced. Second, the contractor may reduce the impact of exchange rate fluctuations by changing the place of procurement; i.e., if the currency of the country where the project locates devalues, the contractor should purchase materials and equipment from local sources as much as possible. Third, the contractor may negotiate with the employer to include additional losses that may be caused by exchange rate fluctuations into the main contract through reasonable adjustments. Fourth, the contractor can choose suitable foreign exchange trading methods, such as forward foreign exchange transactions and foreign currency options.

§4.02   CLIMATIC CONDITIONS RISKS

Climatic conditions that can affect the construction of international projects can be classified into two kinds: normal climatic conditions and abnormal climatic conditions. Normal climatic conditions refer to general climatic conditions of the locality, such as an established regular persistent rainy season, sand storms and continuously high or low temperature for a long time, all of which can affect construction activities to varying degrees. For instances, a persistent rainy season will impair earthwork and civil work, and lasting low temperatures will cut down effective construction time, reduce work efficiency and increase costs. However, abnormal climatic conditions refer to exceptional conditions which are outside of the normal range of established climate patterns. These conditions will hold up regular progress of construction activities and cause damage to the projects. Contractors need to pay special attention to the abovementioned elements.[119]

[A]   Normal Local Climatic Conditions

Case 1: An Airport Runway Expansion and Transformation Project in Country S, Africa, adopting a procurement and build contract procurement model. The contract

---

118. Overseas Engineering Risks of Chinese Engineering Contracting Companies: An Analysis Based on Cases. *See* http://www.sohu.com/a/159226568_168969, last visited May 19, 2018.
119. Xia Zhihong, "Risk Identification and Prevention in International Projects Contracting", China Construction Press, 2004.

provided that the contractor was responsible for the procurement of materials, equipment and construction work. The construction period was 14 weeks, commencing with the transfer of possession of the airport runway from the employer to the contractor. The contractor was liable to pay delay damages at the rate of USD 1,500 for each day of delay beyond the contractually agreed completion date and compensate the employer for all other losses if any.

The employer transferred the airport runway at the end of April and the rainy season began in June. Due to the climatic condition, the progress of fundamental civil work and the following asphalt work were impeded, which led to delay of the construction project. The employer, referring to relevant terms in the contract, demanded the contractor to pay for the delay damages. However, the contractor contended that the delay is attributable to the rainy season which occurred during the contract period, and therefore no delay damages should be paid. Further, the contractor lodged a claim against the employer on the basis that the rainy season had impaired construction progress. In consequence disputes arose.

Remarks: The above scenario in which the normal climatic condition influenced the construction progress frequently occurs in international project contracting.

In this case, the contract provided clearly the completion time and delay liability, but the construction period was delayed because of the normal rainy season. Although the delay caused idling of the construction equipment, machinery and labor force, the contractor should not be exempted from the delay liabilities from the contractual and legal point of view because the rainy season is a normal climatic condition in the local area which cannot be regarded as abnormal or as a defined force majeure event. As an experienced contractor, it should have taken into full consideration the rainy season when signing the contract and setting the construction program. Thus, there is no contractual ground for claims against the employer.

To avoid unnecessary contract disputes and financial loss, the contractor should take into consideration the construction period and relevant elements which influence the completion of the project when making the bid. Drawing lessons from this case, contractors should fully consider the influence of the rainy season while making the bid and ask for further clarification of construction period (influence of rainy season on the construction period) in the clarification meeting before or after the bid in order to ensure an extension of time from the employer in appropriate circumstances. However, if the employer denies any modification to the construction period or contractual provisions, the contractor should take into account fees for accelerating work when making a quote and make out a scientific-based and prudent construction schedule during the execution of the contract to minimize the effect of the rainy season on project progress and profit.

[B]   Abnormal Climatic Conditions

Case: An EPC lump-sum turnkey project contract in the Middle East. The force majeure clause in this contract provided a definition of force majeure events and the extent to which the parties are exempted from assuming liability in case of force majeure.

However, the force majeure clause explicitly excluded atrocious weather from its scope.

As the country was located in the desert, there was only a short-term rainy season with a small amount of rainfall. However, in the year that the contract was performed there was extraordinary rainfall in the rainy season with record-high rainfall amounts and record-long durations. The storm wreaked havoc on the civil work including the foundations, pipe and cable trenches and brought about idling of construction equipment, machinery and the labor force, which caused serious economic losses for the contractor. As a result, the contractor lodged claims for extensions of time and cost compensation.

The employer denied the contractor's claim for time extension as it held that the storm did not constitute a force majeure event as defined in the contract, and it did not conform to the exemption conditions. It also rejected the cost claim as it assumed that the employer should not be to blame for both damages to the site and the idling of equipment, machinery and labor force.

Remarks: In this case, the contractor suffered financial loss and time delay due to the unforeseeable storm. It brought up two claims before the client: One is for the extension of time, the other is for economic compensation.

Whether the two claims can be granted depends on the contractual grounding. More substantial analysis follows.

As regards the claim for extension of time, it depends on whether the exemption conditions for time delay have been met. In this case, as for the damages to the civil work on site brought about by the storm, the contractor should be entitled to a claim only if the storm falls within the scope of a "force majeure" event in the contract. In this case, atrocious weather was not included as a force majeure event in the contract

The claim for compensation for direct economic damages and idling of equipment, machinery and labor force was also ill-founded under the contract, flowing from the above analysis. Indeed, events of force majeure do not typically entitle either party to compensation.

In conclusion, the contractor's claims for time extension and compensation were highly unlikely to be approved by the employer.

[C] Preventive Measures

In the context of international construction projects, the contractor's lack of knowledge about the on-site climatic conditions combined with the uncontrollable nature of the natural climate makes it much more necessary for the contractor to transfer and control climate risks in the following ways.

[1] Environmental Investigation in the Early Stage

Where complex or changing climatic conditions apply, the contractor must conduct an in-depth investigation into the anticipated climatic conditions on site and its neighborhood throughout the project. That investigation should include, but not be limited to, the lowest and highest temperature, the applicable rainy and dry seasons, rainfall and snowfall statistics, the presence and depth of permafrost or other frozen layers, average wind directions and speeds, the frequency of natural disasters such as earthquakes, floods, tsunami, typhoon, windstorms, sand storms and thunderstorms. The Contactor should take account of the results of this survey when preparing its working methods, construction schedule and price. The results of the survey will affect the contractor's allocation of resources and may affect the payment schedule.

[2]   Risk-Sharing Mechanism in the Contract

Some employers will look to limit or remove any entitlement of the contractor to lodge a claim for "exceptional adverse climatic conditions." If the contractor finds out in the early-stage investigation that the climatic conditions of the site and its neighborhood is adverse or unstable, it should in the contract negotiation phase try to ensure that appropriate contractual clauses are included to ensure an appropriate allocation of risks between the two parties.

The traditional way to deal with such issues is the insertion of a force majeure clause in the contract. Such a clause not only deals with the effect of unforeseen weather events (as defined by the contracts) but also the effect of other events beyond the contract of the parties. The clause defines such events like:

- Indicates what notice must be given if such an event occurs.
- The obligations of the parties to mitigate the negative impact of such events.
- Whether the occurrence of the events suspends the obligations of the parties, e.g. the contract to progress the works and the employer's obligation to pay for them in the meantime.
- Whether prolonged occurrence of a defined event can bring the contract to an end, and so on.

Transfer risks to the insurance company. In accordance with international EPC contract, the contractor might need to affect insurance including All Risks Insurance, Design Liability Insurance and Employers Liability Insurance. Contractors' All Risks Insurance, typically includes cover (a) for property damage suffered by the employer/contractor and (b) for injury or damage caused to third parties. The risks which are covered by such insurance may include earthquake, tsunami, thunder, hurricane, typhoon, tornado, windstorm, stormy rain, flood, freeze-up, hail, landfall, landslide, volcanic eruption, land subsidence and other irresistible and disastrous natural phenomenon.[120]

---

120. *See* the last annotation, p. 138.

[3] Claims in Performance Phase

During the performance of project, it is necessary for the contractor to properly preserve relevant evidence. In the event of exceptional adverse climate which influences the completion time or costs, the contractor is expected to negotiate with the employer and make claims for time and costs in line with the contract.

Case: The over-lengthy rainy season in an African country impeded construction progress. A Chinese contractor contracted for a road project in an African country which has two rainy seasons annually, each lasting for three months. During the construction period, the annual rainfall amount surged, severely delaying construction progress. The contractor lodged a claim for an extension of time by reason of "exceptional adverse climatic conditions" and compared the annual rainfall amount experienced with those of the previous 15 years to prove that the situation they had suffered fell into the range of exceptional adverse climatic conditions for the purposes of the extension of time clause.

§4.03 GEOLOGICAL CONDITIONS AND SITE DATA RISKS

The impact of site conditions and climate on construction and work quantities can never be ignored in an EPC contract, especially for large-scale facility projects such as power plants, refineries, crude oil processing plants, airports and wharves. As such projects cover a huge geographic area, if the site conditions do affect construction progress, generally, a large quantity of work will be involved. Similarly, projects which extend over long distances, such as pipelines, roads, railways, underground cable and optical cables are more likely to encounter varied abnormal conditions over or underground.

Under contracts for large international projects, the employer commonly provides (as part of the bidding documents) information about on-site conditions including on-site topography, geology, and such barriers as mountains, rivers and building facilities along with the parameters of the site. However, under standard-form EPC contracts, the contractor is often expected to be responsible for undertaking a site survey. Therefore, the information on the on-site conditions provided by the employer (including the landform and topography, soil texture and barriers over and underground in general) are not conclusive. Without a clear allocation of risk for shortcomings in the material provided by the employer, the contractor may incur increases in work quantity and costs arising from site conditions only discovered after the commencement of the project. Thus, the contractor should pay attention to the risk of adverse site conditions when providing its quote and when negotiating the terms of the contract.

[A] On-Site Topographic Conditions

Case: An EPC contract for a plant project. The on-site topographic map in the contractual documents showed that the landscape on site was relatively stable. On the basis of the on-site elevation shown in the map, the earth volume to be excavated from the higher ground would approximately equal that for filling the lower ground. During the tender process, the employer only organized a quick tour for contractors on site and did not undertake an on-site survey.

In execution of the contract, the contractor conducted an on-site survey only to discover that there were a lot of differences between actual topographic conditions and those presented on the map. As a result, the contractor had to transport materials for earth filling. As the plant covered a huge area, significant extra costs were incurred as a result of the need to import earth from off-site, moving the earth and carry out earth filling activities.

The contractor alleged that due to the difference between the topographic conditions on site and those shown on the map, it had suffered significant additional construction costs for which it should be compensated through the variation machinery in the contract. However, the employer rejected the claim on the basis that the contract provided that the contractor agreed that it had already obtained a whole picture of the on-site conditions when signing the contract. A dispute arose between the two parties.

Case Analysis: Whether the contractor was entitled to compensation depended on the following two points: One was the basis upon which the contractor had bid for the contract, and the other was whether the difference should be counted as a variation or a contractual risk accepted by the contractor.

On the first point, the contractor had not been allowed during the bidding process to conduct an on-site survey. Accordingly, the bid was only based on the earthwork quantity evaluated in accordance with the on-site topographic map. As to the second point, there is no denying that under the express terms of the contract, the contractor was presumed to have understood the on-site conditions and taken responsibility for the accuracy of site data. But in construing this clause, one had to consider the practical situation when the contractor made the bid. On account of the restrictions imposed by the employer, the bidder had been unable to conduct a site survey. As a result, the confirmation by the contractor of its understanding of site conditions was limited to those presented in the bidding documents instead of the practical conditions.

In the circumstances, the employer was found to be liable for a reasonable compensation for additional costs suffered by the contractor.

[B]   Geological Features

Case: An EPC contract for a chemical plant project. It was clearly stated in the contract that there were two potential methods of anode groundbed providing cathodic protection for storage tanks and transmission pipelines: namely deep-shaft mode and horizontal mode. However, instead of specifying which method to adopt, the contract provided that the relevant choice would depend on the grounding resistance measured by the contractor on site. In particular, if the grounding resistance went beyond standard values, the deep-shaft anode groundbed method was to be employed.

Otherwise, the horizontal anode groundbed method should be employed. Moreover, grounding resistance parameters were missing from the contract.

Based on a measurement of the soil texture, the contractor calculated the on-site grounding resistance and thus proposed to choose the deep-shaft anode groundbed method, to which the employer agreed. Consequentially, the deep-shaft method was taken for all the anode groundbeds.

To the contractor's mind, the horizontal method was an available option in line with the contract. But in consideration of the practical on-site grounding resistance, it had to choose the deep-shaft method to effect anti-erosion protection for storage tanks and pipelines. The contractor contended this was a variation to the contract as it resulted in an increased quantity of civil work, cathodic protection material and therefore extra costs. The employer disagreed as it assumed that the contract had explicitly provided that the relevant method depended on the practical grounding resistance measured by the contractor.

Case Analysis: In this case, because of the lack of clarity regarding the method of anode groundbed, disputes arose between the contractor and the employer.

The contractor argued that it was entitled to make a choice between the two methods and that it should be a variation to the contract if the contractor priced the works on the basis of the horizontal method during the tender process, but then employed the deep-shaft method in view of the practical grounding resistance measured following the making of the contract.

However, the employer argued that the contract was not definitive as to the method of groundbed that applied and that if the contractor found it necessary to adopt the deep-shaft mode of anode groundbed out of concern for the protection of plant, that was just one part of the contractor's scope of work instead of a contract variation.

In light of the fact that no ground resistance parameters were present in the contract and the mode of anode groundbed was to be based on the ground resistance values measured on site after the making of the contract, it was difficult for contractor properly to claim from the employer.

[C] Preventive Measures

Without a professional survey, it is difficult to evaluate on-site conditions, especially underground conditions. As a result, uncertain underground conditions often bring about unexpected risks. Generally speaking, only "unforeseeable physical conditions" as defined in the contract entitle the contractor to claim for extension of time or additional costs. "Unforeseeable physical conditions" refer to those conditions including geological conditions, their distribution and type, including the hardness and stratification of the terrain, which do not match with any contractual investigation report. To deal with this, the following measures are available for the contractor.

The contractor should meticulously verify the site data provided by the employer as generally the employer will not be held accountable for the accuracy and completeness of that data. By contrast, the contractor needs both to rely on the data and bear the risk of its lack of accuracy or completeness.

117

The contractor must bring appropriate specialist knowledge to bear in the data review and clarification stages. Those specialist skills may include topography, water hydraulics, soils, civil engineering and earth movement, vegetation and so on.

During the tender process, especially during the clarification process, the bidder should ask for a clarification. In case the employer rejects the requirement for a site survey, the contractor should try to state clearly in the contract that the tender offer is given on the basis of the tender documents and that if a difference arises between the conditions described in the tender documents and the practical site conditions, that should be regarded as a variation for which the contractor is entitled to an extension of time and additional costs. During the tender process for large-scale international projects, the employer is usually unwilling or opposed to any modification of contract conditions by the contractor. Against this background, the contractor should aim for a clear clarification in the contract documents that its offer is based on the tender documents.

The contractor may transfer risks to the employer when necessary. Before setting about a project, the employer normally needs to go through the whole process of putting forward a proposal, conducting feasibility research and making invitations to tender. Underground and geological conditions are usually included in the feasibility research, while other relevant information will be provided later. The contractor thus needs to verify the site data carefully. In these circumstances, if there is not enough time or the underground conditions are complex, the contractor should try to negotiate with the employer to transfer this risk and to reflect this change in the contract price.

Case: A Chinese contractor undertook a superhighway project in Arica. In execution, it was found out that the underground earthwork quantity was far beyond expectations. Consequently, the contractor lodged a claim on account of "unforeseeable physical conditions."

Case: Another Chinese contractor undertook a road project in Arica. According to information offered in the tender documents, the contractor calculated the costs of building materials from the recommended nearby quarry and included it in its tender offer. Later, it emerged that the recommended quarry did not meet the contract requirements. The contractor was forced to find another quarry and made a claim for extension of time on the basis that it had had no time to verify the position prior to making the contract.

§4.04   RISKS IN LAND ACQUISITION AND REMOVAL

[A]   Overview of the Risk

Generally speaking, in overseas engineering contracting practice, employers are responsible for providing construction sites and carrying out land acquisition and removal by working with neighboring residents and local government entities. Factors such as the local government's policies, compensation payments, geographic conditions, local conditions and customs, culture and religion influence whether employers can successfully carry out land acquisition and removal. As a result, employers frequently run into problems in land acquisition and removal, the contractor is unable to start work on time and the project is delayed. These risks are referred to as site risks.

For example, an EPC railway construction project contracted by a Chinese enterprise in Kenya ran into severe site risks during construction. First, as land is privately owned in Kenya, land acquisition and removal there had never been easy. In addition, according to the design drawing, part of the construction had to cross industrial areas. For instance, because the Athi River Super Bridge of the Mombasa Nairobi Railway goes through an area of heavy industry in Athi River Town and Nairobi National Park, it was even more difficult to carry out land acquisition and removal in those locations. The process of land acquisition was so slow that the contractor's construction progress was greatly delayed, causing enormous losses to both parties.[121] Customarily, if the delay to the project results from the employer's failure to accomplish land acquisition and removal within a reasonable period, the contractor is not liable for the delay and can ask the employer for an extension of time to completion and additional costs caused by such delay.

Site risks can trigger many related problems. For instance, the contractor's original evaluation of the project will have taken account of factors affected by the estimated construction period such as capital turnover, local weather, geographical environment, government policies, exchange rate fluctuations, public holidays' influence on workers' working hours and so on. However, if the project is delayed, these considerations may diverge from the conditions originally envisaged for the project: The local climate may change from dry season into rainy season, which would increase cost of the construction; international events in the extension period may cause a change in exchange rates. Thus, project delays can expose contractors to huge risks.

According to the 1999 FIDIC Conditions of Contract for EPC/Turnkey Projects, the employer is required to give the contractor the right of access to and possession of all parts of the Site at the time or times stated in the Particular Conditions. If the contractor suffers delay and/or incurs additional costs due to the employer's failure to provide the site on time, the contractor may give notice to the employer and claim an extension of time and/or payment of any extra costs plus reasonable profit. However, no rules are provided in the Silver Book regarding the calculation of the recoverable costs (save to say that it is all expenditure reasonably incurred (or to be incurred) by the contractor, whether on or off the site, including overhead and similar charges)—and difficult questions may arise where other events, within the contractor's scope of responsibility and having the potential to cause delay, occur in parallel with the employer's failure to give possession of the site. Therefore, during the period of delay caused by the failure to give possession of the site, contractors should guard against other kind of risks, minimize extra expenditure and collect evidence carefully.

---

121. Rui Guo, Fangjie Zhou, "Brief Study on the Construction Progress Control of the Overseas EPC Railway Projects," *Value Engineering*, 2015 (XXXII) pp. 71-73.

[B]   Coping Mechanism

[1]   Background Investigation of the Host Country

Before contracting, the contractor should comprehensively and prudently investigate potential risks brought by local policies, culture and environment and design strategies in response to these potential risks. It is also important for the contractor to ask the employer to provide relevant materials about local situations to predict possible risks when assessing engineering risks and negotiating contract terms.

For example, since the privatization of land employership in East European countries in the 1990s (some of the main employers in overseas contracting projects undertaken by Chinese enterprises), it has become increasingly difficult for employers to acquire land for construction projects. Land acquisition and removal has become one of the main tasks for local employers. An expressway construction project contracted by a Chinese company encountered problems of this type. The expressway construction project was an open bidding project of the Polish government. A joint venture consisting of two Chinese companies won sections A and C of the project of which the overall length was 49 kilometers, the total contract amount was USD 447,000,000 and the total construction time was 32 months. During the early-stage of the construction, the project encountered many obstacles with land removal, resulting in soaring project costs and a slowdown in progress. Furthermore, the engineering progress of the Chinese enterprise was directly affected.[122] In this case, the Chinese contractor won the bidding at the price of PLN 1,300,000,000, less than half of PLN 2,800,000,000, the price estimated by the Polish National Administration of National Roads and Highway. The Chinese contractor proposed such a low tender price because it failed fully to understand the local situation, to duly investigate the construction site and estimate the price of construction materials and to fully consider the difficulty of land acquisition by the employer. Therefore, the Chinese contractor should conduct diligent background investigations of the host country while bidding as well as forecast the difficulty involved in land acquisition in order to estimate engineering costs and decide a reasonable tender price.

[2]   Precautions to Take During Contract Negotiation Stage

Taking Contract Negotiations Seriously

Before signing a contract, contractors shall not only investigate local background but also take contract negotiations seriously in order to avoid risks and protect their interests through the contract. The employer and the contractor are bound by the contract, which also provides the main basis for settlement of later disputes.

---

122. Xiwei Zhang, Lihua Zhang, "Features, Problems and Responses of Construction Project Contracting in Central and Eastern Europe by Chinese Enterprises," *International Economic Cooperation*, 2017 (6) pp. 87-95.

If investigations reveal that substantial risks exist as to land acquisition and removal, the contractor should ensure that the contract terms allocate the risk of delay and additional cost arising from difficulties with providing access to and possession of the site to the employer.

Proposing Specific Engineering Plans

Some Chinese contractors are not cautious enough at the contract negotiation stage and ignore project information. Sometimes they even agree to sign a contract with a mere design concept. This can expose the contractor to severe risks, which are exacerbated if contractors fail to take measures to cope with such risks, adopt a passive position in their dealings with the employer. In these circumstances, the contractor may suffer great losses.

For instance, a Chinese corporation contracted a light rail project in 2010 in a country in the Middle East, when only a design concept was available at contract execution. However, during the construction process, the underground pipe network and land acquisition and removal for which the employer should have been responsible were delayed seriously, which led to a dramatic increase in actual construction quantities. Further, the employer greatly increased its transportation demands in 2010 compared to the stipulations in the contract, which, together with other factors, resulted in a substantial increase in workload and cost and periodic delay to the project.[123] Site risks in this case were caused by the hasty signing of the contract before the design was sufficiently advanced and when it was not possible accurately to forecast the project costs or duration. To avoid such problems, the contractor should avoid estimating the likely cost or duration of a project solely on the basis of its experience, nor should it act with undue haste in pursuing complicated megaprojects. Otherwise, the contractor may lose sight of the bigger picture and neglect to make detailed and specific plans.

[3] Actions to Take After the Occurrence of Site Risks

Calculation on Construction Delay

In cases where land acquisition risks give rise to claims, due to the complexity of the construction, the employer's failure to give possession of all or part of the site will not (or not necessarily) prevent all of the work continuing. For example, the contractor may be able to continue engineering works and investigatory works. In addition, it may be possible to take steps to mitigate the effects of a failure to give possession of part of the site. As a result, the period for which a contractor is entitled to an extension of time does not necessarily correspond to the period between the date when the employer

---

123. Zheng Wang, "Overseas Operational Risks and Precautions to Chinese Engineering Contractors," *International Economics Cooperation*, 2011 (X) pp. 24-27.

should have given possession of the site and the date when possession was actually provided.

Commonly, the employer's requirements will describe (even in general terms) the form of delay analysis which the contractor should provide to support any claim for an extension of time. Further, the Silver Book Conditions of Contract require notice of claims for an extension of time to be provided within 28 days of the failure to give possession. By that time, and indeed by the time that a detailed claim is to be provided, the full impact of the delay in providing possession may not be known. That being so, the contractor will have to make clear that the claim is interim and provide further claims in due course. Following the making of a claim, the contractor should negotiate with the employer to maximize its interests.

Effective Communication with the Employer

When land acquisition and removal runs into obstacles, instead of passively waiting for the result of land acquisition from the employer's side and letting the situation further deteriorate, the contractor should conduct active and effective communications with the employer to prevent the accumulation of losses and accelerate the process of land acquisition and removal.

First, contractors should actively negotiate with the employers to know the current status of land acquisition and removal. Then, contractors should adjust and update their construction plan taking into account the current and estimated site provision situation. This will include revising procurement planning, personnel arrangements and revising and updating the contract program, to minimize the contractor's losses.

Second, contractors should negotiate with employers on the extension of time and payment of extra costs promptly after the risks happen to make clear their positions and to inquire as to the employers' position. As noted above, contractors need to send notices seeking an extension of time and requesting payment of any additional costs promptly and within the time periods specified in the contract. As the land acquisition and removal issues continue, contractors should make adjustments to their claims accordingly. Also, contractors should keep contemporaneous records to substantiate their claims. These will include detailed expenses reports which should be sent to the employers on a regular basis. If employers raise doubts regarding such reports, contractors should actively communicate with them and collect and provide the relevant evidence to support their claims.

Full Play of the Liaison Department's Initiative

Contractors can sometimes assist the employer with land acquisition and removal through their liaison department. Liaison work is an important aspect in overseas engineering contracting and may have a significant influence on the successful conduct of land acquisition and removal. The liaison department in a project should communicate with the employer sufficiently and promote the progress of land acquisition and removal through communications with employers, local governments, land acquisition companies and relevant individuals. For instance, in the railway project undertaken by a Chinese contractor in Kenya mentioned above, in response to the site risks, the contractor's liaison department effectively communicated with the railway administration, local governments and other relevant parties in Kenya. Through such communications, it pushed forward the land acquisition and removal and contributed to the final settlement of site risks.[124]

§4.05 PRICE RISK

Price risk is one of the most critical in undertaking overseas projects. A series of factors including politics, economics, laws and regulations, finance, tax and exchange rate need to be considered in making any tender. It is unimaginably difficult to strike a balance between so many factors with the view of making an optimal tender. However difficult it is, a company should not accept exposure to all the risks only for winning the award. The past years have seen so many Chinese contactors paying heavy prices for making tenders without sensible consideration of the associated risks. Therefore, a company should base its tender on a complete due diligence and market investigation and resort to legal means to protect its legitimate interests when disputes arise.

[A] Risks Worthy of Consideration in Making a Bid

EPC contracts are generally lump-sum contracts in which the contractor undertakes almost all the risks of changes in quantities and price. The main price risks include the following.

[1] Risks in Miscomputation and Omissions

The contract price offered by the contractor should include all the costs and expenses for the execution and completion of the contract. Risks for any omissions will be taken by the contractor. To deal with this, the contractor should read meticulously the drawings and specifications to avoid miscomputation and omissions.

[2] Risks in Miscomputation of Quantities

No matter whether it is the employer who provides the bill of quantities or the contractor who prepares the quantity list itself and bids accordingly, the contractor should verify the quantities and correct the calculations where miscomputation has occurred.

---

124. Rui Guo, Fangjie Zhou, "Brief Study of the Progress Control of the Overseas EPC Railway Project," *Value Engineering*, 2015 (XXXII) pp. 71-73.

[3]   Risks in Rising Prices and Inflation

The contractor should evaluate thoroughly and take account in its pricing of the risk of fluctuation in prices.

At the same time, to prevent risks, the contractor may divert and transfer risks through subcontracting, joint bidding and insurance. Further, to control price risks, thought should be given to including a suitable mechanism for increasing the contract price to take account of inflation.

[4]   Risks Caused by Changes in Legislation

As a project usually lasts for a relatively long period of time and changes in legislation are mostly unforeseeable, there is a limited extent to which the contractor can take into consideration possible legislative changes (for instance, changes to tax regulations or environmental standards or so on) in making a bid.

[5]   Risks in Currency Exchange

The currency exchange rate plays an important role in deciding whether a project is profitable. This is especially true in soft currency countries. If an unsuitable or unstable currency is selected for the contract price, the profits of the contractor may be unduly diluted.

[B]   Preventive Measures for Price Risks

[1]   Price Adjustment in Lump-Sum/Fixed Unit Price Contract Price

The costs of labor, construction materials and construction machinery can climb continuously in overseas projects. Even if the contractor successfully predicts the price trend, the increased costs of labor, materials and machinery can wildly exceed expectations.

Price in lump-sum contracts is not absolutely nonadjustable. If additional costs are incurred by the contractor as a result of inflation or policy adjustments (including those for the price of labor force and plant), the contractor may (depending on the terms of the contract) be entitled to ask for reasonable compensation. An employer who intends to make costs controllable will generally arrange provisions for price adjustment (e.g., the FIDIC conditions). The two parties when drafting a contract may agree on the scope and method of price adjustment. For instance, a contract may provide that if the change in costs goes beyond a certain range, the price will be adjustable while the contractor is liable for risks of costs changes within the range. For risks of costs changes beyond the certain range, it is necessary to provide for the adjustment method to ensure that the contractor is properly compensated.

[2] *Principle of Changes in Circumstance/Principle of Contract Frustration*

If, when executing a contract, there is an abnormal surge in prices of labor, materials or machinery (as opposed to normal market fluctuation), that might amount to an unforeseeable change for which the contractor should not be responsible. Whether such circumstances justify modification or termination of contract will depend upon the contract terms.

Under some common law systems, the contract may be treated as frustrated if an event occurs (without default of either party and for which the contract makes no sufficient provision) which so significantly changes the nature (not merely the expense or onerousness) of the outstanding contractual rights and/or obligations from what the parties could reasonably have contemplated at the time of its execution that it would be unjust to hold them to the literal sense of the contract's stipulations in the new circumstances. Where that is the case, which will be rare, the doctrine of frustration brings the contract to an end automatically.

§4.06 DESIGN RISKS

In the current international contract project market, traditional contracting mode has been gradually replaced by general contracting modes including EPC, DB and so on. General contracting mode which integrates design, procurement and construction comprehensively is the main contracting mode. Design risk is the top risk for contractors in undertaking and executing EPC projects. In terms of design, the work quantities and costs of design only occupy a small part of the whole project; however, design imposes far-reaching influence on cost, period, craftsmanship and material choice of the whole project. The contractor should attach as much importance to design as to resource organization in the early stage.

Design risk mainly presents itself in the following aspects.

[A] Design Capability Risk

In general contracting projects, design director is required to acquire an understanding of the local statutes and broad knowledge on features of materials. With additional problems of difference in language, design capability and architecture style, Chinese contractors in most cases are unable to carry out design independently. This is exactly where the design risks lie. It is necessary for the contractor to make efforts in cultivating professional designer team with international competitiveness and at the same time localize the designer team as much as possible by employing local experienced and capable design consulting company. In the case of design contracting, the contractor should stay alert to mismatch between design in early stage and construction and procurement ability in later stage.

[B]   Uncontrollability Risk of Local Design Institute

In terms of contractors entrusting work to design institutes, local design institutes usually fall short of design capability and prolong the design period, while the European design institutes are not only highly priced but also less controllable and communicative. If the designer of a project sticks to his/her design philosophy, more time may be spent on the study of feasibility and specific design which adds a degree of uncontrollability as to costs and time. Practical lessons have taught us that controllability is the precondition in choosing a design institute. One should learn to foster its strengths and avoid its weakness and combine design contracting and consulting flexibly. The designer team should be localized as far as possible and experienced and capable local design consultancy is much preferred. When there are few local choices available, the contractor may consider forming a consortium between a Chinese design institute and a European design institute.

[C]   Delay Risks in Overdue Design Submittal and Approval

In an EPC project, the contractor is responsible for submitting design to the employer for approval. In most circumstances, the delay in design and that in approval intertwines with each other, causing project delay jointly.

[D]   Risk in Defective Design Drawings

Sometimes, the drawings the employer provides are incomplete and self-contradictory with many details left for further evaluation, thereby creating more cost to the contractor. The contractor should organize timely drawing review and engage in detailed project planning to distinguish underlying risks behind rough drawings.

[E]   Risk in Attribution of Design Liabilities

Before entering into a construction contract, the contractor must realize whether the design liability is attributed to the designer or the contractor in design drawings (under a D&B arrangement) and in shop drawings. The risk allocation should be clearly provided for in the contract in terms of the design liability and its scope such as specifying items and contents, test and inspection, determining the design representative and responsibility for on-site technical service, illustrating the required level of depth and detail (including or not the compiling of shop drawing, bidding documents and as-built drawing) and explaining the liability of designer in the defect liability period, in order to avoid wrangles and disorientation in the absence of advanced plan.

[F]   Risk in the Limited Flexibility of Contractor

In DB contracts, the contractor is endowed with freedom in detailed design, choice of craftsmanship and material provided such designs comply with the employers requirements as contained in the contract documents. By contrast, in the example of a particular housing project, the employer set an all-around limitation on the contractor's freedom in the detailed design. In that case, the technical documents provided by the employer in the early stage were incomplete, the design was barely half-finished and the designation of material and machinery were inapplicable and self-contradictory. After signing the contract, the contractor was left with no choice but to bear all the negative consequence of irrational preliminary design.

[G]   Risk in Application of Varied Specifications and Design Standards

The employer may apply varied standards such as the American Society for Testing Material (ASTM), British Standard (BS), European Norm (EN) and International Standard Organization (ISO) standard, making it more difficult for the contractor. If in the specification the employer puts forward super high-performance requirements which go far beyond the general international standard, in the case of incomprehensive design philosophy, inconsistent and even inapplicable design, the contractor would likely suffer considerable losses in both time and costs and experience difficulty in achieving the necessary employer approvals for completion of its work.

[H]   Risk in Government Examination and Approval

If it is the contractually ascribed responsibility and liability of the contractor to make design drawings in conformity with local specifications and obtain approval from local government, the risks in policies and work efficiency have been transferred to the contractor. In a country with immature specification and ever-changing policies, achieving an approved design may be more difficult. To obtain approval of relevant government department for the project design, sluggish and overdue approval procedures will consume much time, resulting in considerable delay which will be at the contractor's risk. For instance, in an overseas housing project, the aggregated time consumed for approval of the design drawings was nearly two years. In many cases, such delays will be at the contractor's risk. The contractor should obtain experienced local advice at the time of submitting the tender to minimize the risk of serious delay in locations where local regulatory approval is either immature and uncertain or overly complex and difficult to obtain.

[I]   Risk in Application of Mock-Up

Mock-up is a model for design or equipment for education, presentation, evaluation and promotion, scaled down or as big as the real object. To utilize mock-up before finishing the design is a benefit for the employer but a burden for the contractor as it requires the contractor to incur more time and costs. If a mock-up is required under the contract terms, then the contractor should estimate the cost and include it in its tender bid. If a mock-up is not required in the contract but later requested by the employer, this will constitute a variation to the contract and the contractor can claim additional payment.

[J]   Risk in Design Modification

In practice, many changes to the contract will not be defined as contractual variation. Nevertheless, when the employer initiates a variation, the contractor is liable to remind and help the employer to confirm increase in costs and time for the variation. The contractor should establish a process to submit such claims. Failure to do so can result in the contractor's inability to recover costs for serious project delays caused by variations to the project scope. Time and money claims for variations must be documented in a timely manner, to lay foundation for claims for extension of time and increase in costs. The contractor should carefully check and observe any time limits for making claims for variations as stated in the contract, to avoid losing the opportunity to recover its claims for extension of time and increase in costs.

[K]   Risk in Insurance

A contractor may be required to effect design or professional liability insurance, which is quite difficult to put in place given that some insurance companies refuse to provide or lack these types of insurance or impose high premium rates. During the bidding or negotiation process, the employer and the contractor may negotiate putting in place a bond arrangement in lieu of design or professional liability insurance.

Case: In an EPC lump-sum contract, it was provided that the employer was entitled to review the contractor's design documents and the contractor was liable to hand in design documents to the employer for approval. The review time limit for design drawings was 21 days.

The contractor finished PFD design of the plant on February 10th and submitted version A to the employer who responded on March 1st. The contractor revised the PFD design in light of employer's comments and submitted version B on March 11th, to which the employer made comments again on April 3rd. Later on April 22nd, the contractor revised the PFD design and submitted version C, and the employer responded with comments on May 16th. After that, the contractor revised and submitted version D and not until mid-July did the employer approved the final O version.

The contractor took the view that the contract has provided the time limit of 21 days for reviewing the document and the employer's suggested revisions on many occasions resulted in a significant amount of design work and a delay in the design progress. In the contractor's view, this, in turn, delayed the ordering of machinery and construction progress for which the employer should award certain time extension and financial compensation.

The employer took the view that its suggestions were based on specifications and fundamental data in technological design and the contractor itself failed to follow the requirements in the contract when preparing the design. In addition, the employer conducted each round of review within 21 days. The delay in approval should therefore be attributed to the contractor's failure to conform to the contract requirements. On this basis, the employer rejected the contractor's claims. In the circumstances, a dispute arose.

Case Analysis: In this case, putting aside the employer's requirements for revision of the PDF for several times, the contractor should conduct design in strict accordance with contracts and try to pass the review in the first attempt. However, in reviewing the design documents, the employer should put forward all the suggestions for revision at one time to avoid repetitive approvals later. The contract in this case did not set limits on the number of rounds of revision, but in the usual practice of international contracting projects, the employer is expected to cooperate with and give support to contractor in ensuring the timely completion of the project. In this spirit, the employer should try to bring forward suggestions at one time which is also the common practice in international contracting projects.

Considering the practical situation, both the employer and the contractor should be held accountable for the delay. Thus, the employer should provide reasonable compensation, including time extension and costs increase to the extent attributable to the employer's portion of the delay.

§4.07 TRANSPORTATION RISKS

[A] Characteristics of Logistics Management in Overseas Contracting Projects

The supply chain of overseas contracting projects includes the entire process from suppliers to subcontractors and from contractors to project employers. Logistics management permeates all parts of the supply chain and coordinates a series of work in a planned, orderly and step-by-step manner for materials and equipment to go through factory production delivery, cargo collection (port or airport), domestic customs clearance, shipment, customs clearance abroad and inland transportation in the country where the project locates. The international logistics management of overseas contracting projects involves a wide range of aspects and includes many phases. Its main features include the following: (1) there is a longer logistics delivery cycle with more steps; (2) logistics delivery methods are more extensive, including shipping, air transport, land transport, railway, international joint transport, etc.; (3) it involves many phases and entities, including suppliers, subcontractors, general contractors, employers, freight transport agents, shipping companies (or airlines), customs clearance agents at destination ports and customs agencies; (4) logistics transport from long distances are time-consuming and can cause delay to a project; (5) it is affected by different national cultures and customs usage and geographical environment; (6) logistics costs are higher.

[B]   Transportation Contract

Transportation contracts are an indispensable part of international contracting projects and the basis of logistics management in every project. As international contracting projects usually involve cross-border transportation of materials and equipment, there will also be issues related to international transportation contracts. Compared to domestic transportation contracts, international transportation contracts are unique in terms of the subject matter of contract, applicable laws, rights and obligations of the parties and transportation risks. In international contracting projects, contract management is a separate and wide topic. Here, we do not intend to provide a comprehensive and detailed introduction to transportation contracts. Rather, we take two issues, the limitation of the carrier's liability and the carrier's delivery of cargo without the original bill of lading, as examples to shed light on the risks arising from the selection and application of governing laws of transportation contracts.

[1]   Limitation of Carrier's Liability

Take the comparison between land, maritime and air transport systems as an example. The Convention on the Contract for the International Carriage of Goods by Road (hereinafter "the Road Transport Convention") for land transport, the International Convention for the Unification of Certain Rules of Law relating to Bills of Lading (hereinafter "the Hague Rules") for maritime transport and the Convention for the Unification of Certain Rules for International Carriage by Air (hereinafter "the Warsaw Convention") for air transport contain different provisions on the limitation of the carrier's liability. The rules on the attribution of liability and the corresponding distribution of burden of proof are also different. According to the Road Transport Convention, if the loss, damage or delayed delivery of the goods is due to the fault or instructions of the consignor, the inherent defects of the goods (including the defects of the packaging, the nature of being prone to rust or decay, etc.) and/or any other situations and results that the carrier cannot avoid or prevent, then the carrier can be exempted from liabilities. This Convention basically establishes the principle that the carrier can only be exempted from liabilities when it has no fault. Due to the peculiarities of maritime and air transport, the exemption rules are different. According to Article 20 of the Warsaw Convention, if the carrier proves that the loss or damage of the goods is due to its negligence in piloting, aircraft operation or navigation, while in all other aspects the carrier and its agents have taken all necessary measures to avoid the loss or damage, the carrier can be exempted from liabilities. According to Article 4 of the Hague Rules, the carrier may be exempted from liabilities for loss or damage of the goods caused by the act, neglect or default of the captain, mariner, pilot and other employees in navigating or managing the ship. Compared to the Warsaw Convention where the carrier may only be exempted from liabilities caused by negligence in driving, the Hague Rules enlarges the range of circumstances under which the carrier may assert impunity. Even within the maritime transport rules system, the Hamburg Rules stipulate different principles of attribution of liability from the ones in the Hague

Rules and the Visby Rules. The three rules also differ in limitations on the amount of the carrier's compensation liabilities.

In the case *Hunan Zhonglian International Trade Co., Ltd v. Shanghai Jiexi International Freight Forwarding Co., Ltd* concerning carriage of goods by sea,[125] the plaintiff sued the defendant for the loss of the goods. It alleged that the cargo damage was due to improper stowage and lashing of the goods, in other words, the improper management of the goods by the carrier and the actual carrier. The defendant argued that the loss was due to extreme weather (typhoon), bad sea conditions, force majeure and natural disasters. It relied on Article 331 of the PRC Contract Law, which provides that a carrier who can prove that the loss or damage of the goods is due to force majeure, the nature of the goods themselves, reasonable wear and tear or the fault of the consignor or the consignee, there is no compensation liability for the defendant. The Shanghai Maritime Court decided that the PRC Maritime Law, rather than the PRC Contract Law, should apply. The exemption defenses such as natural disasters and shipwrecks under the PRC Maritime Law should not be equated with force majeure and cannot be examined solely under the force majeure criteria. When the court examines extreme weather defenses such as typhoon, predictability should not be a decisive factor, but the focus must be on whether the severity of the sea conditions simply amounts to a normal maritime risk. Wind power and its duration and wave height and ship tonnage are two groups of important indicators, while visibility, roll angle and damage suffered by nearby ships can be used as auxiliary indicators. Defenses such as natural disasters which cause shipwrecks are often intertwined with issues of the ship's seaworthiness as well as navigation and management negligence. Therefore, after determining whether the sea condition constituted a natural disaster or not, causation must be further examined to decide whether the loss was due to the natural disaster, excusable negligence or nonexcusable negligence. In case of a combination of causes, according to the contribution of each cause, the liability shall be allocated proportionally.

In this case, the court especially emphasized that the PRC Maritime Law is a special set of rules that is independent of the principles and rules of general contract law. It is based on international conventions on maritime transport, encompasses nongovernmental rules that reflect common international shipping practice and draws from prevalent standard contracts. Therefore, overseas project contractors, when dealing with international transport contracts, should pay special attention to the applicable law or rules of the contract, for instance, whether it is a national law or an international convention. If it is a national law, the contractors should consider whether the contract is governed by the general contract law or a special set of rules. The same situation may be explained and treated differently under different rules and regulations, which may further affect the allocation of liabilities for potential losses and damage and identify risks to the project.

---

125. *Hunan Zhonglian International Trade Co., Ltd. and Shanghai Jiexi International Freight Forwarding Co., Ltd.* Shanghai First Intermediate People's Court (2012) Hu Hai Fa Shang Chu Zi No. 1208.

[2]   Release of Goods Without the Original Bill of Lading

No global consensus has been reached on the legal liability of the carrier when it releases goods without being presented with the original bill of lading. Applying different governing laws or rules provided in the shipping contracts and bringing lawsuits in courts of different countries may lead to different outcomes as to the carrier's liability. For example, Article 71 of the PRC Maritime Law stipulates that clauses in the bill of lading concerning the release of goods to the nominee, release of goods under instruction or release of goods to the holder of the bill of lading constitute the basis for the carrier to release goods. This provision requires the carrier to release the goods to the consignee based on the original bill of lading, without distinguishing between straight bill of lading and unnamed bill of lading. The 1916 United States Federal Bill of Lading Act (hereinafter "the 1916 Pomerene Act") provides that the carrier may release the goods to the consignee of the straight bill of lading. The carrier is not obliged to ask the named consignee to present or submit the bill of lading.[126] It demonstrates that for the straight bill of lading, U.S. law does not prohibit the carrier from releasing the goods even if the original bill of lading is not presented. In other words, a straight bill of lading does not have the function of a document of title in the U.S.

In the case of *Wanbao Group Guangzhou Feida Electrical Appliances Co., Ltd. v. US Presidential Steamship Co., Ltd.*,[127] the plaintiff sued the defendant for its release of goods to the consignee in Singapore when the consignee presented no proof of employership, let alone the original bill of lading. The plaintiff alleged that this was an infringement of its employership of the goods and violated the defendant's obligations under the transportation contract as the carrier. In this case, the bill of lading indicated that it was governed by the 1936 United States Maritime Transport Act (hereinafter "the 1936 U.S. Act") or the Hague Rules. In the trial at first instance, the Guangzhou Maritime Court held that neither the 1936 U.S. Act nor the Hague Rules specified whether the carrier could release goods to the named consignee without the original bill of lading being shown, and the relevant Singaporean law (which had the closest connection with the dispute) did not apply retrospectively to the bill of lading at hand. Therefore, the bill of lading should be governed by PRC law and relevant common international shipping practice, under which the Guangzhou Maritime Court found that the defendant violated its basic obligations under the transportation contract and infringed plaintiff's employership of the goods. In the trial of second instance, the Guangdong High People's Court came to the same conclusion but differed in its determination of governing law. The Guangdong High People's Court held that a dispute arising from the release of goods without the original bill of lading was a tort

---

126. Section 80110(b) of the Pomerene Bills of Lading Act, 1916, a common carrier may deliver the goods covered by a bill of lading to …(2) the consignee named in a nonnegotiable bill … *See* http://www.kpiclub.or.kr/board/data/file/Library_01/2039258253_mEzXrxBK_POMERENE _BILLS_OF_LADING_ACT.pdf, last visited May 19, 2018.
127. The United States President Steamship Co. v. The Wanbao Group Guangzhou FeiDa Electrical Appliance Factory, Philip Lee (Guangzhou) Industrial Co., Ltd., and China Great Wall Industry Guangzhou Co., Ltd. The Supreme People's Court (1998) Jiao Ti Zi No. 3.

dispute and was not subject to the governing law stipulated in the bill of lading. In this case, China was the place where the result of the tort happened, where the plaintiff resided and where the bill of lading was issued, so PRC law was more closely related to the dispute and should apply. However, in the retrial, the Supreme People's Court overturned both judgments. The Supreme People's Court held that as stated in the bill of lading, it should be governed by the 1936 U.S. Act. Article 3(4) referred to the 1916 Pomerene Act,[128] which, as stated above, did not require the carrier to ask the named consignee to present or submit the bill of lading. Therefore, the defendant should not undertake any liability for breach of contract or tort.

This case once again demonstrates that the application of different governing laws to international transportation contracts may result in far different outcomes as to the carrier's liability. Hence, contractors of overseas projects should fully understand the relevant provisions in the possible governing laws at the early contract negotiation stage and try as much as possible to agree with the carrier on a more favorable governing law for itself. In this case, the Guangdong High People's Court characterized the bill of lading related dispute as a tort dispute, concluding that the dispute was not governed by the law chosen by the parties. This practice actually rendered the law chosen by the parties meaningless, and fortunately, it has been modified by the current PRC law.[129] Despite that, contractors should still pay attention to whether other countries have similar legal practices (treating a bill of lading related dispute as a tort dispute) and take necessary measures to limit any such interpretation in advance.

[C] Customs Clearance

[1] *Domestic Customs Clearance*

Problems arising from domestic customs clearance are mainly about restrictions imposed on the materials and equipment to be exported, as well as qualification requirements on the exporter. For example, some construction machinery equipment or materials need quality certificates issued by the state in order to be exported, whereas an enterprise needs to have import-export operation rights to directly export goods, or it needs to cooperate with a foreign trade enterprise.

Many Chinese enterprises that have contracted overseas projects have purchased materials and equipment in China. If either the goods lack the required certificates of competency or the exporter violates restrictive provisions of the state on export products, customs clearance at domestic ports will face obstacles, which will increase the time and cost of transport and may even constitute a breach of contract with the

---

128. Section1303(4) of the Carriage of Goods by Sea Act, 1936, ... nothing in this chapter shall be construed as repealing or limiting the application of any part of Chapter 801 of title 49 ..., *See* http://www.docin.com/p-212046786.html, last visited 19 May 2018 (Chapter 801 of title 49 is the Pomerene Bills of Lading Act).
129. Article 44 of the PRC Law on Choice of Law for Foreign-related Civil Relationships effective on April 1, 2011: The laws at the place of tort shall apply to liabilities for tort, but if the parties have a mutual habitual residence, the laws at the mutual habitual residence shall apply. If the parties choose the applicable laws by agreement after any tort takes place, the agreement shall prevail.

carrier. More importantly, violation of relevant regulations may bring about the risk of degrading an exporter's previous export qualification level. Once the export qualification level is degraded, the exporter's products will suffer more difficulty in obtaining customs clearance, as the customs authorities will be stricter in the review and approval process.

[2]   Foreign Customs Clearance

Customs clearance procedures in foreign countries may be more complicated and bring about more risks. First, language difference has become a basic problem, resulting in communication barriers for customs clearance abroad. Many customs clearance issues are often caused by poor communication, such as demurrage charges, goods inspections and delay in clearance. In these procedures, logistic teams, third-party logistics companies or customs clearance agents need to communicate and negotiate with local customs authorities to fully understand procedures, costs, etc.

Second, the host country may impose specific legal or policy requirements on certain products, which appear to be just formalities but may nevertheless impede customs clearance. For example, the customs may require formal quality and/or origin certificates for raw materials procured abroad before they can be imported. In an electric power project located in Southeast Asia, in addition to the permanent equipment purchased according to the contract, the Chinese contractor also made many of its own construction tools and materials. These self-made products did not have factory test reports, quality certificates from designated institutions or other quality assurance documents. When all these equipment and materials shipped by the contractor arrived at the port of the host country, they could not successfully obtain customs clearance, because the customs regulations required factory test reports, product quality certificates or other necessary certification documents for all imported mechanical and electrical equipment, tools and materials. In order to satisfy these requirements, the Chinese contractor had to apply for and collect those documents back in China. As a result, all the equipment and materials were detained at the port by the customs authority. The contractor had to assume high demurrage fees and fines, and the project schedule was also seriously affected.[130]

Third, customs clearance obstacles may also come from risks related to letters of credit. The vast majority of overseas EPC projects use letters of credit for payment and collection between buyers and sellers. Due to the huge amount of funds involved in EPC projects, letters of credit, the conditional payment commitments guaranteed by the credit of banks are more secured and safer and fairer to both the buyers and sellers. However, the letter of credit transaction is not entirely free of risks. If the seller conducts transactions with the buyer through letters of credit, once the seller submits a negotiation document (e.g., a certificate or an invoice) that is not compliant with the letter of credit, the buyer may refuse or defer payment. As a result, the buyer cannot

---

130. Overseas Engineering Risks of Chinese Engineering Contracting Companies: An Analysis Based on Cases. *See* http://www.sohu.com/a/159226568_168969, last visited May 19, 2018.

timeously redeem documents such as the bill of lading, invoices, packing lists, certificates of origin from the bank.[131] These documents, however, are necessary for customs clearance, without which the materials and equipment imported cannot be successfully delivered to the project site, and the construction schedule will eventually be affected.

[D] Traffic Conditions of the Host Country

Since most of the construction sites of overseas projects contracted by Chinese enterprises are located in underdeveloped countries and regions and inland areas, the traffic conditions of the host country or region may also bring about transportation risks. The construction of infrastructures such as roads, railways and airports in these countries are far behind developed countries, causing difficulties in the delivery of materials and equipment purchased or provided by the contractor. For example, if the vehicle breaks down or has to slow down because of bad road conditions, the materials and equipment may not be timeously shipped to the project site, and the construction schedule could be delayed. Moreover, some construction projects are even located on plateaus, giving rise to even more transportation difficulties and risks. In conclusion, before the implementation of the project, the contractor should investigate and fully understand the traffic conditions of the host country and formulate a practical transportation plan, so as to successfully ship the materials and equipment to the project site in the host country.

In addition to the transportation infrastructure conditions, the local culture, customs, climatic conditions and prevalence of natural disasters will also affect the transportation of materials and equipment. Examples include the Muslim country's Eid al-Fitr, Eid al-Adha and rainy seasons in Africa. Before delivering the goods, the contractor should learn about local customs and traditions, climate features and customs regulations related to imported goods and try to avoid shipments during where delays are more likely to occur. Given that these problems inevitably involve the host country's social environmental risks and natural environment risks, etc., the contractor should carry out an overall analysis and evaluation of the host country's endemic risks even if only to mitigate transportation risks.

[E] Establishment of a Modern and Holistic Logistics Management System

The contractor should establish a holistic and efficient logistics management system and assign persons specifically responsible for procurement, transportation, storage and distribution. The logistics management department must put forward a detailed and reliable procurement plan at an early stage of the project and implement detailed works such as management of international transportation contracts, cargo declaration

---

131. Article 16 of the Uniform Documentary Credit Management (UCP600). *See* https://wenku. baidu.com/view/2b67794033687e21af45a935.html, last visited May 19, 2018.

at port and container packaging. For instance, the logistics management department should classify and inspect the purchased goods in order to improve the efficiency of customs declaration and container packaging. With regard to the domestic transportation in the host country, the logistics management department should be familiar with the host country's legal or regulatory requirements and traffic conditions, including customs clearance requirements, the ability of vehicles to deliver goods and whether specifications of mechanical equipment such as cranes, forklifts and the like can meet the loading and unloading requirements of container cargoes. Efforts should be made to minimize government charges, transportation costs, loading and unloading costs, manual handling costs and other expenses arising from all stages including transportation, storage and distribution. Through investigating the host country's logistics conditions, the logistics management department can provide feedbacks to the project department back in China, which in turn can then make advance adjustments in both procurement and customs declaration, including the choice of mechanical equipment type (such as the power of transformers and generators) and the choice of container type so as to comply with local machinery and equipment capabilities and reduce customs clearance costs as well as inland transportation costs.

Another approach is to subcontract the logistics management and let logistics subcontractors carry out and strictly monitor the logistics of the entire project in an orderly manner. Generally, logistics subcontractors should be chosen from third-party logistics companies with experience in international cargo transportation and logistics management of projects in the host country, so as to ensure that they make correct judgments under special circumstances, take effective reactive measures and to the fullest extent possible save time and costs. It goes without saying that the contractor must also take the increases in costs, time and human labor arising from logistics subcontracts into consideration.

Lack of comprehensive understanding of modern logistics management inevitably causes risks and losses in the implementation of the project. Taking the export of construction equipment by a domestic cement machinery manufacturing factory as an example, due to the limited experience of the project logistics operators, a large number of steel structures did not have appropriate shipping marks during transportation. The shipping marks of the tower crane equipment were only made of small plastic cards and tied on a shelf, making it difficult to distinguish the tower crane equipment from steel structures. After the goods were unloaded at the port of destination, they scattered on the ground and most of the shipping marks were lost. The local customs could not identify which items were part of the tower crane and which were steel structures. As a result, the customs refused to grant customs clearance, which brought about a lot of trouble to the customs clearance work and incurred unnecessary expenses.[132]

If contractors pay due regard to the importance and key role of logistics management in project implementation and take active and effective measures to

---

132. Liu Xuexin, "Research on Logistics Management Optimization of Z Company's Overseas Projects". *See* https://max.book118.com/html/2015/0128/11830422.shtm, last visited May 19, 2018.

strengthen and improve logistics management, they would benefit immensely. A typical example is the import of second-hand machinery equipment by a domestic heavy steam turbine factory from England, with General Technology Group International Logistics Co., Ltd. as the carrier. A total of 42,000 billed tons of equipment was shipped. Since the beginning of shipment, the steam turbine factory had been working closely with General Technology to facilitate the transportation work of the project. All the stages were connected sequentially from the delivery time to the timely update of the packing lists, from the packaging standard to the making of shipping marks, from the making of documents to the inland transportation arrangements and from the dismantling, packing, sea and land transport to the foreign customs clearance, equipment installation and test, and the entire process of domestic and overseas transportation operations only lasted 10 months. Due to the successful logistics management, the steam turbine factory saved millions of dollars in expenditure.[133]

§4.08 VARIATION RISKS

According to Article 13 "Variations and Adjustments" of Conditions of Contract for Construction for Building and Engineering Works Designed by the employer (the "1999 Version FIDIC Red Book"),[134] a variation is a concept with a broad meaning, including changes in work volume, construction location, construction time and sequence and characteristics of the work etc. Variations can influence the project in many respects. For example, variations may lead to changes in the contract price and require additional time for completion, and the high-frequency of variations will cause increase in workload and difficulties in communications with engineers and contract management.[135] Therefore, variations must be effectively dealt with to avoid leading to increased workload and costs, which may trigger disputes between the contractor and the employer.

[A] Analysis on Legal Risks of Variation

At present, Chinese contractors lack management experience in international engineering projects compared to contractors from mature international contracting markets, like the U.S. and EU. For Chinese contractors, it is not unusual that variation claims are not pursued in accordance with the requirements of the Contract, with the consequence that the claims become difficult to pursue subsequently. Considering the features of variations and cases involving Chinese contractors, the legal risks of variations for Chinese contractors in overseas operations mainly come from the following aspects.

---

133. Zhang Yiping, "Great Expectations of International Engineering Logistics". *See* https://wenku
    .baidu.com/view/4358dbd684254b35eefd3458.html, last visited May 19, 2018.
134. Unless otherwise stated, this article only discusses the 1999 Version FIDIC Red Book.
135. Dezhi Duan, Exploring the Variations in International Construction Contracts, Construction
    Materials and Decoration, November 2015.

Low Bidding Price

"Low-price bid and high-price claim" is a strategy commonly used in the domestic market in China, which means the contractor wins the bid through a price much lower than the reasonable construction budget and then makes a profit by making high-price claims against the employer in later phase.

Unlike domestic projects, international engineering projects often take months, years or even decades, during which raw material costs, exchange rates, and construction conditions may change. Whether the said changes can be recognized as variations under the contract must be judged in accordance with the contract terms. According to 1999 Version FIDIC Red Book, when variations come up, contractors can adjust the contract price only when they obtain relevant instructions from engineers and follow the contractual procedures. Therefore, although some Chinese contractors plan to use the strategy of "low-price bid and high-price claim" in international projects, the variations may not be accepted by the employer for various reasons, and Chinese contractors would be at an unfavorable position in bringing claims at a later phase.[136]

On February 10, 2009, a Chinese company's overseas subsidiary won the bid to build a light rail in Mecca, Saudi Arabia (the "Mecca Light Rail Project"). The company initially quoted USD 2.2 billion and then lowered its quotation to USD 1.77 billion. The price was nearly USD 1 billion lower than the price quoted by a local railway construction company which was very experienced in local infrastructure constructions.[137] Although the Chinese contractor eventually completed the construction, according to the announcement issued by its parent company, it suffered losses of RMB 4.15 billion.[138] Similar to the aforementioned case, in September 2009, a contractor consisting of several Chinese companies won a highway project in an opening bid proposed by the Polish government (the "Polish Highway Project") with a winning price of USD 4.47 billion, which was less than half of the budget calculated by the Polish government. From May 2011 the subcontractors refused to continue to deliver construction materials to the site because the Chinese contractor did not pay on time. Subsequently, the Chinese contractor had to abandon this project.[139]

---

136. Hongwen Zhu, Ru Yan, "Legal Risk and Prevention in International EPC Construction Contract", Chinese Lawyer, November 2011.
137. Pengcheng Xiang, Zhenzhen Wan, "Investigation on the Losses of CRCC Mecca Light Rail Project: A $1 Billion Gambling", Sohu Finance, October 29, 2010, http://business.sohu.com/20101029/n276731841.shtml; The Story behind CRCC's Huge Losses, Sina Finance, December 9, 2010, http://finance.sina.com.cn/chanjing/sdbd/20101108/15278917962.shtml.
138. CRCC Expected to Suffer RMB 4.153 billion Losses on Mecca Light Rail Project, CNTV, November 17, 2010, http://jingji.cntv.cn/20101117/101972.shtml; Shuying Zhu, "Legal Risk Prevention and Control under the 'Belt and Road Initiative,'" Construction Enterprise Management, March 2017.
139. Failure of Low Biding Price Strategy: Polish Highway Project is in Trouble, Ifeng Finance, November 21, 2011, http://finance.ifeng.com/stock/ssgs/20111121/5103791.shtml; Shuying Zhu, "Legal Risk Prevention and Control under the 'Belt and Road Initiative'", Construction Enterprise Management, March 2017; Pengcheng Xiang, Xiaohua Niu, "The Causes and Enlightenments of Failures of International EPC Construction Contract—Taking Polish Highway Project as an Example", International Economic Cooperation, May 2012; Clarifications from Poland Highway Administration on the Termination of Polish Highway Project, Ifeng Finance, July 21, 2011, http://finance.ifeng.com/roll/20110721/4299221.shtml.

Since Chinese contractors won both the Mecca Light Rail Project and the Polish Highway Project with a price far below the reasonable construction budget, they were inevitably going to face financial difficulties and be subject to high risks from the very beginning. As the construction progressed, variations would come up frequently and the management of variations would become difficult due to the low contract price.

Lack of Comprehensive and In-Depth Due Diligence

Under the "Go Global" strategy of China, Chinese contractors should pay attention to the selection and identification of the target market before going global. For a risky target market, due diligence shall be conducted in advance and a corresponding exit mechanism should be established.[140] Comprehensive and in-depth due diligence can allow Chinese contractors to understand the cost of the project, the existing technical difficulties, the credit status of the employer and the macro-environmental risks of the host country. It can also allow the Chinese contractor to anticipate the possibility of occurrence of major variations and revise the contract in advance to mitigate the relevant variation risks. For high-risk projects, if detailed due diligence has not been carried out, when variations subsequently occur, the engineer and the employer may dispute whether the purported changes qualify as variations under the contract and whether the contractor is entitled to make claims.

In a highway project, as the contractor failed to comprehensively study the special geological conditions of the construction site, with the result that the actual work volume of some construction items was far beyond the work volume stipulated in the project description. For example, according to the project description, bridge piles were to be driven into the ground over a distance of 49 kilometers. In actual fact, it turned out that such piling was required over a distance of 60 kilometers.[141] Meanwhile, because the Public Procurement Law of the host country prohibited major price adjustment by a contractor after winning the bid, the key terms relating to price adjustment originally stipulated in the contract were deleted, resulting in a "locked" total contract price. Therefore, when variations occurred, it was difficult to make claims against the employer or require the employer to compensate in the name of variations.[142]

---

140. Yueping Zhou, Xiaochen Ji, Yi Meng, "Risk Identification and Prevention in International EPC Contract", China Architectural Decoration, August 2016.
141. CRCC Failed in Polish Highway Project: Low Price Strategy Cannot Be Copied, Sina Finance, August 23, 2016, http://finance.sina.com.cn/chanjing/gsnews/2016-08-23/doc-ifxvcsrm2267 022.shtml; Pengcheng Xiang, Xiaohua Niu, "The Causes and Enlightenments of Failures of International EPC Project Contract—Taking Polish Highway Project as an Example", International Economic Cooperation, May 2012.
142. Shuying Zhu, "Legal Risk Prevention and Control under the 'Belt and Road Initiative'", Construction Enterprise Management, March 2017; Pengcheng Xiang, Xiaohua Niu, "The Causes and Enlightenments of Failures of International EPC Project Contract — Taking Polish Highway Project as an Example", International Economic Cooperation, May 2012; CRCC Encountered Claims and Terminated the Project to Avoid Worse Results, Sohu Finance, http://business.sohu.com/20110627/n311719997.shtml.

Noncompliance of Variation Procedures

According to the 1999 Version FIDIC Red Book, the engineer can issue a variation instruction or request the contractor to submit a proposal for a variation, and if the engineer requires the contractor to submit such a proposal before issuing any instructions, the contractor shall provide a written response as soon as possible. While the contractor is waiting for the reply, the contractor shall not delay any construction work. A variation instruction must be issued in written form. If the engineer delivers the instruction to the contractor orally and the contractor fails to obtain written confirmation in time, it may be difficult to prove the reasonableness of the variation later.[143]

In addition, variation instructions emanating from the employer/engineer and variation claims emanating from the contractor are two separate concepts and should be handled in different ways. When issuing a variation instruction, the employer or the engineer may negotiate with the contractor to determine the compensation payable pursuant to the variation instruction. In these circumstances, a variation may be more acceptable to both parties and less risky to the contractor in terms of recovering the compensation payable. However, in circumstances where the employer or the engineer has not issued any variation instruction and the contractor seeks to bring claims against the employer on account of a purported variation, it may be very difficult for the parties to reach consensus on whether there has been a variation and one party may have to submit such a dispute to a court or an arbitration institution in the end. contractors often confuse the significance of differences between variations instructions emanating from the employer/engineer and variation claims emanating from the contractor and/or fail to comply with variation procedures. In this regard, the contractors may give up striving for variation compensation in the early stage but treat all variations as part of the claims it brings against the employer later on. In this way, it would be harder and more burdensome for the contractor to bring claims, and the contractor may miss the variation compensation it could have obtained because it chooses the wrong way to request compensation.[144]

Take an example to illustrate the importance of complying with variation procedures. In an overseas project, a Chinese contractor and an employer signed a contract in the form of 1999 Version FIDIC Red Book and started plant installation. During the construction, due to the influence of the worldwide financial crisis, the employer modified the design several times to reduce costs, thereby increasing the work volume and prolonging the construction period. The Chinese contractor promptly submitted a variation proposal to the engineer with supporting evidence to request additional time for completion according to Article 8.4 "Extension of Time for Completion" of the contract. Since the Chinese contractor strictly followed the variation procedures, the proposal was approved by the engineer and the variation was completed smoothly.[145]

---

143. *See* Article 13.3 of the 1999 Version FIDIC Red Book.
144. Weifang Li, "Laughing Inside Confirmation and Control of Variations", Architecture Economy, March 2007.
145. Jinsheng Chen, "Claims and Inspirations of Cases under the Conditions of FIDIC Contracts", 2016 Edition.

[B]   Prevention of Variation Risks

Variations affect the contract price, work volume, time for completion, characteristics of work and claims and can have a domino effect on the whole project. Therefore, variations need to be a focus of contract management. Considering the analysis and cases introduced above, Chinese contractors may consider preventing the legal risks relating to variations in the following ways.

Have a Good Command of FIDIC

FIDIC model contracts are widely accepted and used in the international construction market. If Chinese contractors aim to take a more important role in the international engineering market, they should become more internationalized in terms of legal sense and contract management by achieving a good understanding of FIDIC and utilizing its terms in practice for their own benefits.

Regarding construction variations, Chinese contractors shall understand not only the clauses about variations, but also other clauses that are relevant to variations. For example, the time limits for claims set out in Article 20.1 in the 1999 Version FIDIC Red Book are also applicable to claims arising from disputes over variations and Article 8.4 which concerns time for completion also addresses the extension of time for completion in the event of variations.

Pay More Attention to Contract Clauses

If Chinese contractors fail to pay enough attention to the clauses of the contract when negotiating the contract, they may find themselves accepting procedures for the presentation of variation claims which they are unable to comply with. Chinese contractors should improve their own contract awareness and negotiate and revise the contract clauses before signing the contract.

Whether a change in the course of construction amounts to a variation and whether the contractor will be compensated for such a change in the same manner as variations must be judged in accordance with the contract. Therefore, the contract should include detailed provisions on the nature or scope of all kinds of changes and specify the price adjustment method applicable to price changes caused by changes to the law, inflation and exchange rate fluctuation, etc.[146]

Comply with Variation Procedures Strictly

Generally, variations should be carried out in accordance with the written instructions of the engineer or the approved variation proposals. When the engineer only orally instructs a variation without a written instruction, Chinese contractors should obtain a written instruction as soon as possible or require the engineer to sign a confirmation letter.

---

146. Yueping Zhou, Xiaochen Ji, Yi Meng, "Risk Identification and Prevention in International EPC Project Contract", China Architectural Decoration, August 2016.

In addition, Chinese contractors must pay attention to special clauses relating to variation procedures provided in the contract. For example, according to Article 3.3 of the 1999 Version FIDIC Red Book, if the engineer gives an oral instruction, receives a written confirmation of the instruction from (or on behalf of) the contractor within two working days after giving the instruction, and does not reply by issuing a written rejection and/or instruction within two working days after receiving the confirmation, then the confirmation shall constitute the written instruction of the engineer. Under such provision or other similar provisions in the contract, if the engineer refuses to issue written instructions, Chinese contractors can also send a written confirmation letter to the engineers to avoid the risks arising out of failure to obtain written instructions from the engineers.

Prepare for Claims Early

Chinese contractors with less experience in international projects often lack sufficient understanding of claims. They may not pay due attention to claim issues until they need to make a claim. In the end, the claims are often difficult to realize due to problems like expiry of time limits or lack of accumulation of evidence.[147]

Making claims is a means of self-protection and an effective way to improve income. Chinese contractors should make preparations for claims to be raised for variations early rather than wait until disputes arise. In addition, claims should be raised within the time limits provided in the contracts and sufficient supporting evidentiary materials should be provided. Only in this way can Chinese contractors gain a more favorable position in the process of subsequent dispute settlement.

Record keeping of the daily commercial events in the life of a construction project is fundamental to the ability to bring a claim against an employer. A lack of records may mean that a claim may not be brought successfully. The Chinese contractor must be able to evidence its claims from independent contemporaneous written records. For example, if a Site Instruction is given verbally the contract will often call for the Chinese contractor (not the employer) to provide written confirmation of the instruction it has been given within a short period. Verbal instructions can be denied either because of genuine miscommunication or more devious reasons. Besides written and acknowledged site correspondence, Requests for Instructions, Minutes of Meetings or fully annotated drawings, it is a good idea for all senior staff are instructed to keep a daily diary of interactions with the engineer or employer's representative. The diary should record daily events and out of the ordinary events such as site instructions for the contractor to take or alter a particular course of action. In the event of a claim, these diaries can be used as corroborating evidence supporting other correspondence and records. The importance of site record keeping cannot be emphasized enough.

---

147. Hongwen Zhu, Ru Yan, "Legal Risk and Prevention in International EPC Project Contract", Chinese Lawyer, November 2011.

§4.09 RISKS IN PROJECT DELAY

Delay risks are the most frequent yet the most complicated risks in overseas projects. The project duration directly influences the project's costs and to some degree determines the success of the employer and contractor in achieving their economic objectives. Accordingly, in the event of delay, the employer will look to recover the losses that it may suffer by claiming liquidated "delay damages" from the contractor. By contrast, the contractor will look to claim an extension of time for the period of delay and may also look to recover compensation for its additional costs arising from the delay.

[A]   Principal Causes and Liability Attribution of Project Delay

Project delay usually results from many factors interacting with each other including inadequate capability on the part of the contractor and non-contractor factors. If the contractor causes delay, it is generally attributed to insufficient capabilities in many respects such as design management, construction organization, procurement management, labor management and capital management. Non-contractor factors mainly include interference from the employer or a nominated subcontractor, failure of the employer in satisfying the conditions required for construction progress (including site, technical documents, machinery, necessary approvals and licenses for construction), delay caused by the authority, employer's risks, variations and force majeure.

To differentiate specific liabilities, the liability should be attributed to the employer in the following events: delay in providing drawings; failure in obtaining relevant approvals and licenses; deferred tests on cover-ups; project delay caused by fossils; unqualified construction work caused by employer; delayed conclusion and execution of provisional sum contracts caused by employers; failure in giving instructions promptly and correctly; and default of the employer.

In the following cases, the contractor should be held liable: inadequate survey or insufficient understanding of on-site conditions; disqualification and suspension on the part of the contractor; utilization of materials in disconformity with design; assignment and unlawful subcontracting; delayed execution and default of the contractor. Among others, the contractor should stay alert to the following potential delaying events: inadequate survey or insufficient understanding of on-site conditions; delay of the nominated subcontractor; and delayed receipt of correspondence.

As project delay is caused by both the employer and the contractor, in practice, it is generally quite difficult to allocate and quantify the respective liabilities. Given that the contractor bears the burden of proof when seeking an extension of time, better evidence management is required of the contractor to enable it to be sufficiently prepared for making later claims.

Case: In an overseas project of a Chinese contractor, progress was delayed from the outset. The factors leading to the delay caused by the employer included: delayed provision of access to the site and construction drawings; design modifications during construction; and the absence of construction permits. The contractor should also be

143

held accountable for the following factors: failure in registration of representative office before commencement; delay in authentication of construction qualifications and tax registration; and late arrival of building materials due to a funds shortage. Delaying events attributable to both sides were intertwined, and the employer found the progress severely lagged behind the original program. The two parties terminated the contract and commenced arbitration to resolve disputes and differences relating to delay.

[B]   Risks in Provisions for Project Time Worthy of Special Attention

[1]   *Clarity of Commencement Time and Completion Time*

With reference to the FIDIC conditions, the employer should give the contractor not less than seven days' notice of the commencement date of the project, which commencement date should be within 42 days after the contract taking effect. That is, the employer needs to serve notice of commencement date not later than 35 days after the contract coming into force to avoid claims for additional costs and/or extension of time.

Disputes often occur because of a disjuncture in the understanding of the employer and contractor of the documents required for the acceptance of the works and what constitutes completion under the contract. In extreme cases, the employer has rejected acceptance tests or refused to take over the works for extraneous reasons of its own. Hence, it is necessary to specify clearly in the contract documents the requirements for acceptance of the works and the requirements for completion. A most critical provision is for the contract to provide that if the employer has neither issued a taking-over certificate nor rejected the contractor's application for tests to be conducted on completion within a specified period, the project should be regarded or deemed as having been completed upon the expiration of a specified period following the contractor's application for tests to be undertaken. To obviate the risk of the employer occupying and using the project without conducting tests on completion, the contract should provide for taking-over to be deemed to have occurred after the employer places the project into commercial operation.

[2]   *Rationality of the Arrangement for Project Time and Liquidated Delay Damages*

The contractor should avoid making commitments which go beyond its construction capability in order to be awarded the contract. At the same time, the contractor should try to avoid agreeing to pay delay damages for delayed completion of each phase of the works where there is phased completion. If this is unavoidable, it is advisable to add provisions to the effect that in the event that the contractor catches up and recovers the original progress in respect of one or more phases the paid damages should be returned to the contractor in whole or at least in part.

144

To mitigate the risk of the contractor having to make onerous compensation payments for delay, the rate of delay damages should be reasonable and there should be an upper limit or cap on liability for delay damages(usually 10% of the contract price).

[3]   Conditions for Extension of Time and Procedures

In the event of delay caused by non-contractor factors, the contractor is generally entitled to apply for an extension of time unless the contract provides for the contractor to assume the risk of delay caused by these non-contractor factors. Depending on the terms of the contract, the contractor may be entitled to apply for an extension of time in case of unforeseeable physical conditions or delayed issuance of drawings and instructions by the employer/engineer. When reviewing the contract terms, the contractor should check the completeness and rationality of the terms for extension of time by taking into consideration the project type.

[C]   Critical Path Analysis

The critical path is the sequence of activities through the project from start to finish, the sum of whose durations determines the overall duration of the project.

The critical path of a project is typically dynamic in the sense that it changes over the course of the project. Moreover, there may be one or more critical paths.

In the planning stage, appropriate assessment of the critical path enables the overall time required for the project to be identified and priority to be given to those activities which determine the overall project duration. During the execution of the project, continuous monitoring of the critical path is necessary to ensure the effective allocation of resources and to enable focused attention to the key points of the project so as to ensure the timely completion in accordance with the requirements of the contract. At the claim stage, a critical path analysis enables the detection of those activities which delayed the overall completion of the project. In a case provided by the ICC for this research project, the mistake committed by the operator hired by the employer in the operation of the crane did cause delay, but the arbitral tribunal determined that the incident did not cause delay on the critical path. Therefore, it was not a justifiable ground for the Chinese contractor to advance its claim for delay.

There are typically three steps in any critical path analysis: First (at the relevant point in time), identify the critical path; Second, identify the activity which is alleged to have caused delay and incorporate it into the program (either as a new activity or by extension of the duration of an existing activity) taking account of its known or expected duration; Third, consider whether the activity alleged to have caused delay either (a) affects the activities on the existing critical path and/or (b) affects other (previously sub-critical) activities so as to cause a change to the critical path.

[D]   Concurrent Delay

The term "concurrent delay" is used in two different ways. Sometimes it is used to refer only to two delay events of **approximately equal causative potency**, one of which is the contractor's responsibility and one of which is the responsibility of the employer. More frequently, however, it is used to refer to the situation where there are two delay events occurring over the same time period **regardless of their causative potency** (i.e., regardless of the fact that one cause of delay, say the delay for which the contractor is responsible is critical and the other delay is sub-critical).

Concurrent delay can affect contractor and employer claims in different ways. Moreover different legal systems approach concurrent delay in different ways. In the following examples, delay for which the employer is responsible is referred to as "employer-delay" and delay for which the contractor is responsible is called "contractor-delay:"

Case 1: Where employer-delay affects the critical path and, at the same time (but independently), contractor-delay affects activities which are not on (and do not enter) the critical path, the contractor may be entitled to (a) an extension of time for the entire period of employer-delay; and (b) to the extent provided by the contract, compensation for additional costs which it has incurred due to the employer-delay. Note, given that in this example where there has been parallel (but sub-critical) contractor-delay, the contractor's entitlement to compensation may be limited to compensation for the **additional** period of delay to project completion caused by the employer-delay, i.e., that period for which the employer-delay exceeded the delay that the contractor-delay would have caused in any event.

Case 2: Where contractor-delay affects the critical path and, at the same time (but independently) employer-delay affects activities which are not on (and do not enter) the critical path, the contractor may not be entitled to any extension of time and so may be liable for delay damages for the full period of contractor-delay.

Case 3: Where contractor-delay and employer-delay both affect the critical path equally, the contractor will usually be entitled to an extension of time (and hence avoid having to pay delay damages to the employer) but the contractor will not usually be entitled to any compensation of its own.

[E]   Evidence Management

When carrying out business activities overseas, relevant staff should keep records of the key events that occur during the project, whether those records take the form of instructions from the employer, notices to the employer, evidence of meteorological conditions or labor disturbances, records of workaround or accelerative measures that have been adopted and so on. The project program should be regularly updated to reflect the progress achieved on the project and the contractor's internal and external reporting should accurately reflect the occurrence of events and their effect on the project program. Detailed records should be made of additional labor/staff, material and equipment costs.

It is reasonably frequent for projects of long-duration to experience a significant turnover of staff, including project management and planning staff. Where that is the case, the handover process to new personnel should not be a mere formality. Instead, a detailed list of documents with explanatory notes should be provided to ensure that the new personnel are properly appraised of conditions on the project. Handover should not, however, be merely a document transfer. The person responsible for the handover should inform the person taking over of the works in progress, the procedures to be handled and the experience and resources accumulated during the work. It is prudent (if possible) for the transferor to work together with the transferee for a period before total handover, helping them to understand the manner of handling varied affairs and the details and tips worthy of special attention. The conclusion of the handover process should also not result in a break in connection. The transferor should be prepared to provide any assistance required by the transferee for a certain period even after the transferor returns from abroad.

[F]   Retaining Evidence in Common Situations of Delay

Whenever events occur which the contractor believes might entitle it to an extension of time, the contractor should keep records of the effect of the delay on the project program, including copies of the project program prior to the occurrence of the event and then copies of the program as adjusted following occurrence of the event. Moreover, the contractor should look to retain the following types of documents in the following common situations.

Delay in issuance of drawings and review approvals: To enable the contractor to keep control of any delay by the employer in issuing or reviewing drawings, the contractor should keep a register of drawing issue and revision. The contractor should also maintain records of relevant correspondence and meeting minutes, recording any concerns relating to the impact of any delays on the development of the design and construction progress.

Delay in provision of equipment and materials which should be supplied by the employer: Where delays are encountered in the supply of equipment or materials by the employer, the contractor should keep an eye on relevant correspondence and meeting minutes. The contractor should also seek from the employer records of the employer's dealings with the supplier (including bidding documents, contracts, correspondence and minutes), details of any acceptance tests or other records.

Delay in invitation for bids of nominated subcontractor (professional subcontractor): Where there is delay by the employer in identifying nominated subcontractors, the contractor should seek copies of subcontracting bidding documents issued by the employer, professional tender documents from the subcontractors, bid opening records, letters of acceptance, subcontract document and evidence of preparatory work done by subcontractors, as well as records of arrival on-site (construction log and supervision journal).

Delay in the performance by a nominated subcontractor (professional subcontractor): Where delays are caused by a nominated subcontractor and the employer is

147

responsible for such delay, the contractor should keep relevant correspondence and meeting minutes, any construction program submitted by the subcontractor, records of the transfer of the relevant site location and work interfaces, the material construction logs or supervision logs and documents evidencing specific assistance offered by the general contractor to the subcontractor and records of management measures.

Increase of work quantities and variation instructions: the contractor should keep relevant instructions issued by the employer or supervisor (or confirmed by the contractor), records of the handover of additional drawings, relevant correspondence and meeting minutes concerning the related instruction or increase in quantities, the construction log, management log and any additional acceptance records.

Ceremonial events of the government: the contractor should keep records of relevant media coverage, documents and notices served by the relevant departments of the local or national government or government offices.

Severe weather: the contractor should collect relevant media coverage, pictures and videos, and obtain comparative analysis reports of meteorological records, weather forecasts and meteorological records.

Delay in payment: the contractor should keep records of the contractor's requests for payment (and any accompanying certificates) as well as other relevant correspondence and meeting minutes.

[G] Claim Procedures for Delay

Under the FIDIC Silver Book, special attention should be attached to the following points in the context of claims for extension of time and costs.

First, the contractor must keep and maintain such contemporary records as may be necessary to substantiate any claim. Without substantial evidence of the event that is alleged to have caused delay (and of its effects), the contractor will lack an objective foundation for any claim for time and costs.

Second, where a contractor believes it may be entitled to an extension of time and/or compensation for time and costs, the contractor should review the contract documents. The contractor must be prepared to comply with all contract requirements regarding the substantiation of the delay which it alleges has been or is likely to be caused.

Third, the contractor must give notice of claim to the employer within 28 days (or such other time specified by the contract) after the contractor becomes aware or should have become aware of the event or circumstance giving rise to the claim. There are number of points to note about this requirement:

(a) With respect to the form of notice, it is desirable to title the letter as "Notice of Claim" and to refer to the relevant clause of the contract pursuant to which the claim is made. A letter that mentions the event that causes the delay but does not expressly state that a claim is being made will not be regarded as a notice of claim.

(b) The starting point for counting the time for issuing the notice is the time when the contractor has or should have detected the event or circumstance giving rise to the claim. In practice, a contractor is unlikely to be able to excuse failure to serve a notice on the basis that it failed to detect the occurrence of the relevant event or circumstance.

(c) Unless clearly stated in the contract, a time period stated in days will be calculated on the basis of calendar days.

(d) If the contractor fails to serve the notice within 28 days, it will be deprived ever of the right to ask for extension of time and payment of costs.

Fourth, following service of the initial notice of claim (and typically 42 days after the contractor became aware (or should have become aware) of the event or circumstance giving rise to the claim), the contractor must send to the employer a fully detailed claim which includes full supporting particulars of the basis of the claim and of the extension of time and/or additional payment claimed. If the event or circumstance has a continuing effect, the contractor should send further interim claims on a monthly basis and then a final claim after the end of the effects resulting from the event or circumstance.

In a case provided by the ICC for this research project, the employer terminated the contract based on the Chinese contractor's non-conformity with the notice of correction and delay in the construction period, etc., and claimed for "any additional expenses required for the completion of the project" and other losses in the arbitration. The employer hired a quantum expert who evaluated the additional cost to be approximately three times the remainder of the contract price! The contractor's expert also provided an estimation but it was relatively crude and the evidence it was based on was insufficient. In the end, the arbitral tribunal fully accepted the calculation of the employer's expert in damages for the employer's claims. Section §2.09[A][5] Arbitration (f) Expert Witnesses concentrates on the use of expert in arbitration; please refer to that section for more information.

§4.10 RISK OF SUSPENSION AND TERMINATION

[A] Conditions for Project Suspension

According to the Silver Book, 1999 Edition, the employer may at any time instruct the contractor to suspend progress of part or all of the works,[148] whereas the contractor can only choose to suspend or slow down the works when the employer fails to provide reasonable evidence of its financing arrangements or fails to comply with its payment obligations, in which case the contractor may suspend the work until it has received the reasonable evidence or payment.[149]

---

148. *See* section 8.8 in the Silver Book, 1999 Edition.
149. *See* section 16.1 in the Silver Book, 1999 Edition.

In addition, when certain events or circumstances constituting force majeure arise, either party may notify the other party of the obligations under the contract which it is or will be prevented from performing due to the force majeure. After sending out the notice, this party is relieved from performing such obligations as long as the force majeure continues.[150]

If the contractor suffers delay and incurs increased costs because of a suspension instructed by the employer, the contractor may claim for an extension of time and any relevant cost and (depending on the contract terms) may be able to recover reasonable profit as well. For some, but not all, events of force majeure, the contractor may be able to make similar claims (without claiming profit). Notably, there is no entitlement to compensation for force majeure where the event of force majeure involves natural catastrophes such as earthquake, hurricane, typhoon or volcanic activity.

[B]   Conditions for Contract Termination

According to the Silver Book, 1999 Edition, three general conditions may lead to termination of the contract, namely termination by the employer (section 15), termination by the contractor (section 16), and termination caused by force majeure.

Termination by Employer

Section 15.2 of the Silver Book provides for the situations where the employer may terminate the contract for breaches committed by the contractor, which can be summarized as follows: (a) the contractor failing to comply with the requirement for performance security or a notice to correct,;(b) the contractor abandoning the works or otherwise plainly demonstrating an intention not to continue performance of its obligations under the contract; (c) the contractor failing to proceed with the works following notice of commencement being provided; (d) the contractor subcontracting the whole of the works or assigning the contract without the required agreement; (e) the contractor becoming bankrupt or insolvent or going into liquidation or administration; or (f) the contractor offering to give to any person any bribe or other things of value as an inducement or reward.

Section 15.5 in the Silver Book also grants the employer an unconditional entitlement to terminate for its convenience, even in the absence of any breach committed by the contractor. Given that such termination for convenience would not be regarded as a breach of contract by the employer, the contractor can only claim compensation for the amounts that have already fallen due under the Contract together with certain additional costs, but not other losses that the contractor might suffer as a result of the termination. In this way, the employer may unilaterally terminate the contract with a significant adverse impact on the contractor despite the lack of any breach committed by the contractor, which demonstrates the relatively powerful position held by the employer under the contract.

---

150. *See* section 19.2 in the Silver Book, 1999 Edition.

In practice, it can be difficult to prevent the employer from exercising this entitlement abusively. For example, a Chinese contractor undertook a power project in an African country. However, after the contract went into effect and the work was commenced, the employer company was reorganized and most of its original executive officers were replaced. The new executive officers, after taking office, reviewed the contract and were of the opinion that the original contract price was unreasonably high. They later demanded that the Chinese contractor reduced the price, threatening to terminate the contract if the contractor did not. Although according to the Silver Book, the employer is prohibited from terminating the contract to substitute the contractor, it is hard to prove that the employer has acted with this intention. In the end, the Chinese contractor reluctantly agreed to reduce the price to avoid further losses.[151]

Termination by Contractor

The circumstances where the contractor may terminate the contract are summarized in the section 16.2 of the Silver Book and include the following: (a) the employer failing to comply with the financial and payment arrangements; (b) the employer substantially failing to perform its obligations under the contract; (c) the employer failing to comply with requirements regarding assignment; (d) a prolonged suspension affecting the whole of the works; and (e) the employer becoming bankrupt or insolvent or unable to operate for other reasons. The contractor has no right to terminate for convenience. Thus, the contractor only has a conditional right to terminate the contract under the FIDIC Contract Conditions.

Termination Caused by Force Majeure

The Silver Book provides for two circumstances in which force majeure leads to termination: first, under section 19.6, if the works have been obstructed by force majeure for a certain period, either party may opt for termination; second, under section 19.7, if any event or circumstance outside the control of the parties (including, but not limited to, force majeure) arises which makes it impossible or unlawful for either or both parties to comply with the contract or the governing law the parties are entitled to be released from further performance of the contract. In either case, either party can give notice of termination.

The provisions for force majeure under the FIDIC Contract are similar to those which apply as a matter of PRC law, under which whether an event constitutes force majeure is to be judged from a combined objective and subjective perspective. Under the Silver Book, 1999, "force majeure" means an exceptional event or circumstance: (a) which is beyond a party's control; (b) which such party could not reasonably have provided against before entering into the Contract; (c) which, having arisen, such party could not reasonably have avoided or overcome; and (d) which is not substantially

---

151. Meng Fanyi, "Research on the Legal Issues Relating to Termination of International Construction Contracting Contracts under the FIDIC Conditions", University of International Business and Economics, 2016.

attributable to the other party. The FIDIC Contract explains that force majeure events include, but are not limited to, exceptional events or circumstances such as war, terrorism, riots and strikes and earthquakes, typhoons and so on.[152]

[C]   How to Avoid Suspension and Termination from the Perspective of Chinese Contracting Enterprises

Prudent Selection of the Project

In the face of fierce market competition, many Chinese contracting enterprises have lowered the standard for project selection in order to win a project after entering the international market. Projects carelessly selected tend to be immature and insufficiently financed, and their employers probably are not qualified in terms of creditworthiness. As a result, suspension or termination happens from time to time. Chinese contractors, therefore, should consider the following factors prudently at the project selection stage:[153]

(1) The employer's creditworthiness. The success of a project largely depends on the employer's reliability and capacity to conduct a project. In assessing the employer's creditworthiness, the following aspects deserve further attention: the nature of the company (private or state-owned); whether the company is listed or not; its shareholders' conditions; whether its scope of business covers the area into which the project falls; the reputation of the company; whether and how it has breached contracts; and any ongoing arbitration and litigation.

(2) Maturity of the project. The maturity of a project affects whether the project is executable. While evaluating the maturity of the project, the following aspects deserve further attention: whether the research involved in this project is complete; whether it has passed an environment evaluation; whether the host country has approved the project; and whether the land acquisition has been accomplished.

(3) Financing of the project. Sufficient financing contributes to the success of a project. If projects have insufficient financing at the outset, the contractors may be trapped if the employers turn out to be unable to make progress payments later in the project. To examine the financing of a project, the following aspects shall be considered: the source of the financing (sponsored by the employer itself or the bank); whether the financing has been paid; whether the payment is guaranteed by national bank or in other ways; whether the payment is made via letter of credit; and whether the issuing bank has good credit conditions.

---

152. *See supra* n. 5.
153. *Ibid.*

(4) Conditions of the host country and the site, including the political, economic, and natural conditions of the host country and the site. Special attention should be paid to: whether there are wars and conflicts or the possibility of their occurrence; whether the natural conditions would warrant the operation of the project; whether the economic conditions are stable; whether the host country is subject to sanction; regulations on foreign exchange; and exchange rate fluctuation.

Improving the Project Management

The employer often demands suspension or termination because the contractor breaches the contract. However, breaches committed by the contractor are seldom intentional but rather due to poor project management. Many enterprises use low tender prices to win projects and then suffer huge deficits during the execution phase. As a result, they have to give up the projects entirely. Some enterprises try directly to transplant their experience in managing domestic projects to overseas ones. That can lead to issues such as delay and quality defects and the employer finally choosing to terminate the contract. Self-evidently, if Chinese contractors improve their project management and avoid committing breaches, employers cannot require suspension or termination on account the contractors' breaches.

Raise Awareness of Preventing Contractual Risks

If the contractor defaults and the employer legally terminate the contract, the contractor will have to face serious legal consequences. Therefore, the contractor must be sensitive to and raise awareness of risk prevention and control toward consequences of breach of contract and termination of the contract as stipulated in the contract. In a case provided by the ICC for this research project, the Chinese contractor had a number of defaults, including failing to complete the design work in time, and the employer issued a notice of correction based on Article 15.1 of the EPC contract (based on the FIDIC Silver Book). The notice required the contractor to correct the default within a certain period of time. Since the correction period proposed by the employer was very short, the Chinese contractor believed that it cannot be done within the time period requested and would carry it out at a later time. Instead of making the correction, the contractor argued with the employer multiple times on the reasonableness of the correction period and declared refusal to correct if the employer refused to extend the correction period. The employer terminated the contract on this ground, and the dispute between the two parties accelerated and evolved into arbitration. The arbitral tribunal pointed out that although the correction period specified by the employer may be unreasonable, the contractor did not conduct the correction at all, which in itself constituted further breach of the contract and justified termination of the contract by the employer. Therefore, whether the corrective period was reasonable was unimportant and irrelevant. In this case, if the Chinese contractor had sufficient awareness of risk prevention and control, and had carried out the correction in the first place while simultaneously raising its objection as to the time period or at a later phase in the project, its position in the subsequent arbitration would not have been as negatively affected.

[D]   How to Cope with Suspension and Termination from the Perspective of Chinese Contracting Enterprises

The international engineering contracting market currently is still a buyer's market, where the contractor is in a less powerful position compared to the employer. To cope with suspension and termination, Chinese contractors should learn to take advantage of all remedies available law by studying the contract terms thoroughly and defending their own interests via contracts.

Collecting Evidence and Preparing for Bringing Claims

In conditions where the employer's breaches lead to suspension or termination, Chinese contractors should immediately gather evidence favorable to them and bring claims in time. There is no restriction to the sort of documents that the contractor may rely upon to evidence its claims—such document may include confirmation letters signed by the employer or the engineer, shipping documents (including bills of lading), subcontracts, drawings, emails, proof of payment and so on. If the employer seeks to suspend or terminate the contract on account of the contractor's fault, the contractor should also collect and provide relevant evidence to prove its innocence (or, for example, to show compliance with a notice to correct) in time.

Chinese contractors should arrange for certain members of their staff to be specifically responsible for the collection, retention and management of documents. Chinese contractors have successfully claimed compensation for the employer triggering suspension where the contractors have been able to rely on documents they have gathered during the construction process. For example, a Chinese contractor undertook a five-star hotel project in a country. After the completion of the main structure, the design department of the employer failed to decide the decoration style and ideas and the project was suspended as a result. Later, the employer had to order the Chinese contractor to stop the work. Under such circumstances, the Chinese contractor promptly provided a detailed list of compensation items, including labor costs, material fees, machinery fees, on-site management fees, guarantee extension fees and insurance extension fees, with comprehensive supporting documents. After careful negotiations and explanations, the Chinese contractor obtained approvals from the supervising engineers in relation most of the calculation methods and fee rates it had proposed for compensation items. In the end, the Chinese contractor recovered most of the losses it had suffered due to the suspension.[154]

---

154. Chen Jinsheng Edited, "Project Claims and Case Enlightenment under the FIDIC Contract Conditions", China Planning Press, 1st Edition, October 2016.

Timely-Made Dissatisfaction Regarding the Matters Determined by the Employer

As mentioned above, for the majority of suspension incidents, the contractor is likely to be entitled to claim an extension of time and its extra costs caused by the suspension. However, according to the Silver Book of 1999 Edition, the employer shall determine such matters.[155] Further, in circumstances where the employer terminates the contract, the employer shall also determine (among other things) the valuation as at the date of termination.[156] If the Chinese contractors disagree with the matters determined by the employer, they are required to send NOD with a determination to the employer within 14 days after receiving it and may refer the dispute to the DAB later. If Chinese contractors fail to dissent within the requisite period, the determination made by the employer will be binding upon the parties.

Careful Examination on the Items and Amount of Final Settlement

According to the Silver Book, 1999 Edition, in the event of termination for convenience by the employer or caused by force majeure, the contractor is responsible for presenting to the employer the sums that it calculates to be payable.[157] The contractor shall first check the money items it can claim[158] and verify the amount according to section 19.6 of the Silver Book, 1999 Edition. In addition, where the employer's breaches lead to termination by the contractor, the contractor may claim not only the money items provided in section 19.6 but also the profit loss or other loss or damage it has sustained as a result of the termination according to section 16.4 (though note indirect or consequential losses are excluded by Clause 17.6).

Timely Request for Returning Performance Security

If Chinese contractors choose to terminate the contract due to the employer's breach, Chinese contractors shall require the employer to return the performance security in time. Otherwise, the employer may threaten the contractor in a later dispute resolution process or even require payment from the bank pursuant to such performance security.[159]

---

155. *See* sections 8.9, 16.1 and 19.4 in the Silver Book, 1999 Edition.
156. *See* section 15.3 in the Silver Book, 1999 Edition.
157. *See supra* n. 5.
158. Including:

    (1) the amount payable for any work carried out for which a price is stated in the contract;
    (2) the cost of plant and materials ordered for the works which have been delivered to the contractor, or of which the contractor is liable to accept delivery: this plant and materials shall become the property of (and be at the risk of) the employer when paid for the employer, and the contractor shall place the same at the employer's disposal;
    (3) any other costs or liability which in the circumstances was reasonably incurred by the contractor in the expectation of completing the works;
    (4) the cost of removal of temporary works and contractor's equipment from the site and the return of these items to the contractor's works in his country (or to any other destination at no greater cost); and
    (5) the cost of repatriation of the contractor's staff and labor employed wholly in connection with the works at the date of termination.

159. *See supra* n. 5.

§4.11   RISKS OF INDEPENDENT LETTER OF GUARANTEE

[A]   Legal Source of Independent Letter of Guarantee

Independent Letters of Guarantee are the product of economic globalization. To protect the safety of trade and investment, a party to a transaction often requires a third party to guarantee the performance of the counterparty's obligations. Since banks have traditional advantages in providing credit, one party can earn the trust of the counterparty by providing a bank guarantee for the performance of its obligations. Consequently, bank guarantees are widely used in practice.

In 1978 the International Chamber of Commerce (the "ICC") published *Uniform Rules for Contract Guarantees* (Publication No. 325, "**URCG325**"), which required the beneficiary of the guarantee to produce a judgment or an arbitral award as a condition to payment of the sum guaranteed. In this sense, the guarantee was "dependent" upon establishment of a breach by the contractor.

In 1992, the ICC published *Uniform Rules for Demand Guarantees* (Publication No. 458, "**URDG458**"), pursuant to which the guarantee was considered independent of the underlying relationship between beneficiary and principal. Later, the ICC published the *Uniform Rules for Demand Guarantees: 2010 Revision* (Publication No. 758, hereinafter "**URDG758**").

Apart from the above rules, UNCITRAL promulgated the *United Nations Convention on Independent Guarantees and Stand-by Letters of Credit* (hereinafter "**Convention**") on December 11, 1995. The Convention came into effect on January 1, 2000, formally establishing the basic principles of independent letters of guarantee.

China has not become a party to the Convention or promulgated laws or regulations regarding independent letters of guarantee. The Supreme People's Court promulgated in 2016 the *Provisions of the Supreme People's Court on Several Issues concerning the Trial of Independent Guarantee Dispute Cases* (hereinafter "Provisions"), which came into force on December 1, 2016. The Provisions makes it clear that URDG458 and URDG758 are model rules for transactions of independent letter of guarantee (LG), which are rules of a fixed-type transaction formulated by an international nongovernmental commercial organization and become applicable and binding on parties if the parties agree. Considering that no uniform international custom that is repeatedly applied and universally accepted has formed in the field of independent LG, and the *Uniform Rules for Demand Guarantees*, the *International Standby Practices*, and the *Uniform Custom and Practice for Documentary Credits* all have their market share, and the *Uniform Rules for Demand Guarantees* has not acquired the status of an international custom within the hierarchy of legal authority.

Where an independent LG does not specify the application of any particular model rules or the issuer and the beneficiary have not agreed upon the application of model rules before the end of court debate in the Court of First Instance, a court shall not apply the *Uniform Rules for Demand Guarantees* on its own initiative.[160] That is to

---

160. Article 5 of the Provisions stipulates that "Where an independent guarantee specifies that the ICC Uniform Rules for Demand Guarantees and other model rules for independent guarantee

say, in China, URDG458 or URDG758 apply as part of the guarantee terms according to parties' choice rather than automatically. They have no binding effect on parties in the absence of the election of the parties.

[B]   Features of Independent LG

The principles of independence and abstraction are fundamental to the nature of independent letters of guarantee. Under URDG758,[161] an independent LG is independent of the entrustment contract between the applicant and the issuing bank and the underlying contract between the applicant and the beneficiary. The Supreme People's Court has explained that the independence principle means that, although the purpose of an independent LG is to safeguard the performance of the underlying contract, once such a guarantee has been issued, it becomes a totally independent transaction separate from the underlying transaction and the contract relationship, and its validity and performance shall be decided according to its wording.[162] The abstraction principle (or documentary principle) means that an independent LG bears the abstract nature of a documentary transaction. The issuing bank deals with documents and is only responsible for checking the prima facie authenticity and conformity of documents regardless of whether the obligations in the underlying transaction have been performed or not.[163]

[C]   Several Common Forms of Guarantee, Their Risks and Prevention of Payment

Common types of guarantee in international construction include bid guarantees, advance payment guarantees, performance guarantees and retention guarantees. These guarantees serve different purposes, and the risks vary.

The purpose of a bid guarantee is to protect the employer when the contractor withdraws the bidding documents or refuses to sign the contract after winning the bid. Usually, the amount of bidding guarantee is 1% of the bidding price. In some cases, certain Chinese contractors obtain the project through low-price bidding, but the cost of carrying out the project rises sharply after their winning the bid. In order to avoid greater losses, the contractor has to give up the project, resulting in the confiscation of the guarantee. For instance, the price for steel rose by 65% when a Chinese contractor

---

transactions shall apply, or both the issuer and the beneficiary have referred to them before the end of court debate in the court of first instance, the people's court shall hold that the content of such model rules is an integral part of the terms of the independent guarantee." *See also* Zhang Yongjian, Shen Hongyu, "Interpretations and Applications on Provisions of the Supreme People's Court on Several Issues Concerning the Trial of Independent Guarantee Dispute Case", The People's Judicature (Application), 1st issue 2017.

161. According to Article 5(a) of URDG758, a guarantee is by its nature independent of the underlying relationship and the application, and the guarantor is in no way concerned with or bound by such relationship. A reference in the guarantee to the underlying relationship for the purpose of identifying it does not change the independent nature of the guarantee.
162. *See supra* n. 2.
163. *Ibid.*

was preparing to sign the contract after winning the bid. It would suffer great losses if the contract was signed and performed. Consequently, the Chinese contractor gave up the project which led to the claim for compensation by the employer. Therefore, it is suggested that Chinese contractors fully analyze the market during the bidding process and ascertain the price with great caution to avoid error in the bidding price.

The function of an advance payment guarantee is to make sure the contractor returns the advance payment as prescribed in the contract. It is common practice that the contractor needs to provide an advance payment guarantee to the employer after signing the construction contract, and the contract comes into effect after the employer makes the advance payment and issues a letter of credit. Therefore, the timing that the contractor provides the advance payment guarantee is important, and it is suggested that the contractor submits the guarantee after the funds of employer are safeguarded in order to avoid situations where the employer fails to make advance payment on time and the contractor cannot start construction as a result. For example, in an Ethiopian project, the Chinese contractor submitted the advance payment guarantee in 2005, but the employer only paid the local currency in part due to its economic conditions. The project did not start until the employer paid the remaining part (paid in U.S. dollar) in 2009. During this period, the advance payment guarantee was extended on several occasions, which intensively increased the cost and risk to the contractor. In addition, contractors should pay close attention to the deduction clauses and clarify the rules, time schedule, proportion and procedure of deduction in order to gradually decrease the amount of guarantee and release the credit authorized by the bank, so as to lower the risks of the guarantee and ensure that the authorized credit can be fully used.

The purpose of a performance guarantee is to ensure that the contractor duly performs the contract. Risks for the contractor under a performance guarantee include the breach committed by the contractor itself, the guarantee not being extended after the expiry date as prescribed in the contract, and fraudulent claims. Therefore, on one hand, contractors should improve the project management and duly perform the contract; on the other hand, contractors should be cautious about the claims raised by employers. Furthermore, some employers will transfer or mortgage the guarantee to a bank or other financial institutes in order to obtain project funding. In that case, the contractor would be subject to possible claims brought by third parties unrelated to the construction contract. Therefore, contractors should specify the name of the transferee in the guarantee and limit the times that the guarantee can be transferred in order to control the relevant risks.

A retention money guarantee is to enable the contractors to recover the retention fee in advance, and to guarantee the contractors would duly perform their maintenance obligation during the defect notification period. Employers usually will retain 5%-10% of the contract price as retention money and will pay to the contract after the warranty expires and no defects are found. If the contractor would like the employer to pay the project price in full without withholding the retention, it would need to provide the retention money guarantee for the amount equal to the retention that the employer pays in advance (usually 50% of the whole retention amount). The parties need to agree on either the withholding of the retention or submission of the retention money guarantee in the construction contract. Providing a retention money guarantee enables contractors to recover the full project price in advance and lower the risks of nonpayment by employers. However, sometimes contractors may need to deposit an amount equal to the guaranteed amount in the bank in order to apply the retention money guarantee. In such event, contractors should balance the fee charged by the bank and the risks of recovery by the employer to decide whether to provide the retention guarantee in exchange for early release of the retention money.

[D] Risks of Fraudulent Claim and Its Prevention

[1] Reasons of Risks

Fraudulent claims by the employer (beneficiary) in a project are a significant risk in international construction projects for the following reasons:[164] (1) the independent and documentary nature of an independent LG may prompt some employers to violate the principle of good faith and make fraudulent claims to banks by forging documents or misusing the right to claim despite knowing that their claims lack foundation; (2) laws and regulations on fraud among countries are incomplete and inconsistent, and there is no uniform standard for identifying fraud, abuse of right or lack of fairness, which makes it difficult to determine the nature of claims brought by employers and to take countermeasures.

[2] Determination on Fraudulent Claim by Chinese Courts

Article 12 of the Provisions, based on the principles of good faith and no abuse of right, divides fraudulent claims into three types:[165] no real transaction, document fraud and obvious abuse of right. It also prescribes a clause to cover all possible situations of abuse of right, providing leeway for judges' discretion and judicial practice.

---

164. Lin Yi, "Employers' Fraudulent Claims under Guarantees in International Constructions", International Economic Cooperation, 3rd issue 2014.
165. Article 12 of the Provisions regulates that the people's court shall determine that an independent guarantee fraud is committed under any of the following circumstances:

   (1) The beneficiary makes a false underlying transaction in collusion with the applicant or any other person.
   (2) The third party's documents presented by the beneficiary are forged or contain false information.
   (3) It is held in the court judgment or the arbitral award that the debtor under the underlying transaction has no obligation for payment or compensation.
   (4) The beneficiary confirms that its debt obligation under the underlying transaction has been fulfilled or that the expiry event as specified in the independent guarantee has not yet occurred.
   (5) Other circumstances where the beneficiary knowing that it has no right to demand payment still abuses such right.

Case A: Sinoma Technology & Equipment Group Co., Ltd. v. GHARIBWALCEMENT LIMITED, ET AL.[166]

Although the final judgment was rendered prior to the promulgation of the Provisions, the criteria on identifying fraudulent claim in the final judgment are consistent with the situations prescribed in the Provisions and of referential value. The judges in the first instance summarized the relevant criteria in two points: (1) where the counterparty has duly performed the underlying contract, a party which requests compensation under a guarantee by intentionally making up facts to the guarantor regarding the performance by the counterparty of the underlying contract, or provides forged documents and materials; (2) where the counterparty did breach the underlying contract but such breach was caused by the claiming party's intentional improper behavior.[167]

In this case, Sinoma Technology & Equipment Group Co., Ltd. ("**Sinoma**") signed a contract for construction of a cement plant in Pakistan with GHARIBWAL CEMENT LIMITED, ET AL. ("**GHARIBWAL**"), under which Sinoma was responsible for the design, construction and supply of equipment for the plant. Sinoma provided an unconditional and irrevocable letter of performance guarantee, naming GHARIBWAL as the beneficiary and Industry and Commerce Bank of China (ICBC) Tianjin branch as the guarantor. The claim condition in the performance guarantee stipulated that ICBC SHALL PAY TO GHARIBWAL IN THE AMOUNT OF ... WITHIN 15 DAYS AFTER IT RECEIVES ANY INSTRUCTION FROM GHARIBWAL WITHIN THE VALIDITY OF THIS GUARANTEE STATING THAT SINOMA FAILS TO PERFORM ITS DUTY UNDER THE CONTRACT. GHARIBWAL made a claim against ICBC Tianjin branch on the ground that Sinoma had breached the contract.

The judges determined that the case hinged on whether Sinoma had fully performed its duty in the underlying contract: if the answer was negative, then the claim made by GHARIBWAL was not fraudulent; if Sinoma had duly performed its contract, then GHARIBWAL's claim was fraudulent.

The investigation suggests that, although GHARIBWAL claimed that Sinoma had not finished the basic design, it already made the corresponding payment and could not provide evidence demonstrating that Sinoma had breached the contract during the basic design process. The judges decided that GHARIBWAL had made fraudulent and selective statements in the claim documents regarding the performance of Sinoma and lacked proper reason to exercise the right of claim. Therefore, the judges ruled that ICBC Tianjin branch should stop its payment to GHARIBWAL under the guarantee.

From the Provisions' perspective, GHARIBWAL brought the claim despite knowing that Sinoma has performed the contract. Thus, there was an "abuse of right of claim" within the meaning of the Provisions, i.e., the beneficiary conceals facts on purpose with the knowledge that it is not entitled to bring a claim and submits documents such as request for payment and declaration of violation that are prima

---

166. Tianjin High People's Court (2012) Jin Min Si Zhong Zi No. 3 Civil Judgment.
167. Li Jihong, Wang Liping, Yao Qiang, "Justifiable Causes on Independent LG —Case Study on Sinoma Technology & Equipment Group Co., Ltd. *v.* GHARIBWAL CEMENT LIMITED, ET AL.", The People's Judicature (Cases), 6th Issue 2015.

facie consistent with the guarantee clause, inducing the issuing bank to make wrongful payment.[168]

Case B: Power Links International v. Yuandong Cable Ltd.[169]

In this case, Yuandong Cable Ltd. ("**Yuandong Company**") signed a bid cooperation contract with Power Links International ("**PLI**") dated May 26, 2014 under which the two companies cooperated to bid for the project of Qatar Hydro Corporation. PLI provided a bid guarantee issued by the bank to Qatar Hydro Corporation. According to the contract, Yuandong Company was to provide a performance guarantee of the same amount to PLI.

Yuandong Company issued the performance guarantee on July 15, 2014, naming PLI as the beneficiary. Later, PLI made a claim against Bank of China (BOC) Wuxi branch on the basis that Yuandong Company delayed the issuance of the guarantee which breached the contract.

After reviewing the e-mail correspondence and QQ chat logs, the High People's Court of Jiangsu Province ruled that, although the bid cooperation contract was dated on May 26, 2014, the parties exchanged emails many times regarding the revision of the contract. Until July 4, 2014 when the final version was made, the date on the contract remained the same. It could be determined that the parties forgot to update the date on the contract. Therefore, the parties actually knew that the real signing date of the cooperation contract was July 4, 2014. Starting from August 5, 2014, PLI made four claims against BOC Wuxi branch, alleging that Yuandong Company breached the contract for not applying for the guarantee on May 26, 2014, the date shown on the contract. Following the logic behind PLI's claims, by the time when Yuandong Company signed the final version of the contract and applied for guarantee from the Wuxi branch, it had already breached the contract. PLI, however, never claimed that Yuandong Company had breached the contract during that period or rejected the guarantee. On the contrary, PLI took advantage of Yuandong Company's so-called breach and became the beneficiary under the guarantee which it used to make the claim.

The above behavior indicated that, despite clear knowledge that the date on the contract was not the actual signing date of the cooperation contract, PLI made the claim by taking advantage of the wrong date on the contract, and violated the principle of good faith. On that basis, PLI's claim was found to be fraudulent.

Case C: China Electric Equipment Group (Nanjing) Solar Ltd. v. Alfa Infraprop Pvt[170]

In this case, Alfa Infraprop Pvt ("**Alfa**") signed a procurement contract regarding solar components with China Electric Equipment Group (Nanjing) Solar Ltd. ("**CEEG**").

---

168. Zhang Yongjian, Shen Hongyu, "Interpretations and Applications on Provisions of the Supreme People's Court on Several Issues Concerning the Trial of Independent Guarantee Dispute Case", The People's Judicature (Application), 1st issue 2017.
169. Jiangsu High People's Court (2016) Su Min Zhong Zi No. 932 Civil judgment.
170. Nanjing Intermediate People's Court (2014) Ning Shang Wai Chu Zi No. 2 Civil Judgement.

CEEG provided a quality guarantee to Alfa, stating that CEEG WARRANTS AND CLAIMS THAT THE VALIDITY OF THIS BANK GUARANTEE IS FOR A CONSECUTIVE OF FIVE YEARS (RENEWABLE ANNUALLY) ACCORDING TO THE CLAUSE UNDER THE PROCUREMENT CONTRACT. EXCEPT FOR THE FIFTH YEAR, IT SHALL BE RENEWED 15 DAYS BEFORE ITS EXPIRY DATE FOR EACH YEAR. How to determine the expiry date became the major dispute during the trial. CEEG claimed that, in addition to the period from January 15, 2013 to December 31, 2013, the validity period shall be extended for a two-month claim period, and therefore the expiry date was February 28, 2014. Since CEEG had offered a new guarantee on December 25, 2013 which was more than two months prior to the expiry date, it alleged that Alfa's claim was fraudulent. Alfa contended that the validity period of the guarantee was from January 15, 2013 to December 31, 2013 and it made the claim because CEEG failed to provide the new guarantee 15 days prior to the expiry date of that year (i.e., December 16, 2013).

The judges ruled that the issue in this case was the different understanding between CEEG and Alfa regarding the validity period and the expiry date of each year of the guarantee based on the wordings in the guarantee. Alfa made the claim against Bank of Communication Jiangsu branch because it thought the payment due event occurred as prescribed in the guarantee because CEEG had failed to provide the new guarantee 15 days prior to the expiry date of that year, rather than claiming based on the performance of underlying transactions. CEEG provided no evidence demonstrating that Alfa knew its claim had no legal foundations. Therefore, the judges rejected the contention that Alfa's claim was fraudulent claim under the independent LG.

From above cases and the Provisions, we can see that Chinese courts apply a high standard to recognize fraud and to issue an injunction. Article 14.1 of the Provisions stipulates that for courts to issue an injunction, the following three requirements must be satisfied: (1) the evidence submitted by the applicant proves that the fraudulent situation under Article 12 of the Provisions is highly likely to happen; (2) the applicant must prove the situation is so urgent that it will suffer irreparable damage if the court does not issue an injunction immediately; and; (3) the applicant must provide sufficient guarantee to compensate the possible loss of the respondent. The first requirement is significant on the following three levels: (i) the court will limit its issuance of an injunction only to fraudulent situations as stipulated in Article 12, i.e., no real transaction, document fraud and obvious abuse of right; (ii) the documents submitted by the beneficiary are presumed to be in good faith and without fraud, with the effect that the burden of proof rests on the applicant; (iii) the applicant must prove the fraudulent situation is "highly likely" to happen as it is the applicable standard of proof.[171]

---

171. Zhang Yongjian, Shen Hongyu, "Interpretations and Applications on Provisions of the Supreme People's Court on Several Issues Concerning the Trial of Independent Guarantee Dispute Case", The People's Judicature (Application), 1st issue 2017.

[3] *Preventive Measures*

Employers (beneficiaries) are entitled to make claims under guarantees. Considering the independent and abstract nature and the fact that the court adopts a high standard when determining whether a claim is fraudulent, it is rather difficult for contractors to protect their rights and interests only by resort to ex-post judicial remedies. Therefore, contractors should take preventive measures to lower the risks of fraudulent claims by employers. For example, contractors may specify in the guarantee clauses the documents that employers should submit when asserting claims in order to make it harder for employers to satisfy the prima facie conformity of documents.[172] The Supreme People's Court, when promulgating the Provisions, noticed that the substantive relations between the guarantee and the underlying transaction and the restraints the guarantees impose on the beneficiary can vary on a spectrum from strong to weak.

If the document required in the guarantee clause is only a statement of claim, then this guarantee has the lowest correlation with the underlying contract and the least restriction on the beneficiary. Therefore, it is referred to a "pay on demand guarantee" or (sometimes) "suicidal guarantee." If the documents required include a statement of claim and third-party documents such as certificate or proof of tests on completion issued by architects or engineers, then this guarantee has the middle-level correlation with the underlying contract and a moderate restriction on the beneficiary. If the document required is the judgment or arbitral award, then this guarantee has the highest correlation with the underlying contract and the most stringent restriction on the beneficiary.[173] Therefore, contractors when negotiating with employers at an early stage may require employers to submit documents other than a statement of claim, and specify the type, signatory and submission time of the documents, in order to make it harder for employers to prepare claim documents and lower the possibility of fraudulent claims.

Considering the difficulty in negotiating guarantee clauses, Chinese contractors may also consider regulating the purpose, scope and claim conditions of the guarantee in the underlying contract in order to limit the possibility of abuse of right of claim by the beneficiary.

[E] Risks in the Issuance of Guarantee and Its Prevention

[1] *Reasons for Risks*

The laws in some "Belt and Road" countries (especially Middle East, North Africa, India and Bangladesh) require that employers cannot accept guarantees directly issued

---

172. Lin Yi, "Employers' Fraudulent Claims under Guarantees in International Constructions", International Economic Cooperation, 3rd issue 2014.
173. Zhang Yongjian, Shen Hongyu, "Interpretations and Applications on Provisions of the Supreme People's Court on Several Issues Concerning the Trial of Independent Guarantee Dispute Case", The People's Judicature (Application), 1st issue 2017.

by foreign banks.[174] Instead, the guarantee to the employers must be issued from a local bank or a foreign bank that is accepted by the host state. Therefore, a LG under counter LG is often used in international construction projects.

LG under Counter LG may bring about the following potential risks.

First, the applicable laws for the two guarantees may be different because the instructing bank usually is located in the country of the employer while the reissuing bank is in the country of the employer, which may cause inconvenience if disputes emerge.[175]

Second, for a LG under Counter LG, the exception to the principle of independence would apply only if the beneficiaries of both guarantee (the employer and the reissuing bank) all abuse their right of claim. Therefore, the applicant for the injunction must prove not only the beneficiary-employer made a fraudulent claim under the LG, but also the reissuing bank made the payment to the beneficiary in bad faith, i.e., the reissuing bank, fully aware of the fraudulent nature of beneficiary's claim, still made payment to the beneficiary and requested for payment under the counterguarantee.[176]

[2]   *Preventive Measures*

(1) From the perspective of risk management, contractors should try to persuade employers to accept directly issued guarantees. If the contractor is required to provide LG under Counter LG, then it should make sure that the contents, especially the governing law and dispute resolution clauses, in the guarantee and counterguarantee are consistent.

(2) Contactors should carefully choose the reissuing bank. Given that reissuing bank is directly responsible for making payment to the employer, if the reissuing bank has a bias toward the employer or fails to exercise due diligence when reviewing the documents, then the reissuing bank may become the "accomplice" to fraud committed by the employer when it makes the payment based on the "prima facie conformity of documents."[177]

---

174. Tong Gang, "Protections on Chinese Banks after the Issuance of Guarantee for Overseas Project: Take Libyan War as an Example", published at pkulaw, available at http://article. chinalawinfo.com/ArticleHtml/Article_66894.shtml#10, website serial No. CLI.A.066894.
175. Wan Chengwen, "Several Measures on Increase the Independence of Demand Guarantee", published at Wechat official account of Sky Trade and Finance.
176. Zhang Yongjian, Shen Hongyu, "Interpretations and Applications on Provisions of the Supreme People's Court on Several Issues Concerning the Trial of Independent Guarantee Dispute Case", The People's Judicature (Application), 1st issue 2017.
177. Lin Yi, "Employers' Fraudulent Claims under Guarantees in International Constructions", International Economic Cooperation, 3rd issue 2014.

[F] Risk in Guarantee Provisions and Its Prevention

[1] Validity Provision

It is common in international construction projects that the term of the guarantee is linked to the progress of the project. Sometimes, the employers (beneficiaries) will leave the expiry date in the guarantee clause undetermined in the following two forms:

(1) Although the guarantee provides a definite expiry date, it sets up an auto-circulation or auto-extension clause. For example, a guarantee may stipulate that IT SHALL BE DEEMED AUTOMATICALLY EXTENDED WITHOUT AMENDMENT FOR ONE YEAR FROM THE PRESENT OR ANY FUTURE EXPIRY DATE HEREOF, UNLESS AT LEAST THIRTY DAYS PRIOR TO SUCH DATE WE SHALL NOTIFY YOU BY AUTHENTICATED SWIFT THAT WE ELECT NOT TO CONSIDER THIS LETTER OF CREDIT RENEWED FOR SUCH ADDITIONAL PERIOD.[178]

(2) The guarantee may have an "extend or pay" clause. If the issuer does not agree to extend the expiry date as requested by the beneficiary, it shall pay the amount under the guarantee immediately to the beneficiary. For example, a guarantee may stipulate that THIS COUNTER GUARANTEE ... WILL BE EXTENDED FOR ANY PERIOD ASKED FOR BY [THE EMPLOYER]. SHOULD THE BANK NOT BE IN A POSITION OR DO NOT AGREE TO EXTEND THIS GUARANTEE AND/OR IF [THE CONTRACTOR] FAILS TO PROVIDE THE MEANS FOR ITS EXTENSION AND MAKE THE BANK AGREE TO SUCH EXTENSION, THEN THE BANK UNDERTAKES TO PAY THE AMOUNT RE-FERRED TO ABOVE ... Or a guarantee may write that WE ALSO CONFIRM THAT IF YOUR GUARANTEE IS CALLED BY THE BENEFICIARY FOR FUR-THER EXTENSION IN ITS VALIDITY PERIOD, WE SHALL EITHER IMMEDI-ATELY AUTHORIZE YOU FOR SUCH EXTENSION ... OR SHALL INSTANTLY MAKE PAYMENT TO YOU.

In the case that the expiry date is left undetermined, the employer (beneficiary) may unilaterally decide whether to extend the guarantee, which essentially leads to a guarantee with indefinite term. Sometimes, the contractor may agree to the extension but dispute which party should bear the cost of extension. In an "extend or pay" guarantee, the contractor is put in a disadvantageous position while negotiating with the employer on issues such as cost of extension, since the employer may threaten to demand payment right away if the contractor refuses to extend the expiry date.

Therefore, contractors should pay special attention to the period of validity, the expiry date, conditions on extension when negotiating with employers in the early stage, avoiding providing a guarantee with an indefinite term. If the contractor has to provide a guarantee with open period of validity such as a "extend or pay" guarantee, then it should try to add an absolute expiry date in the guarantee clause, i.e., the guarantee will expire at a certain date no matter what happens.

---

178. Wu Hao, Chang Kun, Li Feifei, Yu Junjun, "Construction Guarantee and Its Prevention in Belt and Road Countries", China Forex, 18th issue 2017.

[2]   Governing Law and Dispute Resolution Provisions

Considering the laws on independent LG vary from country to country, while choosing the governing law of the guarantee, the laws of the country where the employer resides should be avoided. The governing law of the guarantee is of vital importance to determining the responsibility of the bank. As a result applying the laws of the country where the bank is located ensures the greatest predictability and is most beneficial to the contractor. As to the dispute resolution clause, many "Belt and Road" countries choose the court or arbitration institution of the country where the employer (beneficiary) locates or of a third country. Choosing foreign dispute resolution institution may give rise to risks stemming from unfamiliarity with the relevant laws as well as high dispute resolution costs.

[G]   Demand Guarantee

The type of guarantee commonly used in international construction projects is the unconditional, independent demand guarantee, which does not require the employer to provide substantive evidence in order to call on the guarantee. Therefore, in circumstances where a dispute arises between employer and contractor or the employer acts in bad faith, the guarantee applied by the contractor may be under severe danger of being unreasonably cashed.

Although the ICC and UNCITRAL have published rules for demand guarantees, there is no uniform format for the text of the guarantee, nor a single universal standard which applies to all such guarantees.

The construction contract usually sets forth the conditions and format requirements for the guarantee that the Contractor is obliged to arrange. In that regard, matters to which special attention needs to be paid include the guarantee amount, the provisions on the guarantee's transferability or reduction in value, the period of validity, the applicable law and the dispute resolution clause, etc.

[1]   Guarantee Amount

The types of guarantee frequently used in international construction projects are bid guarantees, advance payment guarantees, performance guarantees and retention money guarantees. As described in section §4.11[F] above, bid guarantees are usually demanded by the project employer from the contractor at the time of the bid to prevent the employer suffering losses because the winning bidder refuses to undertake the contract. Generally, the amount of a bid guarantee is 2%-5% of the bidding price, or it could be a fixed amount as well. It is common practice in international construction projects for the employer to pay a certain amount to the contractor in advance as start-up capital for the successful operation of the project. Against that background, an advance payment guarantee is provided by the Contactor ensuring that it will perform its obligations and utilize the advance payment in accordance with the contract. Otherwise, the employer may lodge a claim. Normally the amount of the advance payment guarantee is commensurate with the amount of advance payment. A performance guarantee is issued by the bank on the application of the Contractor and to the employer, to guarantee that the contractor executes the contract in accordance with the time, quality, and quantities provisions in the contract. The amount of a performance guarantee generally will not exceed 10% of the contract price. A retention money guarantee is provided by the contractor to the employer when it intends to collect its retention money in advance. An ordinary amount of retention money guarantee is 5%-10% of the contract price. The guaranteed amounts are substantial and as a result, guarantees are expensive and capital intensive.

[2] Transferability

The concept of transferability in the context of guarantees usually refers to the transferability of the right to make a demand on the beneficiary. If a transfer occurs, the initial beneficiary's position as a party in the legal relations based on the guarantee is transferred to the assignee. Subsequently, the assignee should make a demand in its own name. On account of the non-causative and independent nature of a guarantee, it is always difficult for the bank to refuse payment upon demand by the beneficiary. The addition of transferability further aggravates the risk of the guarantee being unfairly cashed as compared to a non-transferable guarantee. To alleviate the risk, the contractor should request that the employer deletes any unnecessary provision for transferability or should seek to add other restrictive provisions, such as by requiring prior written consent of the contractor in respect of transfers or limiting the scope of the assignee.

[3] Reduction of Guarantee Amount

The amount of any advance payment guarantee should be progressively reduced as interim payments are made. The schedule, percentage and procedure for reduction of the advance payment guarantee should be made clear in the conditions of guarantee. The contractor may also try to negotiate for progressive reduction of any applicable performance guarantee, in line with any reduction in risk that accompanies the progressive completion of the work.

To cut down the expense and risk of providing guarantees, the contractor should obtain written confirmation from the employer and submit it to the bank on a regular basis as the project progress, so that reduction of the guarantee can be secured on a timely basis.

[4] Period of Validity

The period of validity for a bid is usually 120 or 180 days, and that of a bid guarantee is 28 or 30 days after the closing date for submission of the bid. The contractor must submit a bid guarantee when making a bid, and submit a performance guarantee within a certain time period of being awarded the contract. In some cases, the employer will not release the bid guarantee until it receives the performance guarantee.

The effective date for a performance guarantee is its date of issuance, save for circumstances where the contract has not been concluded when the guarantee is issued. In that case, the effective date should be the date when the contract enters into force in order to prevent the beneficiary from advancing a demand before the contract takes effect. The period of validity usually terminates after an agreed period of time (it is advised that this period should not exceed one month) from the expiration of the defects liability period or the issuance of a certificate of performance. To address the risk that the employer indefinitely postpones the issuance of the certificate for performance, contractors can consider the alternative of setting out a specific expiry date based on the addition of a grace period to the notional approximate date of issuance of the certificate for performance under the contract. The contractor can also consider providing in the performance guarantee that its period of validity terminates on the actual date of issuance of the certificate of performance or the specific expiry date, whichever is earlier.

The effective date for a retention money guarantee is usually the date when the contractor receives the money retained, and the expiry date is usually fixed as a date falling after a period of time from the expiration of the defects liability period or the issuance of a certificate of performance.

Although advance payment guarantees, performance guarantees and retention money guarantees are used to provide security for different matters, there are long periods of overlap between them during the execution of the contract which add to the capital risk to the contractor. Without prejudice to the employer's obligation to make interim payment, the expiry date of the advance payment guarantee should be set as early as possible to shorten the overlap between the effective period of the advance payment guarantee and that of the performance guarantee. Further, in view of the overlap between the effective period of a performance guarantee and that of the retention money guarantee during the defects liability period, the contractor may negotiate with the employer to directly transform the performance guarantee still in effect into a retention money guarantee without the need to provide another guarantee so that the retention could be released ahead of time.

[5]   *Dispute Resolution*

The applicable law and dispute resolution mechanism of the guarantee should be clearly stipulated in the text of the guarantee in the first place. Because disputes relating to the guarantee usually accompany serious disputes that arise during the performance of the contract, it is advised that the applicable law and dispute resolution mechanism of the guarantee be identical with those of the underlying contract in order to avoid isolated resolution of the issues in dispute and even inconsistent rulings. Based on international private laws of different countries and international practice such as Uniform Rules of Demand Guarantee ("URDG458" or "URDG758"), if there is no applicable law and dispute resolution clauses imbedded in the guarantee, disputes arising from the guarantee will usually be governed by the court where the place of business of the guarantor's subsidiary that has issued the guarantee is located and subject to the local law of that jurisdiction.

[6] Beware of Bad Faith Demand

In the management of guarantees emphasis should be placed on reduction of the risk of guarantees being confiscated and minimizing the loss incurred by confiscation. To that end, there are three major points that are worth noting. First, the contractor should conduct necessary investigations into the credit status of the employer to avoid fraud by unethical employers and to ensure the safety of the guarantee. Second, unless prohibited by compulsory stipulation of the applicable law, the contractor should try to be allowed to provide an authentication guarantee rather than a counterguarantee or transferable guarantee. Third, an internal system for managing guarantees should be established, which would entail a position to be set up to manage all guarantees of the companies, strengthening dynamic surveillance of guarantees, and setting up a ledger for guarantees. Besides, regular examination should be conducted to check whether there guarantees exist that should be revoked or whose amount should be reduced. If so, a letter of reduction or revocation should be issued to the bank to ensure timely execution thereof.

[7] The Applicant's Approach to Deterring Demand

When the beneficiary has advanced its demand for payment, there are three ways for the applicant of the guarantee to deter the demand. The first is to negotiate with the beneficiary and ask it to revoke its demand. Second, the applicant could work with the bank to examine the letter of demand and documents to see if there is any noncompliance. Last but not least, the applicant could also seek judicial relief by suing the beneficiary and the guaranteeing bank.

In practice, the first approach cannot yield fruitful results unless a huge compromise is made by the applicant. As for the second approach, the applicant does not need to make any compromise or pay for any additional cost because examining the letter of demand and relevant documents is routine work and is conducted with high efficiency. The final approach takes a lot of expense and time, and the result is unpredictable.

Although in comparison with the first and the last approach, the second one is apparently more favorable in terms of efficiency and cost, it is subject to many barriers in practice. First, the requirement for documents in demand guarantees is not a high threshold, which makes it hard to identify any noncompliance to be relied upon to refuse payment. Second, the bank, being concerned about its commercial goodwill, will usually interpret the noncompliance in the interest of the beneficiary, and be inclined to make payment. According to general practice, the bank should make payment within five working days of its receipt of the demand. Therefore, unless the applicant can put forward any substantial noncompliance to justify refusal of payment by the bank, such as the demand was lodged outside the validity period, the guarantee will be cashed.

Case: In a construction project with a contract price of USD 1.5 billion, and the amount of advance payment being USD 200 million, the employer initially agreed to reduce the amount of advance payment guarantee only once a season. However, according to the contract, the parties would settle the financial statements every month. As a result, the pace of reduction of the advance payment guarantee advocated by the employer led unreasonably to an increase in the expense to the contractor of maintaining the guarantee and led to incompatibility between the amount of the guarantee and the remaining amount of the advance payment actually enjoyed by the contractor. Through multiple times of negotiation with the employer, it was finally agreed that the reduction of guarantee amount would adopt the same pace as the issuance of every financial statement. In this way, the project developed a virtuous pattern in which the employer actively hands in a letter of reduction to the bank on time.

Case: In another case, the contractor won the bid and concluded the contract with the employer in 2006. Thereafter, the contractor provided a performance guarantee and advance payment guarantee to the employer in accordance with the contract.

On November 23, 2010, the employer issued a letter through the Supervisor, which demanded the contractor to complete the whole project within 14 days. When negotiations failed, the contractor concluded based on industrial practice that the employer would confiscate the guarantee to make up for its loss resulting from poor market conditions. Accordingly, the contractor applied to the court to issue an injunction freezing all bank guarantees a day before the expiration of the 14-day limit, and the court granted an injunction on the same day. In December, the employer issued a formal letter to the bank requesting the confiscation of all guarantees, while the bank refused payment based on the injunction order granted by the court. The parties later went into arbitration and reached settlement following several rounds of negotiations. The employer returned all guarantees upon its receipt of compensation for part of its losses by the contractor. And the contract was terminated by mutual consent of the parties.

Case: In another case, the contractor did not insist on inserting into the contract a provision of progressive reduction of the amount of the advance payment guarantee with the deduction of advance payment. Accordingly, the contractor was in an extremely disadvantaged position when faced with the employer's bad faith demand on the advance payment guarantee when 99% of the advance payment had already been deducted from progress payment due to the contractor. However, upon realizing the malicious intent of the employer to make a fraudulent demand, the contractor decisively applied for an emergency injunction and was granted the injunction before the time limit elapsed, which secured the safety of guarantee. In this way, the employer was persuaded to negotiate and enter into a settlement agreement with the contractor, leading to the successful and peaceful resolution of the guarantee storm.

§4.12 PARENT COMPANY GUARANTEE

[A] Emergence of Parent Company Guarantee

Prior to 2014, parent company guarantees were rarely used in the field of international construction involving Chinese companies. Since 2014, it has undergone explosive growth and became the common requirement of foreign employers for the following reasons.[179]

[1] *The Increased Scale of Overseas Projects and the Relatively Insufficient Credit of Contractors*

Overseas projects are expanding in scale and EPC (turnkey) has become the main-stream project mode in recent years. These two factors lead to the rapid increase in contract price and there are already a few projects worth billions of USD or even higher.[180] For these large or giant projects, if the contractor in a project is not the group company itself but its subsidiary, the contractor's assets (especially the net assets) and authorized credits will be inadequate compared to the project scale, and the contractor's ability to address risks is severely disproportionate to the risks undertaken by the employer under the EPC contract. To solve this problem, employers have become inclined to require parent companies to provide guarantees.

[2] *From "Prior Approval" to "Registration System": Clear the Way for Parent Company Guarantee*

The People's BOC promulgated the *Procedures for the Administration of Overseas Guarantees By Domestic Institutions* ("**Procedures**") in 1996 and the State Administration of Foreign Exchange promulgated the *Detailed Rules for the Implementation* of *Procedures for the Administration of Overseas Guarantees By Domestic Institutions* in 1997. According to Articles 10 and 11 of the Procedures, domestic institutions are required to acquire approvals from the foreign exchange department prior to providing overseas guarantees. Article 17 prescribes that "if a guarantor provides overseas guarantee without approval, the guarantee agreement it concludes is null and void." Therefore, domestic parent companies need to meet a high legal threshold to provide an overseas guarantee.

The State Administration of Foreign Exchange promulgated the *Provisions on the Foreign Exchange Administration of Overseas Guarantees* ("**Provisions**") in May 2014

---

179. *See* Song Yuxiang, Li Ouwen, "Analysis on Parent Company Guarantee in International Construction", Zhejiang International Construction, 2017.
180. For example, China Gezhouba (Group) Corporation contracted a hydroelectric project worth USD 4.7 billion in Argentina in 2013, a hydroelectric project in Angola worth USD 4.5 billion in 2015; China Railway Construction Corporation contracted a coastal railway project worth USD 11.9 billion in Nigeria in 2014; and China Communication Construction contracted Eastern Railway Project worth RMB 74.5 billion in Malaysia in 2016.

and repealed previous regulations. According to Article 6 of the Provisions, overseas guarantees shall be subject to registration administration, which means that parent companies do not need prior approval by the foreign exchange department to provide overseas guarantees for their subsidiaries but only ex-post registrations. The Provisions clear legal obstacles and open the door for parent companies to provide parent company guarantees.

[3]   Parent Company Guarantee Becomes the Safeguard of Financing for Foreign Employers

Project finance has become a popular choice for foreign employers. It refers to a non-recourse or limited recourse financing or loan secured by the assets, expected benefits or rights of the project. Financiers usually set up the rules in project finance.

Take the power industry as an example. When investing in the construction of a power plant, project finance is commonly used to provide external financing for the investment volume other than capital. Foreign employers are required by financiers (such as financing banks) to mortgage or pledge their entire rights and interests under the EPC contracts and all relevant contracts. Also, financiers may require contractors to relinquish the lien on equipment supplied or construction that is in progress. In this way, as the employer in a project has mortgaged or pledged its entire rights and interests to the financier, the financier may directly intervene in the project and take over the follow-up construction of the project if the contractor violates the obligations under the loan agreement or other contracts.[181] Similarly, in some overseas wind power projects, although the Chinese bank has done an extensive due diligence on the project, it would not fully accept the traditional way of financing considering the complex environment and uncertain risks of different countries. Therefore, Chinese banks tend to combine corporate finance with project finance for the safety of loans, and pay significant attention to the guarantees provided by parent companies of overseas contractors after taking the typical types of guarantee of project finance into consideration.[182]

Financiers will place considerable weight on the nature of the guarantees provided by the contractor when deciding on the bankability of a project. If a project is prematurely aborted prior to actual operation, the financier will face the huge risk of not receiving the principal and interests from the contractor. Consequently, looking for qualified contractors becomes a core concern of financiers. If a contractor does not have the ability to take risks or to indemnify in proportion to the scale of the project, the

---

181. *See* Sun Tingjuan, "Preliminary Study on the Legal Concept of EPC Turnkey Contract in International Power Construction and Other Infrastructure Projects", Legal Thinking and Service on Promoting the "Belt and Road" Construction, Law Press, June 2016.
182. *See* Wang Xianghong, Chen Xiaoping, *Arrangement of Project Finance on Overseas Wind Power Projects*, available at http://law.wkinfo.com.cn/professional-articles/detail/NjAwMDAwMT QzODE%3D?searchId=5695f213357e462c944ed8e2bec03ba0&index=1&q=%E4%B8%AD %E5%9B%BD%E4%BC%81%E4%B8%9A%E6%B5%B7%E5%A4%96%E9%A3%8E%E7 %94%B5%E9%A1%B9%E7%9B%AE%E8%9E%8D%E8%B5%84%E5%AE%89%E6%8E %92.

financier will require the contractor to provide a parent company guarantee in addition to the generally used letter of independent guarantee and require the rights and interests of the employer under the parent company guarantee to be transferrable to it.

[B]   Forms of Parent Company Guarantee and Their Disadvantages

[1]   Forms of Parent Company Guarantee

Taking account of the content of the guarantee, the nature of the guarantee liability assumed by the parent company, and the sequence of guarantee liability, parent company guarantees include the following types:[183]

(1) Completion guarantee: a completion guarantee is used to ensure that a contractor will complete the construction of the project. If the contractor fails, its parent company will continue to implement and complete the project on its behalf.

(2) General guarantee: according to Article 17 of the *Guarantee Law of People's Republic of China*, a general guarantee refers to an arrangement in which the guarantor assumes guarantee liability when the debtor fails to pay the debt. It is common in international construction projects that a parent company will guarantee that the contractor shall perform under the EPC contract. If the contractor refuses or fails to perform its duty, the employer is entitled to claim against the parent company on the guarantee. It should be noted that, in the circumstances of a general guarantee, an employer is required to first request payment or compensation from the contractor. Only after the employer has exhausted legal remedies against the contractor can it claim against the parent company.

(3) Joint liability guarantee: the content of a joint liability guarantee is the same as a general guarantee, but the guarantor may assume the guarantee liability in a different sequence. Under the joint liability guarantee, an employer may first request payment from the contractor, or it can make a direct request that the guarantor (i.e., the parent company) assumes guarantee liability without first exhausting legal remedies against the contractor.[184]

(4) Unconditional independent guarantee: like an independent LG, the unconditional independent guarantee puts parent companies in a position to assume guarantee liability to foreign employers unconditionally. As long as the employer in a project raises claims against the parent company, the latter will assume the liability without considering the validity of the EPC contract or

---

183. *See* Song Yuxiang, Li Ouwen, "Analysis on Parent Company Guarantee in International Construction", Zhejiang International Construction, 2017.
184. Article 18 of the *Guarantee Law of People's Republic of China* regulates that when the deadline as set on the principal contract is passed and the debtor with joint guarantee responsibilities fails to pay the debts, the creditor may demand the debtor to pay the debts or demand the guarantor to assume guarantee liability within the range set in the contract.

whether it has been violated by the contractor. Under the unconditional independent guarantee, the parent company will act as a sole principal obligor for the duty of the contractor under the EPC contract, and it does not enjoy the right of defense the contractor has against the employer under the EPC contract. Therefore, under unconditional independent guarantee, parent companies, as the guarantors, undertake the strictest liability and highest risks.

[2]   Disadvantages of Parent Company Guarantee

[a]   *Parent Company Guarantee May Not Fulfill the Needs to Circumvent Overseas Risks*

Many domestic group companies will set up subsidiaries or Special Purchase Vehicles (SPVs) in the host states and have subsidiaries or SPVs to sign EPC contracts with employers in order to contain the group companies' risks.[185] Under parent company guarantees, parent companies' efforts will be in vain because employers may directly request parent companies to shoulder guarantee liability if contractors fail to complete the projects.

[b]   *Parent Company Guarantee Will Increase the Burden of Parent Companies Which Will Affect the Follow-Up Investment and Financing Ability*

Given that the compensation or indemnity clause is usually included in the parent company guarantee contracts, parent company guarantees are in the nature of financial guarantees, which increase guarantee liabilities and affect the parent company's balance sheet. If a subsidiary is required to provide parent company guarantees on several overseas projects simultaneously, or if several subsidiaries are required simultaneously to provide parent company guarantees on their respective overseas projects, then the parent company will be overwhelmed in terms of its ability to provide the required guarantees and risk management.[186]

As is shown above, with the increase in scale of overseas projects, the amount guaranteed by parent company guarantees continues to increase. The significant change in the balance sheet of the parent company will severely influence its follow-up investment and financing ability, which will impede its operation of other projects.

---

185. *See* Tong Rou, "Protection for Domestic Banks Issuing Overseas Construction Contracting Guarantee: Take Libya War as an Example", available at http://article.chinalawinfo.com/ArticleHtml/Article_66894.shtml#10, 2012.
186. *See* Song Yuxiang, Li Ouwen, "Analysis on Parent Company Guarantee in International Construction", Zhejiang International Construction, 2017.

[c] *A Listed Parent Company Is Required to Disclose the Information of*
Financial Guarantee It Provides to Its Subsidiaries[187]

According to Article 1.5 of the *Notice on Regulating the Overseas Guarantee Provided by Listed Companies*, listed companies are required to publish relevant information to the public in due course in newspapers specified by the China Securities Regulatory Commission, including the total amount guaranteed by listed companies and their controlling subsidiaries as at the date of disclosure, and the total amount guaranteed by listed companies for their controlling subsidiaries as at the date of disclosure. Consequently, parent companies are required to disclose information relating to their guarantee obligations to the public, which may cause much inconvenience to its operations.

[C] **Risks Prevention on Parent Company Guarantee**

Domestic parent companies are faced with a dilemma once foreign employers request for the provision of parent company guarantees: if the parent company agrees, it will face the above disadvantages and the complex procedures for internal approval; however, if the parent company disagrees, the employer may appoint another contractor in place of the parent company's subsidiary. To address this dilemma, parent companies may consider the following measures.

To begin with, contractors should evaluate their asset and credit status in advance and determine the reasonableness of the request for a parent company guarantee in light of the project conditions. First, contractors should analyze the financing structure. If it is project finance, then employers usually have a greater say, leaving little room for contractors to negotiate. Second, contractors should analyze the type and scale of the projects in comparison with their own capacities. If the employer's or financiers' need to control risks can be satisfied by independent LG provided by the contractor, then it is unnecessary to provide a parent company guarantee. For instance, the International Finance Corporation (IFC), part of the World Bank, provided project finance to the contractor in the construction of a PV plant in Egypt. The financier required the contractor to the EPC contract to provide a parent company guarantee in order to ensure that the contractor would pay back the principal and interests. A thorough evaluation indicated that the total assets and net assets of the contractor were significantly larger than the scale of the project. Therefore, the contractor firmly denied the requirement. In the end, IFC gave in and the contractor was only required to provide an independent LG.[188]

Second, contractors should actively face the requirement of providing parent company guarantee. If, after evaluation, the credit of the contractor is limited and disproportionate to the risks undertaken by the employer in the project, then the contractor should fully negotiate with the financier the specific terms in the parent

187. *Ibid.*
188. *Ibid.*

company guarantee contract. The parent company is advised to draw on its strength in credential and capital capacity to participate in the negotiation for the form of guarantee.

Third, parent companies should be well aware that parent company guarantee has become a new trend in recent years, and they should not consider that it is a particularly onerous requirement to provide it in every case. If, after careful evaluation, there is indeed reasonable basis for the project to require the parent company to provide a guarantee, then the parent company should also cooperate with its subsidiary pitching for the project.

Last but not least, in terms of choosing the form of guarantee, contractors should try to limit the scope of guarantee liability and lower the possibility of compensation. Specifically:

(1) Avoid using a monetary guarantee but choose a completion guarantee instead. It may ease the fluctuation on the balance sheet of the parent company. The contractor should try to negotiate that the parent company first assumes the guarantee liability by implementing and completing the project and pays monetary compensation only after the project fails. In this way, the parent company, when facing the breach by its subsidiary, may mobilize resources and workforce from other projects within the group company to continue the implementation and complete the project so as to reduce the burden to directly face monetary compensation and to maintain the integrity and reputation of the group company.[189]

(2) If monetary compensation is inevitable, then a general guarantee is the preferred form as this would require foreign employers to make claims against contractors prior to requesting parent companies to bear guarantee liability. Only when foreign employers have exhausted legal remedies but failed to get compensated from contractors they can make claims against parent companies. In this way, foreign employers will have to invest significant time and money to exhaust their legal remedies against the contractors as a prerequisite to making claims against the parent companies, which will prompt them to negotiate and settle the claims with the parent companies or contractors. If, however, employers insist on the provision of joint liability guarantee, then parent companies should participate more actively in the project and get involved in the control of risks that might give rise to guarantee liability.

(3) Last but not least, parent companies should avoid providing the most stringent and risky form of guarantee, an unconditional independent guarantee. If an unconditional independent guarantee is required, contractors should negotiate with employers or financiers to agree on a lower limit of guarantee liability for the parent company. For example, the parent company is only responsible for the balance of the contractor's liability that is beyond the coverage of any applicable bank guarantee.[190]

---

189. *Ibid.*
190. *Ibid.*

§4.13 COMPLETION AND TAKING-OVER

The completion and taking-over phase of a construction project is of crucial importance in the entire construction cycle. Entrance into this phase indicates the shift of duty of care from the contractor to the employer. The completion and taking-over of a construction project are contingent on various factors and involves multiple parties including the employer, the designer, the Supervisor, the General contractor and the Subcontractor.

The specific types of risks associated with completion and taking-over which the contractor needs to pay attention to should be differentiated based on different stages of the project, namely, the stage before conclusion of the contract, the stage of implementing construction works and the stage of completion and taking-over.

[A] Risks in the Bidding Stage

[1] Definiteness of the Time for Commencing Work

The time of completion of a project is closely related to the time of commencement. Therefore, the contract should make clear the method of fixing the time of commencing. The common practice in international construction contracts is to set the commencement date stipulated in the employer's instruction or order of commencement as the formal commencement date. As far as the FIDIC Silver Book is concerned, the employer is generally under an obligation to issue the order of commencement at least seven days prior to the commencement date. Further, to avoid the incurrence of costs by the contractor while waiting for the commencement date when all the preparatory works have been completed, the commencement date should be within 42 days after the coming into force of the contract.

[2] Reasonableness of the Construction Period and Liquidated Damages for Delay

On the basis that comprehensive consideration has been given to the cost and profit for the project, the ratio used in calculating liquidated damages should be set within a reasonable scale. Further, the upper limit or cap of the liquidated damages should be explicitly stipulated in the contract to ensure that the corresponding risks assumed by the contractor are manageable. In addition, the contract should not impose penalty on delays without due regard to the cause of delay (whether attributable to the employer, contractor or otherwise). Instead, reasonable grounds for extending the period of construction should be provided in the contract.

[3]   Specificity of the Conditions and Time Limit for Completion and Taking-Over

There might be a dispute in relation to fixing the completion date due to different perceptions on documents needed for completion and the status of works completed. Under extraordinary circumstances, such as when the employer is suffering from financial distress affected by economic crisis, the employer might refuse to examine and take over the project for its own extraneous purpose. The provisions on ascertaining the completion time in case of dispute may vary to a large extent according to the applicable laws and terms of the contracts. Therefore, it is advised that the documents needed for completion and taking-over should be specified in the contract, and the contractor should also specify the agreed standard for fixing the completion date, such as the date on which the test for completion is passed, or the date of completion provided in the certificate of taking-over and so on.

In particular, it should be expressly provided in the contract that if the employer does not issue a certificate of taking-over within the stipulated time period without denying the request for taking-over by the contractor, then the project is deemed completed upon the expiration of the stipulated time period after the submission of the request for taking-over. If the employer takes possession and beneficial use of the project without taking-over as required under the contract, then the date on which possession of the project is transferred to the employer should be deemed to constitute the date of completion.

[B]   Risks in the Construction Stage

First, there are risks relating to the employer's inability or unwillingness to furnish the conditions for construction, with respect to the site, materials on technology, equipment, and procedure of examination, approval and license, etc. pursuant to relevant contract provisions. A case on point is where the employer is responsible for land acquisition and resettlement, yet the employer does not hand over the site in a timely manner and thus causing delay of construction progress. In that case, the contractor must lodge a claim for extension of time.

Second, there are risks relating to an insensible construction plan and unscientific organization. The successful completion of a project depends on the strength of the contractor's individual ability. The complexity and difficulty of performing an overseas contract require the contractors to organize the construction works in a scientific way, make out reasonable plans for construction, and optimize the structure of its personnel.

[C]   Risks in the Completion and Taking-Over Stage

In this stage, there are three kinds of conduct of the employer that the contractor should be wary of and act accordingly to mitigate the risks relating to the relevant conduct.

The first is the employer's refusal to take over the project in bad faith. To prevent this from happening, the contractor should send the employer a formal and written request for taking over in accordance with the contract once the project meets the standard of taking-over. In addition, the contractor may also be able to apply for accelerated taking-over in order to push the taking-over party to make prompt preparations, provided that this is within the construction period. Furthermore, the contactor may need to conduct investigations into the underlying attitude and intention of the employer relating to taking-over and be ready to cope with potential adverse circumstances.

The second is that the employer might prefer to have the project handed over to it before conducting the proper taking-over process in accordance with the contract. Generally speaking, conducting a proper taking-over process before handing over the project to the employer is more favorable to the contractor. However, if the contractor is left with no other choice but to hand over the project to the employer before obtaining the certificate or report proving readiness for taking-over, then the contractor must have command of a tool to realize a state of check and balance with the employer, such as control of the key to the technology room.

The third is that the employer might have used certain parts of the project before the issuance of the certificate of taking-over. In these circumstances, the date on which a part of project was first used by the employer should be deemed as the date of taking-over for that part. And from that day onward, the care of the works (i.e., responsibility for damage) in respect of that part should be shifted from the contractor to the employer.

To mitigate the risks relating to the second or third scenario described above, the contractor should collect and preserve relevant evidences.

Case: An employer from a Central Asian country invited a Chinese contractor to participate in the construction of the second phase of a business hotel. While conducting due diligence, the contractor found out that another Chinese enterprise was involved in the first phase of the construction. Communications with the enterprise involved in the first phase revealed that the employer postponed the taking-over based on the alleged failure to fulfill requirements for taking-over, and the employer even did not hesitate to resort to litigation in order to delay payments on construction costs. In view of that, the contractor made a decision to terminate cooperation with the employer, effectively preventing future risks in relation to completion and taking-over.

§4.14 DEFECTS LIABILITY

[A] Features of Defects Liability Period

Defects liability period refers to a period during which a contractor remains liable to rectify defects which appear in the construction project. By reference to FIDIC forms of contract, defects liability period is of the following features:

(1) It commences from the date of completion as certified by the issuance of certificate of taking-over.

(2) The cost of rectifying the defects shall be borne by the party who has caused the defects. Normally, the engineer and the contractor would jointly investigate into reasons behind the defects or damage. If it is proved that the defects are attributable to the contractor, then rectification of the defects and examination should be executed at the cost and risk of the contractor. Similarly, if it was the employer who has caused the defects, then the employer should bear the cost of rectification and examination, in addition to paying the contractor a reasonable amount of profit.

(3) During the defects liability period, the contractor is obliged to complete unfinished works, in addition to its obligation to rectify defects. Pursuant to relevant provisions of the FIDIC forms of contract, finishing touches that would not substantially affect the expected functions of the works or a section may be accomplished during and prior to the expiry of the defects liability period. The contractor shall, with a reasonable time specified by the employer and before the expiration of the defects liability period, complete any work which was unfinished at the time specified in the taking-over certificate.

(4) The duration of defects liability period is normally one year, and can be extended under special circumstances, but would ordinarily not exceed two years.

(5) If the project is suspended due to reasons other than the contractor, the defects liability period would not be affected. Under FIDIC forms of contract, when production and/or material and/or equipment has been suspended based on provisions on suspension of construction or the rights of the contractor to suspend work, any obligations of the contractor shall cease to apply to defects or damage which appear two years after the expiration of the defects liability period.

(6) Obligation of the contractor to ensure quality does not automatically end with the expiry of this period. Under FIDIC forms of contract, it is not until the issuance of certificate of performance by the engineer to the contractor, that the obligation of the contractor is deemed accomplished. In other words, certificate of performance is the final approval for the project.

[B]   Difference Between Defects Liability Period and Warranty Period

During the defects liability period, the contractor is responsible for rectifying any defects in the project, and when that period expires, the contractor would not be held liable for rectifying the defects, but it should still be responsible for significant quality issues in the project. While warranty period refers to the minimum reparation period under normal use after the project was completed and passed acceptance test. During that period, the contractor is only liable for quality issues in the project. A majority of countries in the world have compulsory requirements for the length of warranty period, whereas the length of defects liability period is decided by the parties, and is usually shorter than the former.

[C] Extension and Upper Limit of Defects Liability Period

The employer is only entitled to an extension of the defects liability period when the defects have reached a level that makes the employer unable to use the works or a section for purposes for which they are intended.

The FIDIC forms of contract do impose a limit on the number of rounds of extension, but the upper limit of the total length of the extensions is two years. Thus, assuming that the agreed defects liability period (without extension) is one year, the maximum length of defects liability period is three years.

[D] Ten-Year Liability Insurance

Ten-year liability insurance is a compulsory decennial liability insurance in France, Algeria, UAE and several other countries especially French-speaking countries. This type of insurance is premised on the longevity of construction projects and mobility of international engineering companies. International contractors would evacuate the site and even leave the country where the project is located once the project is completed, but the defects and hidden danger seldom manifest themselves during the one-two years defects liability period. If the contractor has already left the country when the hidden danger emerges, it would be not easy for the employer to receive compensation for defects.

Under French law, the contractor is responsible for the defects of the main body of the construction work that occur within a decade following the completion and acceptance of the work. In France, the contractor is prohibited from executing a project contract unless it has taken out the insurance. After the contractor has taken out the insurance, if defects occur within one year after the project was handed over and put into use, which is within the defects liability period, the contractor should undertake the rectification and bear the ensuing costs. If the defects occur during the rest nine years, then the rectification would be executed at the cost of the insurance company.

In the past, the 10-year liability insurance was primarily covered by French insurance companies. However, insurance companies incorporated in other countries have been entering into this business in recent years. The insurance premium for a construction project is determined by the insurance company taking into account the overall strength of the contractor and the quality of the projects it has contracted. In this type of insurance, the contractor is the policyholder, and the employer is the insured or the beneficiary.

§4.15 LIQUIDATED DAMAGES

Liability for breach of contract, also called civil responsibility for breach of contract, is the responsibility parties to a contract undertake for violating their obligations under the contract. Conduct in breach of the contract can take many forms. Based on whether the contract has been performed, breach of contract can be classified into impossibility of performance, delay of performance, defective performance and refusal of performance. Rules in relation to liquidated damages include the limitation on liability undertaken by the contractor to the employer regarding the project, penalties the contractor should pay to the employer for not having completed the construction works on time and interest the employer should pay for delay in payment for construction works.

[A]   Limitation on Liability of the Contractor

Limitation on liability of the contractor is the maximum amount the contractor ought to pay for breach of contract. Under FIDIC forms of contract, parties are exempted from liability to the other for loss of use of any Works, loss of profit, loss of any contract or any indirect or consequential loss and the total liability of the contractor to the employer under the contract should not exceed the price of the contract. On some occasions, the employer may prefer to cap the liability of the contractor 20%-30% higher than the contract price. In that case, the contractor should negotiate with the employer to limit the liability to the contract price.

[B]   Delay Penalties

Breach of contract by the contractor in international project contracting can be divided into nonperformance and improper performance. Nonperformance, which includes impossibility of performance and refusal of performance, would cause the termination of contract and occurrence of compensatory damages. Improper performance includes defective performance and delay of performance. Generally speaking, based on the contractual provisions commonly found in international project contracts and industry practice, defective performance by the contractor often results in liability for breach of contract caused by delay.

The construction period is of utmost importance in an international construction contract. The contractor would be subject to a severe penalty for delay of the project. If as measured by its own capacity of construction, the contractor envisions it impossible or very difficult to complete the construction works within the overall or sectional construction period, then it should be cautious when making a bid or try to negotiate with the employer to modify the construction period to a reasonable level.

With respect to the penalty, there are two main aspects that should be closely looked into, which are the reasonableness of the method for calculating penalty and the existence of the cumulative upper limit for penalty.

First, delay penalty is generally imposed when the contractor has missed the overall construction period. However, there are contracts that provide for the imposition of delay penalty in cases where the progress of the project cannot meet sectional construction period. The kind of provision should be avoided by the contractor. If it cannot be avoided, then it is advised that the contract permits the contractor to recover in whole or in part the penalty in subsequent construction process provided that the progress has been caught up.

Second, on the basis that comprehensive consideration has been given to the cost and profit for the project, the ratio used in calculating liquidated damages should be set within a reasonable scale. Further, the upper limit of the liquidated damages should be explicitly stipulated in the contract to ensure that the corresponding risks assumed by the contractor are manageable. In international construction contracts, the upper limit for delay penalty is usually 10% of the contract price.

Under FIDIC forms of contract, delay penalty is the only compensation for the employer in case of delay of construction by the contractor in breach of the contract. Therefore, the employer is not entitled to demand the contractor to reimburse other losses, such as loss of rent pursuant to the contract, unless otherwise provided in the local laws.

[C] Interest of Delay Payment

In the context of international construction contracts, the most important obligation of the employer is to pay the contractor on time and in full amount. Being paid progress payment on time is a significant factor which can determine the successful completion of the project, and would affect the expected profit of the contractor for executing the project. Although the obligation of the employer to pay the contractor on time is explicitly provided in the contract, in practice it is not uncommon for the employer to default in making timely progress payment. If this happens, the contractor is entitled to claim interest for delayed payment against the employer. The interest rate should be clearly set out in the contract to avoid disputes as to the applicable rate.

The interest rate for delayed payment should be higher than that of bank loans. Otherwise, the employer would be tempted to expropriate the money that should be paid to the contractor because the cost of doing so is smaller than to get loans from the bank, heightening the risk of the employer's default in payment.

Case: In a large-scale construction project based on an EPC contract, the payment terms for the contract provides that the employer should pay within 30 days after its receipt of the invoice of formal progress payment issued by the contractor.

During the execution of the contract, the employer delayed in its obligation to make timely progress payments 34 times, with each delay ranging from a few days to more than 20 days. Based on the foregoing, the contractor claimed for loss of interest in relation to the delayed payment against the employer in accordance with the interest rate of local bank loans.

The employer argued that it had not delayed in making progress payment, and the alleged delay was mainly caused by the contractor's issuance of invoices that did not reflect the correct amount payable, which did not entitle the contractor to recover late payment interest pursuant to the contract. The employer further contended that there was no basis for the contractor to claim for payment of interest based on the interest rate of bank loans. Therefore, the employer refused to pay the interest for delayed payment.

As later agreed by the parties, in respect of some of the delays relied on by the contractor, the invoices did not reflect the correct amounts payable as there was no deduction on account of liquidated damages for delayed delivery and thus should be corrected—the employer was not liable for delayed payment in respect of these invoices. The employer acknowledged delay in respect of the progress payment forming the subject matter of other invoices and undertook to pay the relevant interest on account of the delay. However, the employer maintained that the interest rate should be at the rate payable by the bank in respect of bank deposits. Given that the contractor could not provide evidence that it had borrowed money from a bank, the interest rate finally adopted was the bank deposit rate.

Comments: In this case, there are two issues concerned in the contractor's claim for delay in progress payment against the employer, namely, liability for delay and calculation of delay interest.

It was provided both in the conditions part of the contract and in the payment conditions and schedule of Attachment 1 that the employer should make progress payment within 30 days of its receipt of effective invoice issued by the contractor. Meanwhile, the Contactor should submit accurate supporting materials and documents to help the employer to review the invoices.

Through further examination by the parties, it was agreed that out of the 34 invoices that the contractor alleged a delay in payment for which the contractor should be compensated with late payment interest, only a few qualified as such. As for the other invoices that did not reflect an appropriate deduction in respect of liquidated damages for delayed completion, the employer made amendments to those invoices and notified the contractor of its approval, and then the employer paid. Although the actual payment was made outside the 30 days provided by the contract, it was exempted from being classified as delay in payment for which late payment interest is payable because the employer should be granted reasonable time to correct the amount of the invoices.

Regarding the second issue, calculation of the interest, the employer contended that the interest rate of bank deposit should be adopted, while the contractor argued for the rate of bank loans. When the contract does not provide for the method of calculating interest, this issue can be approached based on two kinds of scenarios. The first is where delay in payment by the employer caused the contractor to borrow money from the bank to keep up the project progress. In that case, the contractor has incurred loss of interest as its direct economic loss, so the interest for delayed progress payment should be calculated at the rate of bank loans. In the second scenario, the contractor did not borrow money from the bank and was not subject to any kind of third-party claim due to delayed payment. In that case, the loss of the contractor was the interest it could have obtained by depositing the progress payment in a bank, thus the interest rate of delayed payment should be calculated at the rate of bank deposit.

§4.16 INSURANCE

[A] Necessity of Taking Out Insurance

[1] Concerns of Risk

Risk shifting refers to the act of transferring or allocating the risk to other parties through legal documentation or insurance policies. This is not an act of selfishness, the aim of which is to shift the risk to individuals or organizations who are equipped with strong capability of risk tolerance. Insurance in construction projects is a vital instrument to shift the risk associated with the project and to ensure the realization of the project objective. It is usually provided in international construction contracts and/or under the applicable law(s) that the contractor has to take out certain types of insurance, without which the contractor cannot commence its work. Those provisions are primarily in the interest of the employer. However, they can also exert positive influence on the contractor. For example, once damages or losses occur in the project, the contractor can make a claim against the insurance company. In this way, the risk undertaken by the contractor would be covered as well.

Enterprises including financing banks would conduct various kinds of risk evaluation and prevention measures before making an investment decision, yet political risks that are outside the scope of operation risks are hard to control. China Export & Credit Insurance Corporation ("Sinosure") is able to assist enterprises to gain a deep insight into the political, economic and social situations of the host country before they make any investments and to alleviate investment risks. In the event that the risk materializes, enterprises are entitled to financial compensation by Sinosure, which cuts down a great deal of its loss. It is fair to say that political risks insurance has relieved the biggest concern of enterprises when making overseas investment.

[2] Concerns of Financing

A frequent difficulty encountered by enterprises when "going abroad" lies in the difficulty of financing, which would seriously affect the project commencement, progress and/or conclusions. If an overseas project is secured by insurance, banks would be more keen to provide loans, increase the credit amount of the loans, or to loosen the requirements for granting loans to that project. As a result, the financial stability of the enterprise concerned would be greatly enhanced, and its investment potential as well as the appeal of its shares and bonds will increase.

[B] Types of Insurance

The major types of insurance in international construction projects include construction all risk insurance, third-party liability insurance, project and equipment of the contractor insurance, transportation insurance, vehicle insurance, personal insurance, employee insurance of the contractor, most of which are to insure against contractor's risks. As for the risks borne by the employer, unless covered by construction all risks insurance based on industrial practice of host country, it is generally not included in the scope of construction risk insurance. The risks of the employer are of a special nature and entail expensive insurance. If the employer requires the contractor to insurance against the risks of the employer, too, the cost of construction would be extremely high, but the cost-benefit analysis of such requirement will vary depending on the nature of the project and the specifically agreed arrangement between the employer and the contractor.

In international construction projects, it is usually the contractor who would apply for construction insurance to the insurer. Sometimes, the employer and the contractor would respectively be responsible for buying insurance for different types of risks relating to the project. For example, while the employer undertakes insurance for the project, accessory equipment and materials, the contractor is to insure against risks associated with the construction machines and equipment, personnel and third-party claims. The employer would generally require the insurance policy to be in the joint names of the employer and contractor, through which it can gain the following benefits:

(1) As an insurance holder, the employer is entitled to all the rights under the insurance policy.
(2) Situations where the insurer after compensating the insured starts recourse against the employer can be prevented. For example, in a project where collapse caused damage to the property of a third party, if the contractor is the only insurance holder, the insurer is most likely to have recourse to the employer because the third party can claim compensation against the employer who owns the project, and after compensating the third party, the insurance obtains right of recourse against the employer.

[C]   Essential Points in Insurance Policy

The contractor should pay attention to the inclusion of an insurance clause in the construction contract, and the insurance policy issued by the insurance company in accordance with the construction contract can be annexed to the signed contract.

The party bound to apply for insurance, the insured and the beneficiary from a certain type of insurance should be clearly stated in the contract. When reviewing the insurance policy, emphasis should be put on the types of compulsory insurance, insured risks, scope and duration of coverage, insurance premium, the beneficiary and the sufficiency of the insurance proceeds. Besides, the contractor should be aware of any local law requirements on insurance including any restrictions in choosing the insurance company. For example, Bangladesh requires all projects with government investment to buy insurance from its state-owned insurance company to protect its domestic insurance industry. There is only one state-owned insurance company in Bangladesh, which does not offer the contractor any leverage in negotiating the insurance premium. There are other countries that require insurance for construction projects to be bought from domestic insurance companies. In that regard, the contractor should try to sieve out this kind of restrictive provision from the insurance clause of the contract, subject to any mandatory provisions under the applicable law.

Furthermore, the contractor should examine whether the risk type and amount of the insurance conform to specific requirements of the construction contract and whether the insurance has adequately covered the project risks when applying for and reviewing the insurance policy for signing. If requirements in the contract for insurance are not met, the employer would normally be entitled to buy insurance by itself and deduct the relevant cost from the project payment, or to hold the contractor liable when an event that should have been insured against occurs. The insured can simultaneously cover multiple stakeholders including the employer, the contractor, and the lending bank.

The contractor should pay particular attention to the insurance period, exclusions and deductibles. In case of occurrence of modification in the project that has caused change in the information previously provided to the insurance company, timely notice should be sent to the insurance company. If the project is delayed and the project period exceeds the insurance policy period, interested parties should have the insurance policy period extended to prevent refusal of compensation by the insurer.

Further, the contractor should comply with mandatory obligations relating to insurance under the applicable law of the contract, if any. For example, there is a mandatory decennial liability in many countries such as Algeria, Egypt, other Gulf countries, France and many French-speaking countries. Thus, it is mandatory for the contractor to buy 10-year liability insurance in such countries.

[D]   Suggestions

The following suggestions are aimed at contractors who act as insurance holders:

(1) The contractor should try to negotiate with the employer to buy insurance from a Chinese or international insurance company and calculate the insurance premium into the bid price to facilitate insurance claims and amicable resolution of disputes with the insurance company. Besides, the contractor should make thorough bidding inquiry before submitting its bid, and seek proposal on construction insurance from experienced insurance brokers when necessary.

(2) If the employer requires that there should be more than one beneficiary/insured party of the insurance, then the beneficiary should be the employer and the contractor. This could also help to prevent the insurer from compensating to making recourse against one party after it has compensated the other party. Sometimes, the financing bank (project lenders) would ask to be made beneficiary too as per the terms of the finance documents. However, other parties such as other contractors on-site should not be made beneficiary.

(3) When an insured risk occurs, the contractor should immediately send notice to the insurance company in accordance with the insurance policy. Meanwhile, the contractor should take effective measures to mitigate the loss.

Case: In an international construction project, the employer was responsible for taking out the construction all risk insurance. To cut down the insurance premium, the employer opted for deductibles of high amount up to USD 4,00,000 million. During the construction process, part of the construction works and equipment of the contractor were damaged by a flood. Because the monetary compensation was within the scope of deductibles, the contractor was not entitled to compensation from the insurer and the contractor had to bear the relevant costs under the contract. The contractor lost the compensation it should have obtained for lack of knowledge of the conditions in the insurance policy concluded by the employer. Drawing lessons from this case, for the part of insurance that was taken out by the employer, the contractor should closely look into relevant provisions in the contract especially those special conditions, and demand a copy of the insurance policy from the employer to ascertain the amount, deductibles, expiration, procedure for evaluating the loss of insurance. If the contractor contends that the insurance policy is incapable of adequately covering its risks under the project, it should take appropriate remedial measures.

§4.17   FORCE MAJEURE

[A]   Overview of Force Majeure

[1]   Definition of Force Majeure

[a]   PRC Law

PRC law provides for a specific definition of force majeure. Article 180 of *General Provision of the Civil Law of People's Republic of China* provides that: Force majeure refers to unforeseeable, inevitable and insurmountable objective circumstances. *Contract Law of People's Republic of China* sets the same definition. Although PRC law cannot govern international construction contracting practice independently, its understanding of force majeure has significant referential value.

According to PRC law, force majeure consists of four key elements: (1) unforeseeability, which means circumstances cannot be foreseen when the contract is entered into. It is apparently unfair to say an event unforeseeable to one contracting party is unforeseeable as a matter of law. Rather, the foreseeability of an event shall be judged from the perspective of a bona fide third person—if a bona fide third person cannot foresee the situation under the same circumstances, the element of unforeseeability is satisfied; (2) inevitability, which means a party has taken reasonable duty of care but still cannot prevent the situation from happening; (3) insurmountability, which means a party has tried its best but cannot overcome the barriers caused by force majeure to perform its obligations; (4) objectiveness. Objective circumstances refer to circumstances that cannot be changed by human will and which are not exclusive to one party only, which is opposite to subjective circumstances.

[b] FIDIC Conditions of Contract

FIDIC Conditions of Contract is widely applied in Chinese overseas engineering contracting projects. Sub-Clause 19.1 of Conditions of Contract for Construction, published in 1999 sets out a representative definition of force majeure. In this clause, "force majeure" refers to following exceptional events or circumstances: (a) which is beyond a party's control; (b) which such party could not reasonably have provided against before entering into the Contract; (c) which, having arisen, such party could not reasonably have avoided or overcome, and (d) which is not substantially attributable to the other party. Force majeure may include, but is not limited to, exceptional events or circumstances of the kind listed below, so long as conditions (a) to (d) above are satisfied:[191] (i) war, hostilities (whether war be declared or not), invasion, act of foreign enemies; (ii) rebellion, terrorism, revolution, insurrection, military or usurped power, or civil war; (iii) riot, commotion, disorder, strike or lockout by persons other than the contractor's personnel and other employees of the contractor and Subcontractors; (iv) munitions of war, explosive materials, ionizing radiation or contamination by radioactivity, except as may be attributable to the contractor's use of such munitions, explosives, radiation or radioactivity; and (v) natural catastrophes such as earthquake, hurricane, typhoon or volcanic activity.

FIDIC Conditions of Contract lists prerequisites and certain examples of force majeure, without excluding circumstances it has not mentioned, leaving space for stipulating detailed force majeure clause in specific project contracts.

In most Middle East and North Africa (MENA) region countries, the conditions for force majeure match those of the FIDIC and so if an event is *unforeseen, inevitable* and *beyond the aggrieved party's control* it can be characterized as a force majeure event, if it leads to *impossibility of performance* assessed objectively. However, it is worth noting that the regulation of force majeure under MENA laws does not pertain to public policy and the parties are free to agree on the definition, conditions and ramifications of force majeure in their contract, which primarily makes force majeure a creature of contract.

Force majeure generally leads to extinguishing the obligations that become impossible to perform, unless the parties agree in their contract to regulate the ramifications of force majeure differently by allocating the risk of impossibility among

---

191. If it falls into the four categories of events listed below, but does not satisfy the four conditions set force in (a) to (d), then the event does not constitute force majeure. For example, in a case provided by the ICC for this research project, Chinese contractors were forced to stop work due to local mass blockades, which were "riots, uprising, chaos, strikes or closures" as described below, resulting in delays in the construction period. However, the arbitral tribunal held that the main reason for the incident was that the subcontractor of the Chinese contractor did not timely pay the salaries of local employees which did not satisfy the conditions of (a), (b), and (c), and therefore did not constitute force majeure.

themselves as they deem fit.[192] Thus, contractors should be aware of the necessity and importance of addressing and stipulating for force majeure in their contracts.

[2]   Consequences of Force Majeure

[a]   Claims in the Event of Force Majeure

Sub-Clause 19.4 of Conditions of Contract for Construction stipulates "the consequences of force majeure:" if the contractor is prevented from performing any of his obligations under the Contract by force majeure of which notice has been given under Sub-Clause 19.2 [Notice of Force Majeure], and suffers delay and/or incurs Cost by reason of such force majeure, the contractor shall be entitled subject to Sub-Clause 20.1 [contractor's Claims] to: (a) an extension of time for any such delay, if completion is or will be delayed, under Sub-Clause 8.4 [Extension of Time for Completion], and (b) if the event or circumstance is of the kind described in subparagraphs (i) to (iv) of Sub-Clause 19.1 [Definition of Force Majeure] and, in the case of subparagraphs (ii) to (iv), occurs in the country, payment of any such Cost. After receiving this notice, the engineer shall proceed in accordance with Sub-Clause 3.5 [Determinations] to agree or determine these matters.

Therefore, according to Sub-Clause 19, the requirements for bringing claims in the event of force majeure are: (1) force majeure has arisen; (2) a party should notify the other party of the event or circumstance that constitutes force majeure within 14 days after such event or circumstance happens; (3) the contractor shall use all reasonable endeavors to perform his contractual obligation to minimize any delay caused by force majeure; (4) the contractor suffers delay and/or incurs Cost increase due to such force majeure.[193]

[b]   Contractor's Obligation to Send Notice

When force majeure has arisen, the contractor should notify the employer of relevant event or circumstance constituting force majeure in time. Sub-Clause 19.2 of Conditions of Contract for Construction provides that, "If a Party is or will be prevented from performing any of its obligations under the Contract by Force Majeure, then it shall give notice to the other Party of the event or circumstances constituting the Force Majeure and shall specify the obligations, the performance of which is or will be prevented. The notice shall be given within 14 days after the Party became aware, or should have become aware, of the relevant event or circumstance constituting Force Majeure." In

---

192. Article 373 of the Egyptian Civil Code states: *"An obligation is extinguished if the debtor establishes that its performance has become impossible by reason of causes beyond his control."* Similar provisions can be found in Article 307 Algerian Civil Code (1975), Article 364 Bahraini Civil Code (2001), Article 437 Kuwaiti Civil Code (1980), Article 360 Libyan Civil Code (1953), Article 339 Omani Civil Code (2013), Article 402 Qatari Civil Code (2004), Article 371 Syrian Civil Code (1949) and Article 472 UAE Civil Code (1985).
193. Jinsheng Chen., "Engineering Claims and Enlightenment Drawn from Cases under FIDIC Conditions of Contract", China Planning Press, 2016.

other words, it is contractor's obligation to send notice of force majeure within 14 days. Otherwise, the contractor would lose the right to bring relevant claims.

[c] Contractor's Duty to Minimize Delay

According to Sub-Clause 19.3 of Conditions of Contract for Construction, "[e]ach Party shall at all times use all reasonable endeavors to minimize any delay in the performance of the Contract as a result of Force Majeure." When force majeure occurs, it is the contractor's duty to continue the performance of the Contract and take reasonable measures to minimize delay and loss of the employer.

[d] Limits to Force Majeure Clause

Sub-Clause 19.5 of Conditions of Contract for Construction titled as "Force Majeure Affecting Subcontractor" provides that: "If any Subcontractor is entitled under any contract or agreement relating to the works to relief from Force Majeure on terms additional to or broader than those specified in this Clause, such additional or broader Force Majeure events or circumstances shall not excuse the contractor's nonperformance or entitle him to relief under this Clause." This clause means that when force majeure terms between Subcontractor and contractor are additional to or broader than those between contractor and employer, the contractor should bear consequences stemming from the additional terms and continue the performance of Contract. In other words, this Clause is to limit the force majeure terms between Subcontractor and contractor within those between contractor and employer.

[e] Change and Rescission of Contract

When force majeure has arisen, besides causing delay to the project, it may also lead to changes in conditions and purpose of the project, which renders the continuance of the project impossible or meaningless. Therefore, the contractor is entitled to change or terminate the Contract. According to FIDIC Conditions of Contract, when force majeure occurs, the Contract can be partially or entirely rescinded, and the employer shall undertake all losses caused therefrom and make reasonable compensations to the contractor. However, as to force majeure caused by natural disasters such as earthquake, storm, snow, and typhoon, the contractors, subject to any contractual arrangement to the contrary, are only entitled to extension of the project but no compensation for losses caused by it, which demonstrates the spirit of risk sharing.[194]

Sub-Clause 19.6 of Conditions of Contract for Construction provides for the conditions for contracts termination: "If the execution of substantially all the Works in progress is prevented for a continuous period of 84 days by reason of Force Majeure of which notice has been given under Sub-Clause 19.2 [Notice of Force Majeure], or for

---

194. Yinli Gao, "Influence of Force Majeure on Performance of Construction Contract," *Construction Economy*, 2008 (11) pp. 38-40.

multiple periods which total more than 140 days due to the same notified Force Majeure, then either Party may give to the other Party a notice of termination of the Contract. In this event, the termination shall take effect 7 days after the notice is given, and the contractor shall proceed in accordance with Sub-Clause 16.3 [Cessation of Work and Removal of contractor's Equipment]."

Sub-Clause 19.7 of Conditions of Contract for Construction stipulates the conditions for being released from performance: "Notwithstanding any other provision of this Clause, if any event or circumstance outside the control of the Parties (including, but not limited to, Force Majeure) arises which makes it impossible or unlawful for either or both Parties to fulfill its or their contractual obligations or which, under the law governing the Contract, entitles the Parties to be released from further performance of the Contract, then upon notice by either Party to the other Party of such event or circumstance: (a) the Parties shall be discharged from further performance, without prejudice to the rights of either Party in respect of any previous breach of the Contract, and, (b) the sum payable by the employer to the contractor shall be the same as would have been payable under Sub-Clause 19.6 [Optional Termination, Payment and Release] if the Contract had been terminated under Sub-Clause 19.6."

In case of contract termination, consideration shall be given to not only the above provisions in the contract but also other relevant factors especially those of the host country, in order to decide whether it is wise to terminate a contract. When the occurrence of force majeure changes the condition of the contract, making performance almost impossible, the contractor should take full advantage of this clause to seek compensation following the rescission or termination of the contract.

[B]   Response to Force Majeure Risks

[1]   *Recognition as Force Majeure*

In overseas construction projects, suspensions caused by emergencies happen frequently. Only when such event is recognized as force majeure, can the contractor rely on entitlements under the contract in respect of force majeure. Not all emergencies can be recognized as force majeure. Although FIDIC Conditions of Contract provides for the prerequisites and lists certain circumstances for force majeure, whether a given event satisfies the prerequisites still need to be analyzed on a case-by-case basis.

For instance, a construction enterprise from China contracted an electronic power construction project in South Asia. Rainstorms happen frequently in the host country. Considering the frequent rainfall in the rainy season of South Asia, parties agreed on a formula to compute the entitlement to claims for additional payment and extension of time due to the delay caused by heavy rainfall. If the calculation result exceeds the standard, a request to extend the time for completion can be put forward. During construction, many Subcontractors relied on suspensions caused by rainstorms to request extension from the Chinese contractor. Considering rainstorms did render construction impossible, the Chinese construction enterprise, in turn, asserted rain-storms as force majeure and claimed for extension of time for completion from the employer.[195]

In this case, whether rainstorm could constitute force majeure is the key. Rainstorm, being natural weather phenomenon, cannot be manipulated by human. Thus, according to the definition of force majeure provided in Sub-Clause 19.1 of FIDIC Conditions of Contract for Construction, natural weather satisfies the two elements of force majeure, which are "beyond a Party's control" and "not substantially attributable to the other Party." However, whether it satisfies the other two elements which are "such Party could not reasonably have provided against before entering into the Contract" and "having arisen, such Party could not reasonably have avoided or overcome" remains to be discussed.

Here, the destructiveness and frequency of rainstorm should be considered comprehensively. In this case, rainstorm is not uncommon in that area, and as early as at the time of contract execution, the contractor had agreed upon calculation formula regarding extension of completion time, indicating its awareness that the project would possibly be delayed because of the rainstorm. Thus, it is required to take reasonable precautions. However, if the rainstorm is so destructive that the contractor cannot continue the construction, the contractor could not be required to take reasonable precautions. Furthermore, contractors are supposed to comprehensively study the local weather, geography, environment and take countermeasures while undertaking overseas construction projects. Thus, in most cases, natural weather cannot be recognized as force majeure. However, unusual extreme weather does happen. For example, extreme rainstorm may happen during the construction period in a place that seldom rains. Even an experienced contractor cannot foresee this kind of weather, which then satisfies the requirements of "could not reasonably have provided against" and "could not reasonably have avoided or overcome" and constitutes force majeure.

[2]   Specification of Force Majeure Clause

In overseas construction projects involving Chinese contractors, disputes relating to force majeure usually arise due to the indefiniteness of the force majeure clause. Because FIDIC Conditions of Contract just set out the prerequisites and list certain examples for force majeure, it is natural that parties would dispute over whether similar events and circumstances could be recognized as force majeure. Besides, different countries apply different rules regarding force majeure. Thus, without specified stipulations in the contract that certain events shall qualify as force majeure, the interpretation of force majeure insisted by the contractor and favorable to itself may not be supported.

Before contract negotiations, the contractor should carefully investigate and assess natural and social environment of the host country to gain an idea of force

---

195. Jia Zhang, Study of Application of Force Majeure in EPC Engineering Contract (University of International Business and Economics, 2009).

majeure events that may occur there and take relevant factors into consideration in project planning. During contract negotiations, the contractor should actively propose a force majeure clause based on the peculiarity of local situations and the project and reach detailed agreement on the calculation formula of time extension and loss sharing method to alleviate the financial pressure of the contractor and avoid future disputes.

In fact, parties often put more emphasis on core clauses of the contract, such as engineering quality standard, project duration, construction cost and little emphasis on regular terms like force majeure clauses. In most of the cases, the contractors were overly optimistic, believing either that the projects would go well and no force majeure disputes would arise or that the existing force majeure clause has provided sufficient instructions for solving disputes. As a result, the force majeure clauses they agreed upon are not clear and comprehensive enough. Once force majeure has arisen, it is too late for the contractor to seek negotiations and change the wording of the force majeure clause.

For example, a Chinese port construction company won a harbor expansion project in a country in the South Asia through bidding. However, a freighter shipping construction machinery and materials from Tianjin Port encountered a big storm on the sea and had to deviate from its original route for the rest of the trip, resulting in a delay for two and half months. Because of this, the employer requested a compensation of USD 3,600,000 for such delay. The parties failed to settle through negotiations and submitted the case for arbitration. However, because the contract did not stipulate the situations that should be recognized as force majeure and the liability distribution, the arbitral institution ruled that the Chinese construction company should compensate the employer for all losses caused by the delay, totaling USD 2,450,000.[196] In this case, the purported force majeure directly influenced the engineering machinery and materials rather than the project itself but the delay of engineering machinery and materials resulted in the delay of the project. Under such circumstances, parties disagreed on the application of the force majeure clause. If the force majeure clause in the contract is not specific enough, an arbitral tribunal or court may be inclined to adopt a strict interpretation of the relevant provisions and a conservative liability distribution, which may put the contractor at a disadvantage.

While contracting with the employer, the contractor should consider relevant factors and possibilities comprehensively and strive to actively safeguard their interests. In defining the scope of force majeure, the contractor's interests are generally always in conflict with those of the employer. The employer hopes to transfer the risks to the contractor as much as possible, while the contractor expects just the opposite. By all means, the contractor should try its best to set out events that should constitute force majeure. First, the contractor should broaden the scope of force majeure to cover possible circumstances, especially those that may occur during the construction in the host country. Second, specific rules shall be stipulated regarding the allocation of liabilities to reduce future disputes over such issues. The contractor should put more emphasis on force majeure clause, study the law on force majeure in the host country,

---

196. Haixia W, Qidong Huang, "International Project Contractor's Strategy Against Risk of Force Majeure and Its Practice," *Journal of Hohai University*, March 2005 (VII) pp. 8-11.

and adjust the clause to meet the need of the project according to practical situations. Such adjusted terms would facilitate the resolution of disputes and prevent the situations from escalating.

[3] Prevention of Subcontracting Risks

Subcontractors commonly participate in overseas construction projects undertaken by Chinese contractors. Thus, the contract between the contractor and the subcontractor will certainly affect the contractors' control over force majeure risks.

For example, a construction company contracted an EPC project in South Asia and the project contract was modeled on the FIDIC Conditions of Contract, under which the parties agreed to use equipment manufactured by a factory (the "Manufacturing Factory") in the southwest of country S. The construction company signed a Supply Agreement with that factory and agreed on a force majeure clause according to the EPC contract it entered into with the employer: severe natural disasters and catastrophes (like typhoon, flood, earthquake, fire and explosion), war (declared or not), plague, rebellion and turmoil constitute force majeure; if force majeure influence either party's performance of contractual obligations, it would be relieved from performance as long as the force majeure still continues but may not adjust the contract price simply because of the delay caused by force majeure. During the performance of the Supply Agreement, a powerful earthquake in the southwest of country S caused significant losses to the Manufacturing Factory which would consequently miss the delivery date agreed in the Supply Agreement. The Manufacturing Factory requested for delay of the delivery of equipment to be excused according to the force majeure clause in the Supply Agreement. The construction company consent to its request and applied for an extension of the construction period from the employer according to the force majeure clause in the EPC contract.[197]

In this case, since a powerful earthquake is almost indisputably a force majeure, the general contractor's claims for rights provided in the force majeure clause would always be supported. However, in case of an event not indisputably constituting force majeure (like rainstorms mentioned above), even if the subcontractor may successfully request for extension of completion time under the contract with the contractor, which explicitly provides that such event constitutes force majeure, the same request brought by the contractor against the employer would not necessarily succeed if the force majeure clause in the contract between them does not cover such event. The reason is, the agreement between the contractor and subcontractor that such event constitutes force majeure is not binding upon the employer due to the privity of contract. Only the contract signed by the contractor and the employer is binding on the employer. As a result, the subcontractor's liability exemption not necessarily leads to the contractor's exemption of liability.

---

197. Jia Zhang, "Legal Study on the Application of Force Majeure in EPC Engineering Contract", University of International Business and Economics, 2009.

According to Sub-Clause 19.5 of FIDIC Conditions of Contract for Construction, "if any Subcontractor is entitled under any contract or agreement relating to the Works to relief from Force Majeure on terms additional to or broader than those specified in this Clause, such additional or broader force majeure events or circumstances shall not excuse the contractor's nonperformance or entitle him to relief under this Clause." Therefore, while contracting with the subcontractor, the contractor should ensure the scope of force majeure clause would not be broader than that in the contract with the employer, or it would end up undertaking obligations of the subcontract on its own.

[4]   Response after Force Majeure

Once force majeure has arisen, the contractor should send notice of force majeure promptly and request suspension of construction to lay the foundation for the incoming works. For example, a Chinese company contracted a highway construction project financed by World Bank under FIDIC Conditions of Contract, and the consulting engineer was an employee from a long-established consulting firm in Britain. During construction, a dispute upon the free trade agreement broke out between the host country and its neighboring country, which unilaterally shut down the border and stopped fuel supply to the host country, causing the main part of the project to stop for nine months and a half, amounting to 39.58% of the total construction period. The Chinese company sent notice to the consulting engineer right after the occurrence of the fuel crisis, requested him to send suspension order under Clause 40.1, provided legal basis for making financial claims and further work, and stopped unnecessary expenditure.[198]

After the occurrence of major risks, the contractor should try its best to avoid further losses to be suffered by the employer and urge the parties to solve claims through peaceful negotiations. If the contractor is neither permitted to stop the work nor can continue the construction work, losses of the parties would be enlarged and procedural issues like contractor's suspension without authorization would come up, setting obstacles for the contractor to make claims later.

In addition, generally speaking, when force majeure arises, the parties would consult the consulting engineer about claims and take his/her advice into consideration. However, it is possible due to lack of professional competence, or lack of comprehensive understanding of the project, or bias toward one party, the consulting engineer would give improper suggestions. Therefore, although the contractor should take the consulting engineer's advice into account, it cannot blindly adopt all the advice. Equipped with comprehensive knowledge of the project, the contractor would better determine the reasonableness of the consulting engineer's suggestion. In the case mentioned above, the consulting engineer advised the employer to pay USD 1,750,000 in response to the Chinese contractor's claims. Through prudent analysis, the Chinese contractor refused to follow the consulting engineer's advice and prepared

---

198. Haixia Wang, Qidong Huang, "International Project Contractor's Strategy and Practice on Coping with Risk of Force Majeure," *Journal of Hehai University*, March 2005 (VII) pp. 8-11.

to submit the case to international arbitration, which forced the employer to soften its attitude, admit the fuel crisis caused negative influence and show its willingness to settle the disputes through amicable negotiation. Finally, the Chinese contractor received compensation of USD 4,400,000, more than twice the amount the consulting engineer suggested.[199]

Thus, coping with force majeure risks, one should consider various factors comprehensively and make different responsive policies according to the practical situations of the project in order to yield positive results in the end.

§4.18 FAILURE TO SUBMIT CLAIMS WITHIN THE TIME PERIOD PRESCRIBED UNDER THE CONTRACT

[A] Causes of the Risk

An engineering claim usually refers to a claim in terms of money or time legally raised by a party to the contract which suffers actual loss or damage due to reasons not attributable to it during the performance of the contract.[200] A contractor loses its right of claim due to its failure to submit a claim that meets requirements in formality and content within the time limit set for the party to make certain claims, including requests for compensation or reimbursement.[201] Several reasons may contribute to such failure: (1) Chinese enterprises value technique but ignore management in overseas projects;[202] (2) Chinese enterprises have a weak sense on contract management or bringing claims; (3) many Chinese enterprises worry that making claims will affect the relationship with employers so that they voluntarily give up their right to claim.[203]

[B] Statute of Limitation under FIDIC Contract Conditions

The most widely used contract conditions in the field of international construction are Conditions of Contract for Construction, Conditions of Contract for Plant and DB and Conditions of Contract for EPC/Turnkey Projects published in 1999 (hereinafter collectively referred to as "1999 FIDIC Contract Conditions"). FIDIC released the newly revised version of the above three contract conditions in December 2017 (hereinafter collectively referred to as "2017 FIDIC Contract Conditions").

---

199. *Ibid.*
200. Chen Jinsheng, "FIDIC Contract Conditions: Engineering Claim and Case Study", China Planning Press, October 2016, p. 3.
201. Yao Jie, "Legal Practice on Construction Contract Price (Newly Addition)", Law Press, 2011, pp. 257-261.
202. Cui Jun, "Statue of Limitation the Influence of FIDIC Contract", Legal Article, 2nd issue 2015.
203. Ren Xueqiang, "Rights and Technology: Contractor's Claim under FIDIC Contract Conditions", International Economic Cooperation, 1st issue 2006.

[1]   *1999 FIDIC Contract Conditions: Rules and Analysis*

Article 20 of 1999 FIDIC Contract Conditions governs "Claims, Disputes and Arbitration," and Article 20.1 [contractor's Claim] provides the following detailed rules on the procedure of claims: (1) it sets the time limit for a contractor to file the notice of claim—the right of claim may likely be waived if the contractor fails to meet such time limit; (2) it requires a contractor shall keep contemporary records as instructed by the engineer; (3) it prescribes the content requirements and time limit for a contractor to submit claim report; and (4) it stipulates the time limit of approval and the regulations for an engineer to comply with.

The procedure of contractors' claim can be shown as follows.

Figure 4.1   Claims Procedure for the Contractors

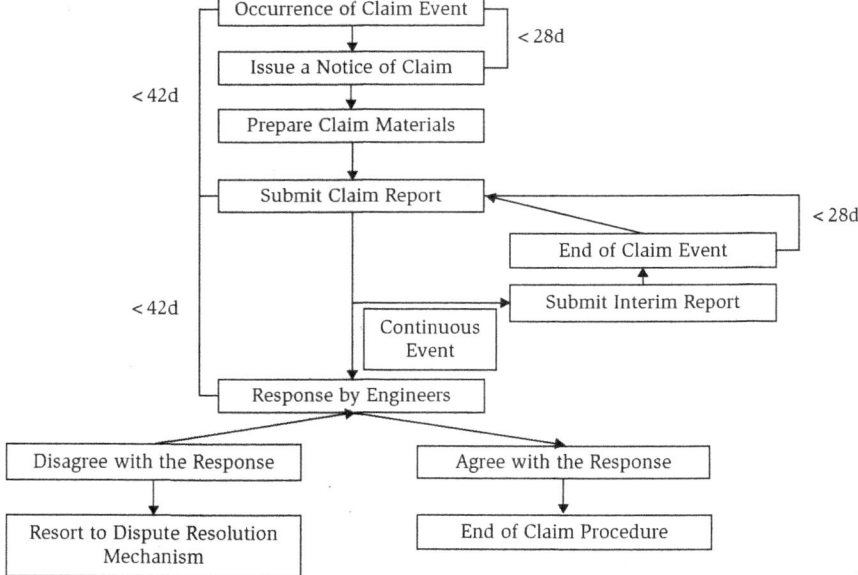

Contractors should pay special attention to three time limits: (1) the notice of claim shall be issued within 28 days after the occurrence of the claim event; (2) the claim report shall be submitted within 42 days after the occurrence of the claim event; (3) regarding continuous events, contractors shall submit the final claim reports within 28 days after the termination of impact of claim events.[204] In addition, Article 20.1 prescribes that the engineer may request the contractor to further supplement materials, but it still needs to give a general response to the claim within the specified time.

---

204. Chen Jinsheng: "FIDIC Contract Conditions: Engineering Claim and Case Study", China Planning Press, October 2016, p. 31.

In practical terms, this rule is beneficial to contractors because sometimes the engineer in a project may postpone its approval of the claim on the basis that the contractor provides insufficient evidence and wait to reject the claim until the contractor has completed major parts of the work and no longer has as much leverage over the employer. This rule may help to avoid such behavior of engineers.[205]

[2] 2017 FIDIC Contract Conditions: Rules and Analysis

Under 1999 FIDIC Contract Conditions, no rule is made concerning the time limit of employer's claim. It only mentions that "the employer shall issue the notice of claim to the contractor as soon as practicable after it becomes aware of the claim event or circumstance." Quite a few experts and scholars believe it may violate the principle of equality and justice.[206]

2017 FIDIC Contract Conditions combines the contractor's claims and employer's claims into one article (Article 20). Under 2017 FIDIC Contract Conditions, the time limit to issue the notice of claim for both employers and contractors is 28 days, and the time limit to submit claim report is 42 days (starting from the date on which the employer or the contractor knows or should have known the occurrence of the claim event). Therefore, employers should follow the time limit when making claims as well. Chinese contractors should also pay attention to the 28 days and 42 days limits when making claims under 2017 FIDIC Contract Conditions.

In addition, according to 2017 FIDIC Contract Conditions, if the engineer, after receiving the notice of claim, considers that the party which makes claim does not fulfill the requirement of 28-day time limit, then it shall send a notice to that party within 14 days. Otherwise, the 28-day time limit shall be treated as satisfied. This new rule is beneficial to contractors.

[C] Preventive Measures for Risks of Statute of Limitation

[1] Submit Notice of Claim and Other Documents in Time

The most important measure to prevent the risks of statute of limitation is to strictly follow the time limit as prescribed in the contract, submitting notice of claim, contemporary records, claim reports and other documents in time. There are quite a few cases where Chinese contractors lose the rights of claim due to failure to issue notice of claim in time.

For instance, in a project for the construction of an international airport in a Middle Eastern country, the project was delayed due to the fault of the employer. However, the Chinese contractor did not file a claim. In the end, not only did it fail to

---

205. Zhang Shuibo, He Bosen, "New FIDIC Contract Conditions: Introduction and Analysis", China Building Industry Press, February 2003, p. 170.
206. Zhang Lixia, Shi Guoqing, "Claim Procedure Comparison Between Employers and Contractors under FIDIC Contract Conditions", Economists, 3rd issue 2007.

claim damages from the employer, but the performance LG provided by it in the sum of USD 70 million was confiscated by the employer.[207]

In another project for road construction in Ethiopia, the Chinese contractor failed to issue a notice of claim within 28 days as stipulated in the contract and lost its right of claim due to its frequent change of personnel in charge and its poor document management.[208]

Of course, there are several cases where Chinese contractors successfully get compensated or initiate the dispute resolution proceedings by duly complying with the contractually prescribed time limits in respect of the relevant claims. In a project for the upgrade of a 112 kilometer road in an African country, the Chinese contractor encountered variations in design and project scope. The Chinese contractor strictly followed the rules under the FIDIC Contract Conditions and issued the notice of claim in time. For instance, the Chinese contractor issued a written notice of claim to the engineer within 10 days after the occurrence of the claim event of "setting off data error". Besides, the Chinese contractor gathered abundant evidence thanks to its sophisticated document management system, and it duly sent contemporary records following the instructions of the engineer. Finally, it submitted the completed claim report and was successfully compensated.[209]

In another case for the construction of main pumping pipe for a Sewerage Bureau of the Public Utilities Department, the contract stipulated that the imported materials used in the construction may be exempt from customs duties. The Chinese contractor thought that oil material should also be imported and requested a tax exemption certificate from the employer, which was rejected. The Chinese contractor filed a formal claim to the engineer regarding the custom duties levied on oil material on the 15th day after the request for a tax exemption was rejected by the employer. The engineer provided a formal response after reviewing the claim report. Because the employer insisted on not issuing the tax exemption certificate after examining the response of the engineer and the claim report, the case escalated to a real dispute, and finally, the Chinese contractor initiated the dispute resolution procedure.

[2]   *Determine the Claim Event and the Timing of Its Occurrence Correctly*

[a]   *Determine the Claim Event*

According to the nature of the event, claim events can be divided into conspicuous events and inconspicuous events. Conspicuous events refer to the claim events or

207. Zhou Yueping, Ji Xiaochen, Meng Yi, "Risks Identification and the Prevention in International Construction (Part One)", available at http://www.zhonglun.com/Content/2017/01-05/1720 572537.html.
208. Cui Jun, "Contract Management and Claim in an Ethiopia Road Project", International Construction and Labor Service, 11th issue 2016.
209. Cheng Jian, Zhang Huipu, Hu Ming, "Claim Management under FIDIC Contract Conditions: Case Study and Analysis on an African Road Project", International Economic Cooperation, 9th issue 2007.

circumstances that are easier for contractors to spot, such as disturbance of local residents, delay of payment, explosion, war or terrorist activities. Inconspicuous events refer to the claim events or circumstances that are not easily discovered by the contractors, such as construction efficiency loss, change of construction method, claim events resulting from technical problems and variation damage.[210]

Chinese contractors usually will issue the notice of claim for conspicuous events in time. But for inconspicuous ones, they sometimes lose the rights of claim due to their failure to send the notice of claim within 28 days.

Therefore, Chinese contractors should take inconspicuous events seriously and send proper notice of claim within 28 days of the occurrence of such events.

[b] *Determine When Claim Events Occur*

Based on the time period of events, claim events may be categorized as instant events (or short-term events) and continuous events. Chinese contractors are usually able to issue notice of claim for instant events (such as abrupt disturbance of local residents or rainstorm). However, the question as to when a continuous event happens has resulted in major disputes between the contractor and the employer. In previous cases, both employers and (supervising) engineers rejected the idea that the contractors could submit the notice of claim during the happening of continuous event (i.e., after 28 days of its first occurrence) or after the termination of continuous event.[211] Therefore, Chinese contractors should preferably issue the notice of claim right within 28 days after the commencement of the occurrence of the claim events rather than waiting until the end of the event, insofar as the event is capable of being ascertained at such point in time. They also should keep a close eye on the development of events.

[3] **Standardize Formality and Content of the Notice of Claim**

Although Article 20.1 of 1999 FIDIC Contract Conditions and Article 20 of 2017 FIDIC Contract Conditions regulate that the contractor (or the party who makes the claim) shall issue a notice of claim within certain time limit, they do not specify the formality or content of a notice of claim. Therefore, it is not uncommon in practice that the engineer refuses to recognize the documents provided by the contractor as the notice of claim, which brings difficulties to contractors to make claims.

Precedents suggest that the followings may be seen as a proper notice of claim: (1) it is entitled "notice of claim," or "notice of intent of claim"; (2) although the title is not "notice of claim" or "notice of intent of claim," there includes wordings such as "the contractor reserves its right to claim," "this letter shall be deemed as a notice of

---

210. Cui Jun, "Statue of Limitation under FIDIC Contract and Its Influence", Legal Article, 2nd issue 2015.
211. *Ibid.*

claim under Article 20.1," or "claim is inevitable"; (3) somewhere in the letter mentions "claim" or "request for compensation."[212]

Chinese contractors usually will write letters to employers after becoming aware of the claim events. However, because Chinese contractors are unwilling to break their relationship with employers, the letters usually describe the events or situations without using the word "claim," and the letters usually will not be titled as "notice of claim" or "notice of intent of claim." Generally speaking, if contractors only describe the event or situations without clearly making claims on compensation, then such letters may likely not be considered as notice of claim, subject to the prevailing circumstances. Some scholars bring the concept of "presumable notice" which considers meeting minutes, revisions of schedules or on-site construction logs that contain descriptions of claim events or contractor's right of claim as valid notice of claim.[213] However, under 2017 FIDIC Contract Conditions, a valid notice must describe the claim event itself and state the specific reference to the contract clause. This new rule intends to enhance transparency and to avoid situations where parties use "informal" notice (such as reference letters or meeting minutes) as notice of claim to circumvent the statute of limitation.[214] Therefore, "presumable notice" should be applied with caution in case engineers or employers refuse to acknowledge "informal" notice.

[4]   Beware of Special Requirements in the Contract

In current international construction engineering practice, some employers directly make detailed provisions on the form and content of a qualified notice of claim notice in the contract. One example is to explicitly require for the notice to be accompanied by an account of the claim event and the relevant supporting evidence. This places higher demand on the contractor's project management ability and risk prevention and control awareness. If the Chinese contractor is unable to exclude these additional requirements through negotiation, then it must see to it that the notice of claim was timely sent after the occurrence of the claim event, so as not to lose its substantive rights. In a case provided by the ICC for this research project, the Chinese contractor failed to submit a qualified notice of claim in accordance with the contract. As a result, it lost its rights to rely on the fact that the employer had prevented the contractor from entering the site on time and that additional customs clearance fees, due to the employer's conduct.

In sum, Chinese contractors are recommended to issue a letter titled "notice of claim" or "notice of intent of claim" after becoming aware of the claim events in order to avoid disputes over whether the letter constitutes a notice of claim and the contractor's intent as to claiming for such events or not. At the same time, apart from

---

212. *Ibid.*
213. Zhang Mingfeng, "Remedies on Statue of Limitation in International Constructions", International Construction and Labor Services, 1st issue 2015.
214. Claim, Dispute and Arbitration under the New 2017 FIDIC Contract Conditions, published on 14 November 2017 at CCOIC, available at: http://www.ccpit.org/Contents/Channel_3466/2017/1114/912885/content_912885.htm.

describing the claim event, the notice should also set out the specific request of claim and the contract clause it relies on. Also, it is recommended to include wordings such as "contractor shall reserve the right of claim" or "this notice of claim is made in accordance with Article 20.1 of the FIDIC Contract Conditions."

CHAPTER 5

Internal Risks of Contractors

External risks are sometimes caused by internal risks when Chinese contractors carry on construction projects overseas. In this chapter, we're trying to analyze contractor's internal risks and give some advice from the perspective of management decision-making and contractors' compliance management.

§5.01 RISKS OF MANAGEMENT DECISION

"Risks of Decision" in this report means those risks which are difficult to be prevented by regular methods. Once this kind of risks eventuate severe crises and serious consequences are likely to follow.

At the background of "the Belt and Road," there are many different ways to confirm the scope and categories of "Risks of Decision." According to summaries and reflection of past empirical cases in this area, we regard that the top four "Risks of Decision" which should be of concern to management decision-makers are: risks of National Markets' Selection; risks of Dealing with Relations between Political Interests and Marketing Interests; risks of Operating Cross-Profession Projects; risks of General Contract Capacity Developing Path.

[A]   Risks of National Markets' Selection

First, Chinese enterprises' decision-makers should keep a rational understanding of target countries' risks before they choose to enter a country's market. The "National Risk Analysis Report" and "Global Investment Risk Analysis Report" published annually by China Export & Credit Insurance Corporation are effective guidelines for Chinese enterprises to identify and avoid national risks. This part in the report adopt countries along "the Belt and Road" and "six major international economic corridors" as objects of analysis, in an attempt to raise an easy method to recognize a target country's national risk from the perspective of judicial remedy. We can judge a target country's national risks through finding out information about three indexes measured by the "barometers" of international relations: whether the country is a member of "the New York Convention" (1958); whether the country is a member of "the Washington Convention" (1965); and whether the country signed a bilateral investment protection agreement with China.

In fact, these three "barometers" are basic aspects of Legal Environment Due Diligence for a Host Country which is important in the making reasonable decisions by Chinese enterprises' decision-makers.

[1]   About "the New York Convention" (1958)

"The New York Convention on the Recognition and Enforcement of Foreign Arbitral Awards" is the formal name of "the New York Convention." Accordance with the Convention, each contracting state shall recognize arbitral awards made by any other contracting states as binding and enforce them. Until now, there are 159 countries participating in "the New York Convention" including China.[215]

Considering the important status and effect of "the New York Convention" in the field of international commercial arbitration, we can say that whether the target country is a member of the Convention or not is a basic condition to forming a judgment on whether the country would accept the international market's game rules, for example, international commercial arbitration. The target country not being a contracting state of "the New York Convention" may preclude recourse to international commercial arbitration. This "structural risk" deserves to be considered seriously by any foreign enterprises including Chinese enterprises.

For example, we found out a Chinese contractor signed a contract to construct an industrial product line in Pakistan and parties agreed to adopt Dubai as contractual arbitration place at the end of 2004. Pakistan, where the project was located, signed to an accession of "the New York Convention" at 1958. However, the Convention was not certified in Pakistan until 2005. Further, the place of the arbitration, UAE, had no participation in the Convention until 2006. So the place of the arbitration and the country where main property was located were not valid members of "the New York Convention" when the contract was signed. The Chinese contractor's oversight of this risk would have resulted in severe consequences if the disputes arose in the early part of the project. Fortunately, disputes only arose in 2008 when the country where the project was located had already became a member of "the New York Convention," avoiding fatal deficiencies in the agreed dispute resolution process.

According to this report's statistics about the situation of whether each country along "the Belt and Road" and along the "six major international economic corridors" become a "the New York Convention" member or not, we find the nations who have not join in the Convention until now, including: East Timor (11 countries in Southeast Asia), Maldives (seven countries in South Asia), Turkmenistan (six countries in Central

---

215. The 158th member of "the New York Convention" is Sudan in March 26, 2018.

Asia), Iraq, Yemen (18 countries in West Asia), we will call these countries "5 non-members of 'the New York Convention'" below.

Chinese enterprises' decision-makers should consider the structural risks that "5 non-members of 'the New York Convention'" have yet to join the Convention, and consider the design of alternative plans to resolve disputes under multilateral or bilateral legal constraints. The dispute resolution process, which is the "last line of defense" for risk management of overseas projects, should be properly addressed in advance.

[2]   About "the Washington Convention" (1965)

The "Convention on the Settlement of Investment Disputes between States and Nationals of Other States" is the formal name of "the Washington Convention" (1965), which is established by International Bank for Reconstruction and Development (World Bank). The Convention aims to provide convenience of mediation and arbitration of investment disputes between members of the Convention and nationals from the other contractual states, and hopes to eliminate political interference and diplomatic interference, with the view of improving the investment atmosphere.

While the applicability of "the New York Convention" (1958) in the target countries is a reflection of whether the target country in question accepts the basic game rules in the international commercial market, the applicability of "the Washington Convention" (1965) in the relevant target country is more of a reflection of the level of protection of foreign investor's interests afforded by a target country's government. Currently, there are 161 countries which have joined "the Washington Convention" (1965) including China, but there are eight countries who participate in the Convention but have yet to certify it (contain three countries along the "the Belt and Road" —Russia, Kyrgyzstan and Thailand).

Projects under initiative of "the Belt and Road" mainly are energy and transportation infrastructure construction and these kind of projects are always executed based on many kinds of Public-Private Partnership (PPP) modes. In these circumstances, Chinese enterprises often need to negotiate with the target country's government as an investor. The importance of "the Washington Convention" (1965) in protecting the interests of Chinese enterprises in overseas investment projects is of greater significance in light of the foregoing. If the target country is not a member of "the Washington Convention," the Chinese enterprises' interests would not be sufficiently protected by the system of investment disputes resolution under "the Washington Convention."

According to this report's statistics about the situation of whether each country along "the Belt and Road" and along the "six major international economic corridors" is a "the Washington Convention" member or not, the countries which have not joined the Convention include the following: Thailand, Laos, Myanmar (11 countries in Southeast Asia), Bhutan, India, Maldives (7 countries in South Asia), Kyrgyzstan, Tajikistan (6 countries in Central Asia), Iran, Palestine (18 countries in West Asia), Poland (16 countries in Central and Eastern Europe), Russia (4 countries of the

Commonwealth of Independent States), we will call these countries "12 non-members of 'the Washington Convention'" below.

In summary, Chinese enterprises should evaluate the structural risk relating to whether the target country is a member of "the Washington Convention" before they enter the country's market.

[3]   Sino-Foreign Bilateral Investment Protection Agreement

We mentioned that "the New York Convention" and "the Washington Convention" are "barometers" that reflect a target country's overall international relations. By contrast, a Sino-foreign bilateral investment protection agreement is a barometer which can reflect whether the economic and trade cooperation between a target country and China is normal.

According to this report's statistics of countries along "the Belt and Road" and along the "six major international economic corridors," we find that a significant number of countries have not signed a bilateral investment protection agreement, including: East Timor, Maldives, Kyrgyzstan, Afghanistan, Iraq, Palestine, Montenegro, we will call them "7 non-bilateral investment protection agreement countries."

These three kinds of barometers form the basis for Chinese enterprises' decision-makers overall identification of the target country's national risk level and would guide reasonable decision-making. If a target does not fulfill the three conditions above, the decision-makers should be cautious and design plans of preventing risks in advance.

For example, before the outbreak of the civil war in Libya in 2011, there was almost no evaluation agency who added Libya to the list of countries with high risk. In fact, Libya is neither a member of "the New York Convention" (1958) nor a member of "the Washington Convention" (1965), and Libya does not have a bilateral investment protection agreement with China. Based on these three conditions, the structural risk of Libya, especially the risk of breaking "the last line of defense" i.e., the path of judicial relief, does indeed exist.

After the outbreak of the civil war in Libya, a large scale of Chinese companies with large number of engineering contracting projects in the country were forced to withdraw with huge losses. Except for a minority of these Chinese enterprises which recovered part of the loss by insuring export credit insurance, most of them realized that they nearly did not have any means to obtain effective international legal remedies. The reason of that is Libya is a country who is neither a member of "the New York Convention" (1958) nor a member of "the Washington Convention" (1965), and it has not signed a bilateral investment protection agreement with China.

Table 5.1   Summary of Situation about Countries along "the Belt and Road" and along the "Six Major International Economic Corridors" Joining Conventions and Signing Bilateral Investment Protection Agreement

	Countries along "the Belt and Road"		
Country	*The New York Convention*	*The Washington Convention*	*Bilateral Investment Protection Agreement*
11 Countries in Southeast Asia			
Indonesia	√	√	√
Malaysia	√	√	√
The Philippines	√	√	√
Singapore	√	√	√
Thailand	√	o	√
Brunei	√	√	o
Vietnam	√	—	√
Laos	√	—	√
Myanmar	√	—	√
Cambodia	√	√	√
East Timor	—	√	—
7 Countries in South Asia			
Nepal	√	√	—
Bhutan	√	—	—
India	√	—	√
Pakistan	√	√	√
Bangladesh	√	√	√
Sri Lanka	√	√	√
Maldives	—	—	—
6 Countries in Central Asia			
That Central Asian Country	√	√	√
Turkmenistan	—	√	√
Kyrgyzstan.	√	o	—
Uzbekistan	√	√	√
Tajikistan	√	—	√
Afghanistan	√	√	—

Countries along "the Belt and Road"			
Country	The New York Convention	The Washington Convention	Bilateral Investment Protection Agreement
18 Countries in West Asia			
Iran	√	—	√
Iraq	—	√	—
Georgia	√	√	√
Armenia	√	√	√
Azerbaijan	√	√	√
Turkey	√	√	√
Syria	√	√	√
Jordan	√	√	o
Israel	√	√	√
Palestine	√	—	—
Saudi Arabia	√	√	√
Bahrain	√	√	√
Qatar	√	√	√
Yemen	—	√	√
Oman	√	√	√
UAE	√	√	√
Kuwait	√	√	√
Lebanon	√	√	√
16 Countries in Central and Eastern Europe			
Albania	√	√	√
Bosnia and Herzegovina	√	√	√
Bulgaria	√	√	√
Croatia	√	√	√
Czech Republic	√	√	√
Estonia	√	√	√
Hungary	√	√	√
Latvia	√	√	√
Lithuania	√	√	√
Macedonia	√	√	√
Montenegro	√	√	—
Romania	√	√	√
Poland	√	—	√
Serbia	√	√	√

Countries along "the Belt and Road"			
Country	The New York Convention	The Washington Convention	Bilateral Investment Protection Agreement
Slovakia	√	√	√
Slovenia	√	√	√

4 Countries of the Commonwealth of Independent States

Russia	√	o	√
Belarus	√	√	√
Ukraine	√	√	√
Moldova	√	√	√

Mongolia

Mongolia	√	√	√

Egypt

Egypt	√	√	√

Countries Long the "Six Major International Economic Corridors"			
Country	The New York Convention	The Washington Convention	Bilateral Investment Protection Agreement

China-Mongolia-Russia Economic Cooperation Corridor

Mongolia	√	√	√
Russia	√	o	√

New Eurasian Continental Bridge

That Central Asian Country	√	√	√
Uzbekistan	√	√	√
Russia	√	o	√
Belarus	√	√	√
Poland	√	—	√
Ukraine	√	√	√
Slovakia	√	√	√
Hungary	√	√	√
Kyrgyzstan	√	o	—
Turkmenistan	—	√	√

Countries Long the "Six Major International Economic Corridors"			
Country	The New York Convention	The Washington Convention	Bilateral Investment Protection Agreement
Azerbaijan	√	√	√
Georgia	√	√	√
Bulgaria	√	√	√
Romania	√	√	√
Hungary	√	√	√
Iran	√	—	√
Turkey	√	√	√
Czech republic	√	√	√
Austria	√	√	√
Switzerland	√	√	√
Germany	√	√	√
France	√	√	√
Belgium	√	√	√
Italy	√	√	√
England	√	√	√

China-Central Asia-West Asia Economic Corridor

That Central Asian Country	√	√	√
Kyrgyzstan	√	o	—
Tajikistan	√	—	√
Uzbekistan	√	√	√
Turkmenistan	—	√	√
Iran	√	—	√
Turkey	√	√	√

China-Indochina Economic Corridor

Vietnam	√	—	√
Laos	√	—	√
Cambodia	√	√	√
Thailand	√	o	√
Malaysia	√	√	√
Singapore	√	√	√

Countries Long the "Six Major International Economic Corridors"			
Country	The New York Convention	The Washington Convention	Bilateral Investment Protection Agreement
China-Bargain Economic Corridor			
Pakistan	√	√	√
Meng Zhong-Indian-Myanmar Economic Corridor			
Myanmar	√	—	√
India	√	—	√
Bangladesh	√	√	√

Note:

"√" are countries that have signed up and taken effect;

"o" are countries that have signed but have not taken effect;

"—" are countries that have not signed.

Description:

Updated time for above information is September 7, 2018.

The internet site of conventions and bilateral investment protection agreement mentioned above:

The New York Convention

http://www.uncitral.org/uncitral/zh/uncitral_texts/arbitration/NYConvention_status.html.

The Washington Convention

https://icsid.worldbank.org/en/Pages/about/Database-of-Member-States.aspx.

Bilateral investment protection agreement with China.

https://investmentpolicyhubold.unctad.org/IIA/CountryBits/42#iiaInnerMenu.

[B] Risks of Dealing with Relations Between Political Interests and Marketing Interests

Projects about "the Belt and Road" always have some connection with the market and politics. The connection with market dictates that the project should be carried out under the commercial game rules by obeying contracts and laws. Decision-makers of Chinese enterprises need to pursue the market interests while considering how to satisfy any political interests.

Market interests and political interests may complement each other but can sometimes be conflicting. It should be an innate advantage for Chinese companies to participate in the initiative of "the Belt and Road" given its strong political support. However, in the process, we should balance market interests and political interests. Every project must be evaluated on its commercial merits before it is undertaken. Chinese companies should not offer a low price with low-risk margins only because a project is politically desirable. Careful project evaluation, including thorough risk assessment and cost-estimating, must always be made, irrespective of any political interests.

In the survey, we found that China signed a "Cooperation Agreement on Strengthening Infrastructure Construction" with a West Asia country's government in 2008. The first big transport infrastructure project undertaken pursuant to this agreement was given attention by these two countries' governments as the first intergovernmental cooperation project. The project also had a strong political connection. In this project, the Chinese contractor adopted PPP mode to construct. During the process of this project, the employer from where the project located made a serious interference to Chinese company's right of design choice, which caused a large number of problems like design changes and serious cost overrun. In response, the Chinese contractor formed a team of consultants with extensive experience in international engineering contract management and raised claims to the employer. The employer who was well aware of their unreasonable conduct complained directly to Chinese government's relevant department about Chinese contractor instead of discussing the same with the Chinese contractor in accordance with game rules of the market. Under the pressure of diplomacy and politics, the Chinese enterprise's management had to invest a large number of resources to carry out large-scale urgent works. Although the project was finished eventually, the Chinese enterprise suffered a huge number of economic losses and the management had to be in a difficult situation.

In fact, there are many cases like the above example, and there is a trend formed in recent years of many enterprises finding themselves in a dilemma between market and political interests. The most driving factor is that more and more foreign governments and employers recognize that Chinese contractors are typically bonded by political interests which differentiates them from other nations in the world. As a result, foreign governments are able to advance their interests through political channels instead of market channels. It is important for Chinese contractors to establish a reputation in the international markets that they act as independent and professional business enterprises and that they are not driven by political interests.

Under the background of "the Belt and Road," projects always have more significant connections with politics. As such, there is an enhanced importance for the Chinese enterprises to design plans to address this kind of special risks in advance to strike a balance between political interests and market interests. This becomes especially pertinent when any event which could seriously interfere with the enterprise's interests, such as major changes or claims, take place. If the enterprise is a listed company, it should work within the framework of legal functions of the securities trading market, independent directors and other project stakeholders to ensure strict compliance with the relevant legal systems of listed companies. If the enterprise is a non-listed company, it should take an independent legal expert's opinion on the basis of any board decision based on the Company Law.

[C]   Risks of Operating Cross-Profession Projects

Qualification level licensing system is a basic system for accessing the construction market in China. Although there are many disadvantages in operating this system, the system actually solves the problem of specialized division. In most countries, conditions of market access usually exist but they are not always as strict as those in China. This creates an opportunity for Chinese contractors to operate cross-profession projects overseas.

Chinese overseas EPC general contractors currently fall within four main categories: commercial general contractors, construction general contractors, design general contractors and manufacturing general contractors.

Given that a commercial general contractor is always taking business and financing capabilities as the core competitiveness, its dependence on its own profession is relatively low. Therefore, a commercial general contractor's operation of cross-profession projects is usually easier than the others. The typical example of a case of failure is that of Chinese provincial international economic cooperate corporation (a listed company) constructing a hydropower project in Africa. The company is one of the earliest provincial companies in China who became a listed company and continued to enter the first 225 of U.S. ENR for many years. The company was running in East Africa for 14 years starting from the provision financial assistance for an African country's gym and have gained economic benefits in East Africa. When their projects in East Africa were almost finished, the company's management fought for the hydropower project and wanted to get its follow-up projects. This company's main business experience was focused on building construction and road construction and the company lacked experience in constructing a hydropower project. However, its management was unreasonably confident because they had not suffered have any losses in East Africa at that time. As a result of the absence of hydropower constructing experience and the lack of sufficient knowledge, the project's design requirement is relatively high with a cross-use of many standards, which contain some American standards like ASTM and General Services Administration (GSA) and some Canadian standards, even including some process requirements which were in the experimental stage in Western countries. The company did not conduct detailed research about the host country's material supply and processing capacity and accepted some difficult technical requirements. During the process, the high technical standards caused rough communication between western supervising engineer and the Chinese enterprise which intensify conflicts. There was a shortage of project managers as none of them could cover management experience, professional knowledge and language capability. The chief engineer was replaced for five times. The amount of labor required for the project increased rapidly beyond the estimated amount. Further, notwithstanding that labor was taken from 91 different entities few of them had hydropower professional knowledge, with a larger number of them having low technical capabilities. The project was eventually terminated by the employer due to serious delays in the progress, and the performance guarantee for a significant sum was confiscated. The company suffered direct losses of more than RMB 200 million and other indirect losses.

The construction contractor's risk of operating cross-profession projects is bigger. The more professional expertise required, the stricter conditions should be imposed for its cross-profession projects. There are many substantive obstacles in aspects of construction technology, design capacity resource reserve, supply chain resource reserve, professional engineering management system, etc. For example, a Chinese international contractor mainly operates energy and transportation infrastructure, which usually operates in African market. The company decided to operate a cross-profession sewage collection project for entering the high-end market in the Gulf. The project became their first project in Middle East market and the first big sewage collection project awarded to an overseas contractor. Given the shortage of experience in constructing these kind of projects, serious insufficiency of management personnel, technical personnel and workers, the company could not satisfy objective requirements of these kind of projects. This was exacerbated by the difficulty in communication and conflict relating to design responsibility interface, completion acceptance between the contractor, the employer and the consulting engineers, which caused time delay and increased costs. Another example is a Chinese international contractor who has a leading position in the area of building construction trying to construct a large-scale petroleum refining project for their first time. Although the contractor has much reliable experience in civil engineering installation, it apparently lacked resource reserve in all aspects of complex petroleum refining equipment and process. This kind of structural defect cannot be resolved by professional subcontracting. Fortunately, the decision-makers in this company did not rush into the field and instead pursued the contract with a conscious mind.

There are relatively few cases in which the design general contractor operate cross-profession projects. However, with the downturn and fierce competition in the international market in recent years, design contractors have more incentive to operate cross-profession projects. Compared with constructing contractors, design contractors are more dependent on their own profession, such that the risks of operate cross-profession projects are higher to them. There is an example of a Chinese contractor not having sufficient experience in the area of energy and industrial engineering and having to become extremely dependent on its professional design subcontractor such that it lacked effective control. This was in relation to a water supply project with a low contract price in a Central Asian country. During the operation, the company met a series of difficulties in supply resources and construction organization management, which caused the progress to be seriously delayed. In the end, the project became the company's only project which leads to a serious loss.

Among the above four types of enterprises, instances of manufacturing contractors operating cross-profession projects are relatively uncommon. An example includes a Chinese contractor who is a leader in the area of port machinery. The management decided to enter the offshore wind power area. Unfortunately, the enterprise faced a huge lawsuit because of quality defects in an overseas offshore wind power project.

216

As stated above, careful project evaluation, including thorough risk assessment and cost-estimating, must always be made, irrespective of the company size and previous experience. Every project is unique and before bidding on a project, the contractor must always ensure that it does not only have the overall strength and resources but the special expertise in the relevant technical field. Although special expertise can often be obtained through subcontractors, the Chinese contractor must have itself the sufficient expertise in the relevant field in order to be able to select the right subcontractors and to manage and supervise them.

[D] Risks of EPC Capacity Developing Path

Risks of operating cross-profession projects should be emphasized by the management. For the enterprises who just entered or be ready to enter the "the Belt and Road" market, decision-makers need to design an EPC capacity developing path according to the actual condition at the start of overseas business.

[1] *Cultivate an International Talent Team by Professional Subcontracting*

For any international contractor, how to cultivate a talent team is always a main challenge. Seizing the main challenge will make sure the enterprise keeping a correct direction from the start.

Considering this principle, if enterprises' decision-makers could make medium or long-term strategic planning rather than be limited to short-term interests, we recommend enterprises getting involved in overseas business by starting as a professional subcontractor. Operating professional subcontract projects would help Chinese enterprises control the risks into a limited scope by the cooperation with Chinese contractors who have more overseas experience or international contractor with more mature management systems. The most important consideration is for the enterprise to cultivate a group of overseas project management talents with core competitiveness. If the enterprise does not have the requisite talent, entering the general contract market is likely to result in failure which will not only causing significant losses but also strike a fatal blow to the overseas development strategy.

For example, a Chinese contractor earned a good reputation by constructing a series of landmark projects with international influence in China. However, at the start of their overseas development strategy's execution, the management did not realize the complexity of international projects, decided to enter general contract market directly. The contractor bidded for a project of capital airport terminal construction situated in West Asia. Because of the absence of commercial staff, technicians and managers, the project was delayed and caused a serious cost overrun. The contract was eventually terminated by the employer, and the performance guarantee of a significant sum was confiscated.

[2]   Joint Venture Contracting

The scale of projects is getting bigger and bigger under initiative of "Belt and Road." Generally, project size is directly proportional to risk level. In this circumstance, individual general contract mode may be equivalent to "putting all eggs in the same basket," which is undesirable for an enterprise seeking to diversify its risk portfolio. If enterprises could use the joint venture mode and operate an overseas project together with another entity, the risks would be spread and a win-win outcome may be achieved by members of the joint venture. Enterprises should design a reasonable and scientific joint venture mode, considering the interior legal risks of relationship of the joint venture. Under initiative of "the Belt and Road," energy and transportation infrastructure projects account for a large proportion of all overseas construction projects. Traffic infrastructure projects such as highways have the characteristics of linear engineering, and it is easier to divide the tenders. It creates objectively favorable conditions for the formation of joint ventures between similar contractors. The energy infrastructure projects such as power stations have the characteristics of point engineering, and the connection between design, procurement, construction and trial operation is relatively close, which makes it more suitable for professional contractors to form a joint venture.

[3]   Micro-Investment and Micro-Financing Promote General Contracting

Recently, with the intensified competition in the international construction market, the environment of investment and financing have changed. More and more Chinese contractors have started to adopt the use of micro-investment and micro-financing to promote general contracting, for conducting and developing overseas operations.

A Chinese contractor who is one of the earliest central state-owned enterprises entered the overseas engineering market. The company promoted general contracting work of a large-scale tourism development project by adopting the use of micro-investment and micro-financing to promote general contracting for expanding their overseas market. But the Chinese contractor did not assess risks of the project and major shareholders including the "investor" and did not design the minority shareholder's decision-making rights in relation to major matters of the employer's project company scientifically. Further, the contractor did not realize the balance of rights and obligations between financing bank, major shareholder and the contractor. Eventually, the project ended with the employer's bankruptcy which was caused by the employer's insufficient capacity to operate the project and a Chinese financing bank was forced to accept the project.

This case sounded the alarm for the decision-makers of the enterprise that has already started or is about to start small investment to promote the general contracting. Investment and contracting have their own logic. If the logic of investment is to promote general contracting, then it is necessary to improve the resource reserves of enterprise investment, especially the scientific design of the relationship between small shareholders and general contractors to achieve a balance of interests. Otherwise, not only the inherent risks of general contracting cannot be effectively controlled, but the investment risk is also further increased.

Management's decision is the key to determining the direction and destiny of the company, and the structural risks of the above four aspects must be fully considered in the decision-making process. "the Belt and Road" is generally good to enterprises, but a company cannot be relaxed and burden the risk prevention and control on the government, which is not objective and unrealistic.

§5.02 COMPLIANCE RISK

Compliance refers to the requirements for enterprises and their staff to abide by laws, regulations and conventions of China and the host country, obeying the internal rules, regulations and enterprise's self-regulation rules. Further, compliance means enterprises and their staff should comply with industry-recognized professional ethics and code of conduct requirements.

Effective compliance is essential for the overseas operations of Chinese companies in order to realize their corporate development strategies and participate in the "the Belt and Road" construction. It is also essential for promoting mutual benefit and reaching a consequence of win-win between China and the other countries of the world. Strengthening the awareness of compliance management is the prerequisite for the company's overseas operations to be stable and far-reaching.

[A] Present Situation and Development Trend of Domestic and Foreign Compliance Supervision

In recent years, with the implementation of China's "the Belt and Road" policy, more and more Chinese enterprises have begun to go abroad and undertake overseas projects. However, due to unfamiliarity with the international compliance and supervision environment, incidents in which Chinese companies have been punished by multilateral development banks or local governments have occurred, and Chinese companies suffered considerable losses. According to statistics, until February 23, 2018, a total of about 120 Chinese companies (statistics including its subsidiaries) and six individuals listed in the Ineligible Firms & Individuals of fraud and corruption by the World Bank. In these enterprises, there are 75 state-owned enterprises at least. Moreover, Chinese companies listed in the anti-fraud and corruption sanctions list by the World Bank have increased per year recently, and the duration for sanction periods has also increased, the maximum of which is up to 10 years.

There are five potential sanctions under the World Bank combating anti-corruption mechanism: debarment, debarment with conditional release, conditional non debarment, restitution and reprimand. Debarment renders an entity ineligible, either indefinitely or for a stated period, to be awarded or benefit from a new bank-financed contract, be a nominated subcontractor or supplier in a bank-financed contract, receive the proceeds of bank financing or otherwise participate in the preparation or implementation of a bank-financed project. Debarment with conditional release has the same effect as fixed-term debarment but ends only if the entity fulfills stated remedial, preventive or other conditions for release from sanction. Restitution requires the entity to make financial or other restitution to the affected World Bank Group (WBG) Borrower or some other entity. A reprimand comes in the form of a letter admonishing the entity for its misconduct.

There are also sanctions imposed by multiple multilateral development banks and international agencies, which has caused huge losses to the sanctioned companies. The sanctions are often happened because of fraud and corruption incidents caused by imperfect internal corporate compliance regulatory systems.

From the perspective of governments around the world, regulation for fraud and corruption has also been strengthened. The countries with traditionally strong regulatory compliance such as the U.S. and some Western countries in Europe, continue to implement strong regulatory policies, and compliance regulation in some emerging countries is becoming stricter. For example, Brazil reached 183 international anti-corruption cooperation agreements with dozens of countries and initiated 1,765 investigation procedures from 2014 to 2017. Among them, the largest builder in Brazil, Odebrecht, has been investigated by many governments for bribery in many projects. The company has already paid a fine of USD 2.6 billion to Brazilian, Swiss and U.S. authorities. Now it is negotiating a plea agreement with regulators in other countries, including Argentina, Chile, Colombia, Ecuador, Mexico, Peru, the Dominican Republic, Venezuela, Panama and Portugal.

The State-owned Assets Supervision and Administration Commission of China issued policy documents including "Opinions on the Construction of State-Owned Enterprises under the Rule of Law," which emphasis on legal compliance operations and strengthening corporate compliance responsibilities in December 2015. More and more state-owned enterprises have begun to establish or improve their internal compliance systems from 2016.

It could be seen that no matter domestic or foreign, integrity and compliance have become the basic requirements for enterprises around the world. The supervision of international organizations, countries and industry organizations will become stricter and stricter.

[B]   "Three Levels" in the Construction of Compliance System and Practical Suggestions

[1]   *The First Level in Construction of Compliance System: Institutional Deficiency and External Barriers in the Compliance Department*

Before embarking on the establishment and implementation of a specific compliance system, the first thing a company needs to do is to fix institutional deficiencies and external barriers of the compliance department. This is the first level of realizing a proper compliance system.

[a] *Institutional Deficiencies of the Compliance Department*

Compliance departments need to operate the compliance system throughout the company and supervise the work of company's business department. As compared to the traditional legal department, the compliance department needs more staff in the organizational structure. However, Chinese enterprises typically underestimate the amount of compliance work which results in a lack of professional personnel who have experience to form a compliance department. In addition, the financial investments in Chinese companies' compliance department are not comparable to that of advanced international companies. In this context, the shortage of compliance personnel is inevitable.

In practice, many enterprises have adopted the method of forming a compliance department by one or two persons with legal experience, and in some enterprises, compliance personnel have been transferred from various departments of the company. These compliance personnel may come from the financial department, even the business department, and some of them take part in the compliance work while keeping their original job scope. These kind of solutions may be effective for a short period, but do not meet the needs of corporate compliance work in a substantial enterprise in the long term. The short-term solution cannot fully implement the aim of forming a fully effective corporate compliance system. Enterprises should establish a specialized, professional compliance department as soon as possible.

[b] *External Barriers of the Compliance Department*

Differing from the other departments, the compliance department will often be considered as a "trouble maker" by other departments' staff. For example, "Compliance in China" network released a report called "China Compliance Management Survey Report (2017)" in early 2018 which states that 22% of the compliance officers believe the biggest difficulty is failure of cooperation with business departments.

In this regard, our recommendation is to improve the status of the compliance department of the company. First, management in the company should pay attention to the compliance work, giving the compliance department and the responsible person a higher management level. Second, the importance of compliance work should be promoted within the company, for example, implementing typical cases' training to improve staff's awareness of compliance at all levels of the enterprise.

[2] **The Second Level in Construction of Compliance System Grasp the Main Risk Points**

After the establishment of compliance department, enterprises should set out their compliance rules. In this process, the compliance department should start to sort out the company's business and find the main risk points in the company's business. According to our research, compared to foreign companies, common risk points for

Chinese engineering companies include corruption risks, agent risks, gift and entertainment risks, bidding risks, cash payment risks, contract risks, etc. We will analyze the agent risks and bidding risks briefly here.

During the process of conduct business overseas, Chinese enterprises often hire local third-party consultants and commercial agents, it is a common approach to develop markets. Although in most of countries, commercial agents are not illegal and in some Middle Eastern countries commercial agents are protected by special legislation, there are also commercial agents who often become intermediaries who help companies pay bribes or seek illegitimate interests. This is an important risk to Chinese engineering enterprises in the course of their overseas business operation.

Conducting due diligence on the third parties and avoiding any cooperation with high-risk third parties is an effective measure to prevent the risks of agents. During the process of due diligence, it is important to investigate high-risk signals. For example, it is important to consider whether the third party has some connection with government officers, whether they asked for excessive compensation, whether they can provide evidence of the specific services they are engaged to provide, and whether they have a record of corruption.

Risks in the bidding process and any relative behavior during the bidding process is always scrutinized by international regulatory agency, especially multilateral development banks. In addition, Chinese engineering companies should also pay special attention to ensuring the truthfulness, accuracy and completeness of the tender documents. According to our research, some Chinese engineering enterprises declare the performance of their affiliates or subsidiaries for bidding. This is likely to cause penalties by multilateral development banks. Further, if the enterprises hire local agents in the bidding process, they should ensure complete disclosure of this fact.

[3]   The Third Level in Construction of Compliance System: Implementation and Enforcement

After the establishment of the compliance department and the compliance rules, the process comes to the third stage, which is the implementation and enforcement of compliance rules.

[a]   Tests of Compliance Rules' Implementation

Currently, many large-scale Chinese corporations have established multi-dimensional, multi-layered systems. As such, in addition to regular compliance work which is carried out by compliance staff in accordance with compliance rules, compliance departments must also supervise compliance work of various companies in the corporation. The aim is to understand the implementation of compliance work and continuously improve the company's compliance system.

The common method to test a company's compliance system is compliance examination, which is performed through reviewing documents, interviewing personnel, investigating sites, unscheduled examinations and opening reporting channels.

Contents of the examination include the personnel of the company under review, the financial and project status, the implementation of the compliance system, the configuration of the compliance personnel of the company under review, the status of compliance consultation records, the occurrence and handling of violations, and the reduction in the frequency and severity of violations.

When a multilateral development bank considers whether to lift sanctions against a company, it is not sufficient that the company's compliance system and compliance department have been established. The implementation of the compliance system in the enterprise is also an aspect of the review. And an internal corporate compliance examination is the most important and direct way to verify that the compliance system is implemented, and is an integral part of the compliance system.

[b] Propaganda of Enterprises' Culture

Chinese enterprises should further establish the values of credit management and compliance management and the corporate compliance culture. Through internal training or external training, the company should inform all employees of the importance of compliance work that how valuable it is to the company's long-term development. This helps the company establishing a corporate culture that everyone should operate legally and compliantly, which are agreed from the management to general employees.

In recent years, more and more Chinese companies who "go out" have faced the test of the international compliance system. Chinese enterprises have encountered many obstacles in the process of establishing a compliance system, but they have also achieved certain results.

For example, in the process of an African engineering project operated by a Chinese state-owned enterprise and its subsidiaries, the African Development Bank (AFDB) as an investor of the project initiated the investigation procedure and proposed sanctions. This had the effect that the enterprise could not take part in any projects which are invested by AFDB while the sanction remains in place. Further, as a result of cross-institutional linkages, sanctions agreement were reached between several multilateral development banks in 2010. If the company is sanctioned by AFDB, it will automatically enter the blacklist of several other multilateral development banks.

Subsequently, the state-owned enterprise, with the assistance of external lawyers, negotiated with AFDB and reached a settlement agreement, which significantly reduced the amount of fines and the time for punishment. In the two-year period, the company established a compliance system that complies with international standards for the entire corporation's overseas business sector and obtained recognition of AFDB. Finally, the sanctions were released in advance.

This is the first example of a Chinese company establishing and operating a compliance system which satisfies the standard of a multilateral development bank through conducting compliance surveys and by cooperating with the multilateral development bank. Officials at World Bank also expressed their appreciation for the fact that the early release of the state-owned enterprise indicates that it has made significant progress in anti-corruption compliance.

A similar case is the sanction by World Bank of Hunan Construction Engineering Group in 2013. After the sanction was imposed, the corporation set out the establishment and enforcement of the interior compliance system. Eventually, Hunan Construction Engineering Group accepted a notification from World Bank about releasing their sanction.

We believe that Chinese enterprises could have a longer and farther path in the way of "the Belt and Road" and "Go out" after establishment of compliance system. "The Belt and Road" advocated by China will also promote development of international cooperation about anti-corruption and compliance.

§5.03   INTERNAL ORGANIZATIONAL MANAGEMENT AND AWARENESS OF RISKS

[A]   Risks of Capacity of Managing Contracts

As compared to the environment of domestic engineering market, international engineering is limited by many different factors such as languages, habits and the culture. In the international engineering market, the parties should pay more attention to the contract and rely on the contract more. To Chinese contractors, one of progress made from decades of development of construction expertise is that more and more enterprises can focus more on the development of contract management capabilities. However, we should be consciously aware that although the progress is in place, the lack of contract management capability is still a relatively common phenomenon, which fundamentally restricts the ability of Chinese contractors to resist risks.

This is mainly reflected in the aspects set out below.

First, there is insufficient awareness of the international engineering contract. This takes the form of the lack of careful evaluation of contract documents before tender which results in the quotation not being fully and accurately reflected in the contract terms, ignorance of contract documents, and implementing a project based on the contractors' own practices and one-sided understanding which may not be consistent with the contract.

Second, there is poor ability in preparing and updating schedules. Preparing and updating schedules is not only a necessary prerequisite to proper management of the schedule but also a necessary basis to claim for delay and for expenses related to the delay. However, due to the absence of domestic engineering management in the education system and in practice, Chinese contractors generally lack the ability to prepare and update schedules in accordance with international good practices.

Third, the absence of contemporaneous records. Records, especially contemporaneous records, always play an important role in international engineering contract management, claims and dispute resolution practices. However, constrained by work habits and the lack of legal awareness, Chinese contractors' record keeping practices fall short.

Investments in the bidding phase, project preparation and contract management are often seen as investments in "administration" or "bureaucracy." contractors often spend much too little time and money on these areas and spend most of their focus on the actual construction activities. However, a common feature of successful projects is that a lot of resources have been spent on the front-end work (cost-estimating, risk analysis, preliminary design, etc.) and on the contract management.

[B] Risks of Stereotyped Thinking Pattern and Empiricism

The lessons Chinese contractors learned in overseas failed projects are always similar. The "Bodies went out, brains are still in China" is a very vivid and profound summary of the root causes to the above problems, and the root cause is a series of subjective limitations which commonly exist in Chinese contractors.

Chinese contractors have created a series of engineering miracles in the domestic market in terms of technology and speed, such as Olympic engineering and high-speed railways. This gives Chinese contractors the confidence and courage to rise up to the challenge of large international complex projects. However, we must be soberly aware that these "miracles" are created by China's unique market environment, which occupies "time, place, and harmony." In the absence of this familiar market environment in which the "miracle" is created, it is difficult for Chinese contractors to replicate the "China speed."

However, the Chinese construction industry generally lacks the tradition of respecting contracts and laws and often relies on "Chinese-style" communication to resolve various disputes during contract performance. This "Chinese-style" communication experience maybe still work in some low-end markets, but in some high-end or quasi-high-end markets, it will always not work.

Chinese contractors often enter the international engineering market with the mentality of "crossing the river while feeling the stones," and Chinese contractors are often evaluated as "risk-takers" by international risk advisory agencies. This is obviously not a positive evaluation.

The phrase "crossing the river by feeling the stones" is a well-known saying to the Chinese people and has played a huge guiding role in the success of China's reform and open up policy. But can this experience be copied into the international engineering market? The answer is negative. China does not have any ready-made experience to draw on when the "reform and open up" policy operates. This objective condition determines that the only thing we could do is "cross the river by feeling the stones" at that time in China. However, the international engineering market has its mature objective development regular patterns, game rules and systems. Under such conditions, the essence of the "crossing the river by feeling the stones" is ignorance.

Overseas EPC projects have an obvious "high-risk" feature, and any experienced international contractor must carefully identify and assess project risks and consider whether the "risk fees" can be matched to "high risk" Notwithstanding that Chinese contractors' cost advantage is shrinking and closing to international contractors, Chinese contractors still often win the bid at ultra-low prices. This is a reflection of many Chinese contractors' failure to pay attention to identifying and respecting the objective regular patterns of international EPC projects. The "high-risk" EPC project is carried out with the "gambling" way and the "take a chance" mentality, so it is not difficult to image the likely ending.

The experience of Chinese contractors in the "go out" process for decades is often at the expense of high costs. In the more risky and more costly international EPC projects, if Chinese contractors cannot break through the "weird circle" that is constantly repeating the same mistakes, the "tuition fee" paid by Chinese contractors will be even more alarming.

Chinese contractors are not efficient in ensuring the high costs of overseas projects translate into valuable experience that benefits subsequent projects. It is often individuals involved in the project who gain experience, and personal experience is difficult to transfer into an enterprise risk management system. Frequently, the people with experience leave the company, taking their experience with them. This has the effect that the company has to re-learn and accumulate experience from ground-zero. It is rare for Chinese contractors to consolidate experience and draw learning points in time to form a knowledge base for future projects, unlike most of mature international contractors. Further, it is difficult for Chinese contractors to establish an effective communication mechanism with other contractors within the industry such that each individual company is unable to tap on the know-how of other contractors within the industry.

The international project management experience formed by Chinese contractors in practice is often immature and resistant to change. The international engineering market is developing very fast, and past experience that was feasible under the traditional construction contracting model may not be applicable at all in the EPC general contracting model. Further, international engineering project management, especially in contract and claims management, usually requires a solid grounding of common law or civil law. In the absence of such grounding, there may be inaccurate and incomplete understanding of key issues and people have a tendency to make a mindset error of "knowing that without knowing why." Experience has to be adaptable to become part of best practices. The failure to adapt is also the key reason that the so-called successful experience of Chinese contractors on some projects cannot always be replicated effectively in other projects.

China's existing international engineering management knowledge system is mainly based on a summary of the experience and knowledge of traditional construction contracting projects. Although a small number of scholars at the forefront of international engineering management practice have written excellent monographs and articles on EPC, in general, the practical experience and theoretical knowledge system of China's international EPC projects are still immature. It is unable to effectively guide the overseas contractor's EPC contracting management practices.

[C] Risks of Not Being Good at Getting Help from "Outside Brain"

One of the most striking features of the international engineering market is the refinement of the social division of labor. In the international engineering market, a group of "outside brains" who have acquired professional knowledge and skills in different fields, providing professional advisory services for financing institutions, investors and general contractors of international engineering projects. These "outside brains" include legal counsel, tax consultants, insurance consultants, cost and delay claims consultants, and technical experts. These "outside brains" use their practice experience and professional resources to bring considerable economic benefits to the parties.

However, most Chinese contractors often do not understand the objective regular patterns of the refinement of division of labor in the international market, and are accustomed to "self-reliance." They always neglect the necessity of investing in external professional resources (the decision-makers even think the functional department is shirking responsibility). The result often is "saving a little money with a big loss." We generalize this phenomenon as a self-reliance of "small-scale peasant economy," which obviously does not accord with the essential characteristics and objective regular patterns of the refinement of division of labor in international engineering.

The various subjective limitations of Chinese contractors make it is difficult for Chinese contractors to improve their overseas EPC project management capabilities and improve their risk management systems in a short period of time through self-development. Even if it is possible to improve these capabilities and systems eventually over a long period, the price paid is beyond imagination.

Under above background, how to use the power of the "outside brain" effectively to make up for the lack of professional competence become an important indicator for measuring the maturity of a contractor's overseas project management, and it is the only way which help Chinese contractors to achieve good sustainable development overseas.

The value of "outside brain" to Chinese contractors mainly focus on aspects below.

First, the "outside brain" provides best practices and work methods. A world-leading professional consultant or independent expert often holds best practices in the field. Communicating and cooperating with these "outside brains" on specific matters can help Chinese contractors to get and understand best practices about international engineering law, contract, project management, etc. in the shortest time, lowest actual cost and obtain best effect. It could help Chinese contractors avoid taking a wrong way and having to overcome the shortcomings of high cost, low efficiency, and immature traditional experience accumulation methods. This best practice sharing mechanism not only brings considerable economic benefits to Chinese contractors in specific projects but also trains a group of talents who are truly familiar with international engineering best practices for Chinese contractors.

Second, it provides a rich knowledge base and a case library. A world-leading professional consultant agency or expert often has a strong database of rich case resources. This is especially valuable for Chinese contractors who are not good at summarizing experience and absorb lessons.

Third, it provides efficient global professional network resources. Although various types of international professional consultant agencies have different professional fields, they formed global professional network resources because they often provide support and cooperation with different parties in different professional directions. In this way, through one of the consultant agencies and experts, it is possible to acquire a strong global network of professional resources, which is undoubtedly the high commercial value existed for Chinese contractors who generally have "short-board" in this respect.

In summary, overseas engineering projects of ever-increasing size and complexity pose more intensive challenges to Chinese contractors than ever. In order to achieve China's "going out" strategy and realize healthy and sustainable development, Chinese contractors should face, reflect on and overcome their own limitations. However, they also need to use high-quality "outside brain" resources to promote the improvement of the company's own project management capabilities, with the view of eventually promoting the level of the enterprises' risk management system construction.

Index